Addiction

A Philosophical Perspective

Candice L. Shelby
University of Colorado Denver, USA

palgrave
macmillan

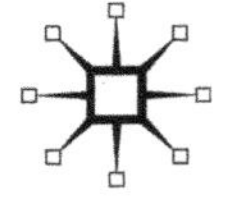

First published 2016 by
PALGRAVE MACMILLAN

Palgrave Macmillan in the UK is an imprint of Macmillan Publishers Limited, registered in England, company number 785998, of Houndmills, Basingstoke, Hampshire RG21 6XS.

Palgrave Macmillan in the US is a division of St Martin's Press LLC, 175 Fifth Avenue, New York, NY 10010.

Palgrave Macmillan is the global academic imprint of the above companies and has companies and representatives throughout the world.

Palgrave® and Macmillan® are registered trademarks in the United States, the United Kingdom, Europe and other countries.

ISBN: 978–1–137–55284–6

This book is printed on paper suitable for recycling and made from fully managed and sustained forest sources. Logging, pulping and manufacturing processes are expected to conform to the environmental regulations of the country of origin.

A catalogue record for this book is available from the British Library.

Library of Congress Cataloging-in-Publication Data

Names: Shelby, Candice L.

Title: Addiction : a philosophical perspective / Candice L. Shelby, University of Colorado Denver, USA.

Description: New York : Palgrave Macmillan, 2016. | Includes index.

Identifiers: LCCN 2015037382 | ISBN 9781137552846 (hardback)

Subjects: LCSH: Compulsive behavior. | Substance abuse–Philosophical aspects.

Classification: LCC RC533.S534 2016 | DDC 616.86—dc23
LC record available at http://lccn.loc.gov/2015037382

For Makenna and Nicholas (in alphabetical order)

Contents

Preface

In 2001, my father dropped dead of a heart attack while shaving. His doctors had told him for 50 years that he needed to quit smoking, and he did, at least a thousand times. Pipes, cigars, plastic straws...all led back to cigarettes. Increasing blood pressure readings had no effect on the puffing. In 2006, my sister died at a bus stop from cardiac arrest, brought on by a fractured skull, which happened as a result of a fall during a seizure, which happened because not enough drugs were in her system to keep her upright. In 2009, it was my mother, following three months on life support after aspirating into her lungs, as a result of taking an overdose of prescription drugs that were brought into the hospital by outside friends. My mother and sister had both been through innumerable addiction treatment centers, and my sister through two years of prison, with no effect whatsoever. These experiences left me with a firm belief that addiction is not what the treatment industry says it is, and it certainly isn't reliably treated with the approaches typically offered.

Although most contemporary clinicians working in the addictions recovery field typically refer to addiction as a "biopsychosocial disorder," when it comes to action, the profession seems deaf to its own characterization. Instead of addressing the triad of biological, psychological, and sociological disturbances that according to their own definition addicts suffer, what we see in the addiction treatment world is a proliferation of treatment centers based on 12-step programs. These programs are self-described as "spiritual," which may be the explanation for why little high-quality medical or psychological treatment makes its way into these facilities. Instead, most are staffed by former addicts with little formal education. When patients of these centers relapse following their release, they are invited to return for another "round of treatment." My mother did, over and over again, to the tune of hundreds of thousands of dollars of my grandfather's and my father's money. The response? "It works if you work it." Regardless of how much is spent by patients' families, or what claims are made on the front end by the rehab facilities, few people make successful life changes based on the model of having a disease for which one needs treatment. Nor, despite popular belief, do a significant proportion of those who try 12-step programs succeed over the long haul. If addiction is a spiritual disease, then work needs to be done to shore up the spiritual cure. I think that what we need to do to increase addicts' chances of living happy, productive lives goes much deeper and is much more radical than most have imagined.

Acknowledgments

People have asked me many times over the years why, if everyone else in my family of origin is dead due to one addiction or another, I am a tenured professor writing a book on addiction rather than living under a bridge with a needle in my arm. The reasons are mostly people. Mitchell Aboulafia, while a professor at the University of Houston-Clear Lake, encouraged and supported me in the study of philosophy, and in making the decision to apply to graduate school. He has remained a great friend and advisor. Likewise, Richard Grandy, Mark Kulstad, and Steven Crowell at Rice University convinced me that I had something to contribute to the intellectual world, and helped make that claim come true with years of continuing support. My colleagues at the University of Colorado Denver encouraged and supported my work, and many internal grants awarded by the College of Liberal Arts and Sciences and by the university made it possible for me to take the time to learn an entirely new area of philosophy. Mark Bauer pushed me in both his Philosophy of Biology class and in personal exchanges. Likewise, the international Code Biology community provided me with the opportunity to interact with accomplished scholars and exposed me to sophisticated ideas, without which I would not have been able to move forward. Kathleen Gargan arranged invitations for me to speak at national meetings of the LifeRing Secular Recovery organization as I was trying out new ideas about ways of understanding and addressing addiction. Finally, Matt Pike provided me with endless hours of discussions, helpful suggestions, and invaluable critiques of my ideas.

With respect to the production of the book, many heartfelt thanks go to my editor, Liz Stillwaggon-Swan, whose quick work, insightful commentaries, and sharp eye improved the manuscript immeasurably. Esme Chapman answered questions, offered guidance, and provided a gracious and patient presence at Palgrave Macmillan. Walter Freeman supplied me with photos of myself that I can actually share. Finally, I would have been nowhere without my research assistant, Rachael Boice, who began our association as a graduate assistant, but became at many points in the process my lifeline. She researched, read, pushed, prodded, and kept me accountable to my plan. Without her, this book would not exist. I am forever grateful.

1
Introduction – Dismantling the Catch Phrase

Human addiction involves a complex dynamic interaction of many systems in which physical responses, emotions, self-judgment, social relations, and a variety of institutions are all critical players. Even when addictive problems are not treated merely as personal failings, the rehabilitative path tends to focus on the individual, and at most on the individual and her closest circle of support. Addictive patterns tend to be separated from their social and civil institutional elements. More recently, as social theorists have begun to examine the social structures that contribute to addictive patterns, a similar mistake is made: those structures are pointed to as "the real cause" of problems in this area. Addiction is a deep-seated and systemic human problem, and yet it continues to be treated piecemeal, both in research and in treatment. In the scientific research literature, it is treated purely as a biochemical disorder involving characteristic brain changes. Although numerous species have been known to compulsively self-administer certain drugs in laboratory settings, (1) animal addiction does not happen in the wild, despite reports of some animals apparently becoming intoxicated on fermented fruit when they come upon it, and (2) even when animals do exhibit addictive behaviors and brain changes in laboratory settings, there is no reason to believe that their compulsive lever pressing or morphine water drinking involves the angst, remorse, or psychological trauma that human addiction does. Although other mammals' physiological reactions may be able to tell us something about human addiction, the phenomenon exhibited here, limited as it is to characteristic brain changes and compulsive repetitive behavior, would not count as addiction in the robust sense in which it is addressed in this book.

Understood better as a process than as a state, addiction is essentially a temporal phenomenon, involving the whole person and long stretches of time in at least these two ways: (1) addicts' wishes to avoid use and their plans for using are temporally distinct, and (2) it takes time for human addiction to develop, and to dissipate. No one is instantly an addict, even when he or she seems to be hooked on a substance or activity from the first time he or she indulges. What's more, even though neuroscientists can point to changes in structure and function in the brain that occur when people become addicted, these results require interpretation. Scans themselves are pictures; they cannot provide evidence that the brain changes they document are *caused by* the addiction, rather than resulting from addictive behaviors that are caused by something else, as yet unanalyzed. One thing that is clear is that addiction develops over time and in an extremely complex way that involves not just brain chemistry, nor just behavior, and certainly not just spiritual dysfunction. Rather, it develops as a pattern that is determined by and pervades the whole life of a person.

Addiction, as it is treated in this book, is not simply substance abuse or chemical dependence, regardless of whether those chemicals come from the inside or the outside. As we consider it here, addiction requires self-consciousness and human social experience, in addition to a brain with neural systems and neurotransmitters associated with seeking, learning, and pleasure. Thus, for us, the models of addiction developed using laboratory animals, although not without usefulness, are of limited value. Laboratory animals are incapable, for example (at least as far as we know), of experiencing what this book will refer to as the "semantic" level of addiction, since they lack the requisite conceptual tools, and they lack the sophistication necessary for the social construction of the meanings of their behaviors and feelings. At the human level, the set of relations defining the addict's global scheme of concepts is shaped by his addiction, and undergoes a revolutionary shift when the addict enters into remission. What's more, even in humans, and even when all of these elements are present, it is not clear where the line demarcating addiction lies. Some people use "addictive" substances or engage in gambling or overeating every day, yet do not feel, nor do others see them as addicted, while others use these substances or engage in these behaviors only infrequently, but feel addicted and are characterized in those terms by those close to them. With addiction we seem to be faced with what is known in the philosophical tradition as a sorites paradox: we can agree when someone clearly is an addict (living under a bridge begging for money for heroin), and when someone clearly is not (never had a taste of an addictive substance or activity), but just where the cutoff point is seems impossible to say in a nonarbitrary way. And this is not simply an academic matter. Although psychologists, neuroscientists, and addiction counselors certainly have criteria, necessary and sufficient conditions, and checklists to help them separate addicts from nonaddicts, these tools address particular aspects of addiction, and various tools will characterize the same person in different ways.

The problems with consistently distinguishing addicts from nonaddicts arise because until now there has been no single, coherent theory of human addiction. Rather, there are in operation at least two primary definitions, or rather, there are many variations on these two types of definitions. For over forty years, the phenomenon has been widely characterized on the one hand as a disease. That language, largely because of advances in imaging capabilities, has come in recent years to be basically the received view. As we will see, first because of discoveries about how the brain's reward pathways can be changed by repeated exposure to certain drugs and stimulating activities, and also because of later discoveries regarding the actions of certain neurotransmitters, as well as salience detection pathways, addiction research talk has come to be framed increasingly in physical terms. Certainly in some ways that is a good thing, as increasing focus on physical characterizations of the "disease" has lessened the stigma and blame associated with addiction. But does it make sense? Do brain changes necessitate addictive behavior? Are humans whose brains are changed in particular ways incapable of self-determination? Given how many people recover from addictions, the answer seems to be "no." If brain changes aren't responsible for behaviors, then are researchers correct in defining addiction in terms of the brain changes involved, or should we instead be defining addiction also in terms of individuals' experiences, or in terms of their behavior, or all of these? Although the latest edition of the *Diagnostic and Statistical Manual* (DSM) of the American Psychiatric Association speaks of a set of symptoms that result in drug taking despite bad consequences,[1] it is not clear whether this definition is focused on the symptoms *that result in* behavior that creates problems, or on the behavior that creates the problems. If it is the first, then we need a specification of those symptoms, and if the behavior is the crux of addiction, then we are left with a quite peculiar disease. It is a disease the recovery from which, as addiction researcher Gene Heyman puts it, is not correlated with the kinds of things that are correlated with recovery from "the diseases addiction is said to be like, such as Alzheimer's, schizophrenia, diabetes, heart disease, cancer, and so on."[2] Recovery, or, put more objectively, transition out of addiction is instead correlated with ordinary concerns, such as care for children or parents, professional responsibilities, and, quite reasonably, fear of judicial prosecution. If it is a disease, it is a disease that puts hundreds of thousands of people behind bars every year, and recovery from it is associated with all kinds of things other than treatment.[3]

There are further problems with conceiving of addiction as a disease, particularly as the term "disease" seems to be popularly used in connection with self-help programs, and in particular, with 12-step programs. How could submitting one's will to God, taking a moral inventory, and making amends, all of which are involved in these treatment frameworks, operate to cure a disease? Conventional wisdom among those who practice this form of cure says that addiction is a disease of the spirit, but again, it is unclear what that can mean in modern terms. What are other diseases of the spirit? Evil? Immaturity? Greediness? None of these characteristics are spoken of in contemporary terms as diseases, or as spiritual. In fact, nothing else denoted by the word "disease" in English concerns the spirit. Although this characterization of addiction is commonplace in the recovery community, we would have to do some serious work to account for it without abandoning all that science has given us.

Standing in contrast to the disease model(s) of addiction is the choice model, of which philosophers, psychologists, and behavioral economists have developed numerous versions. The element tying together the various types of choice theory is rationality. Theorists here either attempt to explain how addicts can be rational in repeatedly choosing something that is harmful to them, or they try to explain how a rational being can consistently choose irrationally. This view has more in common with the spiritual disease model than it does with the physical disease model because both the choice view and the spiritual disease view suggest that mind (or spirit) is separate from body, and that it is free choices that are responsible for the havoc that addiction wreaks. The physical disease model, in contrast, which focuses on physical dependency and brain changes, suggests that the addicted person is much less free with respect to her addiction. None of these views in isolation is able to provide an adequate account of all the complex interacting aspects of addiction. In order to understand this phenomenon and have any hope of developing broadly successful approaches to helping those who suffer from it, we have to undertake a much deeper and broader investigation of the pattern that is addiction than has been done in the past. We have to consider it from genesis to expression in the world, and from unique experience to social context. We need to employ a completely different framework from any that has been offered before.

The analysis has to provide an account of how a psychological and social issue can be at the same time a physical reality. It has to provide, in other words, some way of understanding the relation between the mind and the body. According to one perspective, minds are believed to be nothing other than the brain in action. This perspective raises the question of how mental experience can happen, given that minds seem to be very different from the gray and white goo that sits inside our skulls, even if understood at a deeper level as an ongoing electrical storm. However, to suggest that minds are completely different sorts of things than bodies is to make mentality a mystery, seemingly coming from nowhere, and having no way to connect to the physical world. This is a problem first introduced by René Descartes 300 years ago: if I can clearly and distinctly conceive of myself without appeal to my body, then it seems that my mind is all that I need to be me. My body is a substance with which I am "mixed," but it is not me. I am my experiencing mind. But if my body is so indubitably an extended material thing, with no trace of the mental in it, then how can my mind and brain/body work together to provide me with the human experience of living as an embodied individual? And more importantly for our purposes, how can a person, a mind independent of body, be addicted so that she feels driven by forces that are nevertheless based within herself? A physical sort of answer to these questions would seem to drive us to a deterministic understanding of addiction, since, if all mental experiences are caused by the brain's cells, or the molecules comprising those cells (or pick your level), then whatever choices, yearnings, or fears that one has must be caused by those tiny parts. So, the argument goes, if minds are brains and addicted brains are dysfunctional, then it is not clear how the addicted person could do anything about it. Whether one became addicted or transitioned out of addiction would seem to be the result of purely physical causes. The dualist response, in contrast, would seem to make addiction a free choice. That characterization, though, dismisses the sense of helplessness and yearning to not be addicted that addicts often describe themselves as having. A better response would show that there need be no difference in kind between mental events and physical events, and that emotional, physical, and cognitive elements can all be ways of understanding the patterns that constitute the life of an addict.

The central argument of this book is that, to understand addiction correctly, we need to dismantle the catchphrase. We need to see that addiction, rather than being one thing, whether a way of thinking or a physiological condition, is a set of interacting physical, mental, and social patterns that develops, persists, and dissipates as the patterns from which it emerges and with which it interacts undergo changes. Human beings, with our conscious lives and the problems that arise from them, are natural processes embedded in our environments, experiencing further, emergent natural processes. Our minds are neither soul-like entities, as Descartes would say, nor are they a fundamental but unknown kind, to be discovered by a radically new kind of science. However, neither are our minds identical with the brain's neurons, neurotransmitters, and electrical impulses, otiose in itself and thus eliminable as a category.[4] The philosophical problem of the mind's relation to the body, like a number of other philosophical puzzles, seems to arise from adherence to an old, substance-based metaphysics. From a complex dynamic systems approach resting on a metaphysics sometimes described as structural realism, rather than on a physical object ontology, it will be argued that these problems need not arise. From the perspective that will be presented in this book, human beings are neither responsible for their addictions in the way that we are responsible for choosing between a banana and an apple, nor are we determined by physical forces to become alcoholics, smokers, or gamblers. We are singularly complex, dynamic, self-aware organisms, emerging from lower-level complex processes, within the context of an environment that simultaneously shapes us and is shaped by us. We are susceptible to addictions, some of us more than others, due to processes beyond our control, but we have power to avoid them and to overcome them as well – again, some more than others. Understanding human addictions from a complex dynamic systems perspective, with its characteristic features of emergent properties, hierarchical organization, and "lever points," places at which small changes in inputs can result in large changes in the system offers us the opportunity to see how it is that an addicted mind could change itself, and how a wide variety of approaches can be used to help that process.

Even though it is an analysis of addiction, this book begins with and rests crucially on a metaphysical position. It begins with the premise that mind emerges from the physical, but not in the same way that wholes result from parts. This means that emotional and psychological experiences need neither be explained away nor accepted as brute independent facts. Physicists have for decades accepted the concepts of emergent entities and complex dynamic systems, but neuroscientists and philosophers have been slow to come around. The advantages of taking that approach, however, are many. For instance, even if we trace the brain down through its neural systems to its individually acting neurons, with their particular shapes and internal and external chemical properties, and trace those in turn even further to their molecular makeup, we are not going to see how the nonmental creates the mental, as we see how bricks create a building. But there is a way to understand how the mind and the brain are connected in a single physical system: by conceiving of mind as an emergent process, arising from physical processes, but with autonomous causal and other properties of its own. Assuming this kind of emergence theory allows us to understand the mind as a process both arising from and contributing to more complex processes, and we can understand addiction as a process organized from simpler biological processes within the context of larger personal and social processes. As Terrence Deacon frames it, this discussion is going to be about "processes dependent on processes dependent on processes."[5] Adopting this view of our physiological and psychological selves, together with some reconfigured attendant concepts of meaning and value, will allow us to understand addiction in a different and far more complete way than has been done before.

This means that we can and must address addiction at many different levels of analysis, because there is no question of one "level" based at the "root" of addiction, no one way of understanding what causes it, how it feels, or how it can be treated. The very concept of *causation* that we will have to employ will in and of itself require serious rethinking. This is not to deny the tremendous importance of recent scientific developments in understanding the neural pathways, neurotransmitters, plasticity, and synaptic changes characteristic to addiction. Quite on the contrary, each of the individual levels of organization at which addiction has been analyzed is valuable, both in its own right, and in terms of its connections to other levels of organization. This book therefore begins with a philosophical discussion of just what addiction is, outlining the conceptual clarifications that need to be made in order to coherently carry forward our discussion. Chapter 1 introduces the framework that is used to understand the interrelations of the various levels of organization at which addiction manifests. From there, we turn in Chapter 2 to a discussion of the latest theories of addiction as a biological process, examining the physiological events and changes characteristically associated with addiction. Chapter 3 addresses addiction as a psychological phenomenon, examining some empirical theories that try to capture which environments and behaviors predict addiction. In this chapter, we also consider some theoretical explanations of how and why addiction arises, focusing principally on attachment theory and trauma theory.

Chapter 4 addresses the history and social construction of addiction, expanding the irreducibility thesis yet further, examining the contexts in which addiction emerges as a diagnosis and a social phenomenon. Whatever the physiological, psychological, and/or spiritual nature of addiction, no one gets addicted or recovers from addiction in a vacuum. Human beings are essentially social animals; without others, one cannot become an addict any more than one can become a person.

All of the systems so far discussed also contribute to the system of meanings that shapes the addict's world, and to the ways in which his world is different from the worlds of individuals who are not addicted. Chapter 5 focuses on how the set of meanings that form an individual's world can change as one becomes addicted. It also provides an account of how one's system of meanings changes when "something clicks" and one sees the world in a different light, shifting into a new gestalt. This chapter also explains why those who are not addicted often see those who are as irrational, ill, or spiritually bankrupt. The phenomenology of addiction, the subject of Chapter 6, is the least examined aspect of the syndrome, and understandably so, because the qualitative description of the experience of addiction and recovery varies so much from individual to individual that it is difficult to derive generalities. Even less effectively have the theories that are currently on offer been able to explain how we can consider this wide range of experiences as cases of the same phenomenon. Nevertheless, this may well be one of the most important chapters of this book, as we move beyond third-person objective explanations of what might be going on in addicts to first-person accounts in order illuminate our understanding of both addiction and recovery of a multidimensional, complex human phenomenon. A full exploration of this phenomenology shows the inadequacy of the accounts of addiction offered to date. Chapter 7 considers where promise exists for transitioning out of addiction and into a happier, fuller life. While addiction cannot simply be arrested, as some recent headlines have claimed, by "addiction vaccines," talk therapy, or any other single-pronged approach, understanding the richness and variety of the physiological effects, environments, and ideological frameworks in which addiction survives or fades can assist us in finding positive ways out of an increasingly pervasive problem.

Finally, the concluding chapter explains what this multilevel, dynamic, and complex analysis means for understanding addicts' attitudes and actions, and shows how this view provides a coherent position from which to develop more sensitive, insightful, and successful research agendas and treatment approaches than have so far been offered.

Standard linear causal approaches will be shown to be inadequate both for assessing why a person got into addiction, and how he might get out of it. Although we are very good at giving causal analyses after the fact, direct attempts to change an addict's behaviors, attitudes, and feelings have been notoriously unsuccessful. One cannot stop addiction by merely identifying "triggers" or negative emotions, any more than one can end it by administering drugs, either those that act as antagonists to the addict's drug of choice, or those that make him violently ill in its presence, although any of these methods might help in a given case. Neither can we expect to overcome the social structures from which addictions emerge and within which they make sense – at least not completely, and not immediately. Because addiction is a process, and indeed not a single process but a complex system of processes that are essentially constrained by and that constrain larger and smaller dynamic systems, exposure to a variety of causal influences, sometimes oblique in nature, promises to be a more helpful approach to easing the addict's suffering than any single direct attempt to control addictive responses. Addiction is an irreducibly complex reality, and we shouldn't expect something different of the processes that can effectively address it.

2

Some Philosophical Questions (and a New Theory)

Conversations about the worst social ills facing our age often focus on global climate change, or on the stunning inequalities between the rich and the poor. Many people, though, point to the escalating problem of addiction as our most challenging, both because of its personal costs to health and relationships and because of its economic costs to our own generation and to that of our children. So much has been said about addiction and its related social ills in the past few decades that one might think that the concept is clear and our attitudes uniform. The pervasive "war on drugs" refrain, popular over the past 40 years, seems to suggest that everyone is on the same page. Terms such as "addiction," "disease," "compulsion," and "recovery" are thrown around as though everyone were in agreement about both the existence and the meanings of these occurrences in human lives. In fact, though, the ideas behind these terms are more problematic than they first appear. In fact, each is the subject of controversy.

Some significant ground clearing is called for, then, before discussions can begin about how we as a society might want to address the increasingly pervasive phenomenon of addiction. Let us start by considering a variety of responses to the simple question of what addiction is. Over the past 40 years or so, a generally unchallenged and standard view has arisen that addiction is a psychiatric disease. The *Diagnostic and Statistical Manual of Mental Disorders* (DSM)[1] has included addiction among its categories of mental disorders since the 2nd edition was released in 1968. Since it has come to be coded in accordance with the World Health Organization's International Classification of Diseases,[2] even the medical and insurance industries officially accept the characterization of addiction as a mental disorder, or disease, along with depression, anxiety, and schizophrenia. I say "officially," because although the language of disease is the current mode of discourse, testimony from addicts consistently suggests that social behavior doesn't necessarily follow its talk. Even in the face of general acceptance of the disease model, addicts continue to be treated with derision, blame, and distaste, not to mention legal prosecution. This issue is discussed in later chapters.

For the moment, note that labeling addiction a disease does not in any case resolve anything. A name, as philosopher William James noted, is not a stopping point or a solution. Rather, it is a beginning: attributing a name to a phenomenon simply opens the door to begin asking questions. "You have tonsillitis" does not suggest that the meeting with the doctor is over; instead, it suggests the directions in which she might begin to look for treatment options. Likewise, labeling addiction a disease (rather than, say, a moral failing) provides direction for asking questions, some of which will penetrate to the very foundations of our assumptions about humanity and mentality. What would it mean for addiction to be a mental illness? In most cases that we would call illness, or disease, we find a genetic aberration, or a viral or bacterial infection, or a failure or defect of an organ or system. In the case of addiction, none of these necessarily exist. Although arguments for a genetic predisposition to addiction have been made (to great media fanfare[3]) and supported by adoption and twin studies,[4] there is no gene for addiction, and the impact that genetic factors can have is a topic of some controversy. One might argue on other grounds that addiction is a disease, though, for the evidence is clear that as addiction progresses, changes in brain function and structure do occur. Not everyone agrees, however, that structural or functional changes occurring in brains imply that addiction is a mental illness, since it can be argued that nearly everything we do changes our brains, and some activities that we choose to pursue, such as learning a new language or meditation, make beneficial structural and functional brain changes. Moreover, connecting brain changes, which are physical changes, to *mental* illness is not such a short step as is generally imagined. We could take this line of reasoning even further, and ask what makes anything count as mental at all, but we will for the moment leave aside the deeply philosophical issues and accept for the moment a general conception of this category.

The DSM IV-TR, the psychiatric profession's authoritative reference volume,[5] might be expected to give us a good definition of addiction. The manual does not take the approach of definition, however, but instead provides behavioral criteria for diagnosing what it calls Substance Use Disorders, divided into two subclasses, Substance Dependence and

Substance Abuse, with the first intended to cover more serious cases than the second. The first, as we will see, refers to behaviors that are represented by neuroscientists in physiological models. The DSM's approach on the one hand seems sound, since a definition of something as diverse, complicated, and vaguely bounded as addiction would inevitably be contentious and not much help for diagnostic purposes. At worst, given the pervasively popular mind/brain dualistic metaphysics, such a definition would be doomed to either circularity or incoherence.[6] On the other hand, the DSM's checklist method for determining addiction by characterizing two things, neither of which is identical with what is generally understood by "addiction," leaves the discipline's highest authority in the awkward position of authorizing the diagnosis and treatment of a generally recognized "disease" without ever saying what it is.

The criterion method for diagnosis illuminates an important truth, however, which is that there are no bright lines demarcating where addiction starts and where it stops, and there is no definitive list of kinds of addiction that might exist. Substances only begin to tell the tale, if current research is any indication.[7] First, gambling was recognized as an activity that, as engaged in by certain people, exhibits the hallmarks of addiction.[8] Then research indicated that there could also be addiction to food,[9] then video games,[10] then shopping, tanning, and other non-substance-related foci characterized by similar behavior patterns. The newest version of the DSM, the 5th edition, proposes revisions that include adding the category "behavior addictions,"[11] and foregoing the current subcategories of substance abuse and dependence, in favor of the new category "addiction and related disorders." So, as research on addiction takes off, so does the scope of the phenomenon included under the rubric. What might count as an addiction in another 50 years is anyone's guess. The line keeps moving.

Even within the set of specific addictions included under the DSM IV-TR's list of substance disorders, there is no clear line separating addicts from nonaddicts. According to the DSM IV-TR, the "essential feature" of substance dependence, the more serious of the two subclasses of substance use disorders, is "a cluster of cognitive, behavioral, and physiological symptoms indicating that the individual continues use of the substance despite significant substance-related problems."[12] This description includes so much that it is of little help, although with respect to the most general and paradigmatic cases, it seems to capture what is wanted. The description delineates neither necessary nor sufficient conditions, however, for what could be meant by "addiction." It does not capture necessary conditions, because it excludes any cases in which drugs or alcohol are used without "significant substance-related problems," as happens in early nicotine addiction, for example. The mere fact that a teenaged smoker has not yet experienced chronic lung illness or high blood pressure, or even any difficulty ceasing the practice (because she hasn't tried) does not justify a conclusion that the teen is not addicted. And it seems that that same teenager could smoke marijuana for some time, despite significant substance-related problems, without being addicted to it. The teenager's substance-related problems might have to do with school authorities or parents, indicating that the roots of her problems lie in defiance rather than in addiction. If addiction is a disease, then we need to figure out on what grounds and of what type it is.

Choice theories

At the other end of the spectrum of characterizations of addiction are choice theories. The most forthright of these theories is put forward by psychologist Gene Heyman, in his book *Addiction: A Disorder of Choice.*[13] According to Heyman, the key component to the DSM IV-TR's definition of addiction is the criterion noted above, that "the individual continues use of the substance despite significant substance-related problems." So, behavior, rather than the cluster of physiological and cognitive symptoms indicating this behavior, is the key to the concept of addiction. Drug seeking is voluntary and rational, says Heyman, and neither a genetic predisposition to addiction nor the neural changes that come with the chronic abuse of certain drugs proves otherwise. Based on four large epidemiological surveys, he argues that most addicts stop using drugs by their mid-30s without seeking treatment, most likely because of adult "responsibilities, incentives, penalties and cultural values that stress sobriety."[14] That is, addicts freely and with reason choose their addictive behaviors, and we can tell that this is true, because when incentives shift, so do the behaviors, at least when they are unaccompanied by other mental disorders. On this account, addicts can control themselves, but choose not to, as long as the utilities are in their favor. When the utilities change, suggests the research that Heyman cites, so does the behavior, all other things being equal.

But that may be just the point: whether all other things in the cases of those whom we might label as "addicted" *are* equal. Those who seek treatment for addiction in clinics, for instance, are less likely to achieve and maintain abstinence than those who do not, and it may be that the additional presence of some other non-drug-related mental illness accounts for the lack of success of those addicts who seek treatment in clinics. More than twice as many people who are diagnosed as drug dependent are likely to seek treatment if they also meet the criteria for another mental illness, and that number is probably conservative.[15] The question arises, then, why so many of those who don't have complicating diagnoses simply quit their drug use by their mid-30s. Other than the fact that using drugs interferes with other things that most adults value, Heyman admits that he has no account of this large remission rate. The fact may simply be that he is begging the question here with respect to addiction. Of course, it is true that most people stop drug use when they mature beyond their reckless teen-to-twenties mentality. But are *those* people *really* ever addicted? Perhaps they fit the DSM IV-TR's category of substance abuser, but not that of substance dependence. And perhaps they even fit the criteria for dependence for a time, but nevertheless fail to fit our conception of addiction, since dependence, as we noted above, isn't sufficient to establish addiction. Heyman and many others cite a highly influential study that showed that 90% of the large number of soldiers who returned home from Vietnam with opiate dependency stopped using or "became controlled opiate users" once they left the wartime environment.[16] While disease-model researchers would say that these were precisely the users who weren't true addicts (the conventional wisdom is that about 10% of the population will at some point suffer addiction), Heyman believes that this study, together with numerous others that illustrate, among other things, how incentives can change drug-dependent behavior,[17] shows that people are addicts by choice.

Heyman's is not an uninformed, "free will" argument. He is familiar with the body of brain scan studies showing that brains change with repeated drug use. What he denies is that the brain changes observed in persons identified as addicts rob them of choice, and he denies this for at least two reasons. First, note that those changes follow the drug use – they do not antecede it, and second, there is no reason to believe that these observable changes preclude choice. Like numerous thinkers from a variety of disciplines, Heyman is unimpressed by arguments that the brain determines the mind in any straightforward way, or that one can read mentality from physicality. What is more, if the brain's plasticity allows for changes consistent with becoming dependent on drugs, Heyman argues, that same plasticity can allow for it to change back, and it often does. We consider the arguments regarding the specific brain changes that are used by neuroscientists and research psychologists to define addiction, and to argue against the choice model, in the next chapter. For the present, what is important is that at the root of the disagreement between the disease and the choice models of addiction is the nature of the addict's failure to control his behavior. What causes a person to continue using a substance or participating in an activity when that indulgence is accompanied by problems clearly related to use? Is this failure voluntary or involuntary, or somewhere in between? It would seem that either the addict must be compelled to continue to use – that is, he is simply unable to stop, as those who uphold the disease model maintain[18] – or he is unwilling to do so, as choice theorists believe. Even Heyman notes that, his arguments against the disease/compulsion model of addiction notwithstanding, many addicts struggle. Although he is quicker than many to blame addicts for their use, and to attribute to them excuse making and self-indulgence rather than incapacity, he does recognize that many times addicts hope and believe that they will not use in the future. They make plans not to use, and yet they do. Others, such as neuroscientists George Ainslie and John Monterosso who have no vested interested in Heyman's position, have observed in addicts strong inner turmoil and intrapersonal bargaining,[19] in which sufferers agonize over their plight, recognize what is good for them and what is bad, plan not to use, and have every intention of not using in the future, yet, when confronted with an opportunity, repeatedly do exactly the thing that they have judged to be bad for them. People will often, these researchers note, even while saying such things as "I know that I shouldn't do this," take a drink, light up, or place a bet. So, is the addict compelled in these cases to indulge her addiction, or does she just repeatedly make bad choices?

Compulsion or weakness of will?

Let us consider the last possibility first, that addiction is persistent choosing to use a substance or engage in a behavior. The addict on this account is not totally without control. She does know the difference between what is good for her and what is bad, and she is not forced to choose the worse, but nevertheless does so. This phenomenon is a familiar one in human history, recognized in philosophy long ago by Aristotle, who called it *akrasia*, or weakness of will. As opposed to the virtuous citizen, who restrains his indulgence of pleasurable things to within a moderate range, the akratic character, Aristotle tells us, knows the good and *wants to do it*, yet, irrationally, is led by his weakness to do something else.[20] The akratic character is therefore not wicked, since he knows good from evil, but neither is he guided to action by what he knows to be best. The akratic character gives in to some call other than that of reason, perhaps appetite or emotional impulse. That this kind of weakness is recognized is clear from social institutions put into place in both ancient Greek and current American culture for the specific purpose of shoring up people's resistance to overindulgence in pleasurable goods. The Greeks, for instance, held out Temperance (or moderation) as one of the four cardinal virtues valued in any good citizen. Today, commercially sold food plans, such as the Jenny Craig system, as well as public policies, including citywide bans on supersized soft drinks, serve to discourage overindulgence.

Contemporary philosophers, in contrast to the ancients, often focus on the *irrational* nature of akratic behavior. Rather than recognizing the good but not being able to constrain oneself to follow it, on this version the akratic person behaves paradoxically, for he intentionally does what he judges not to be best. According to philosopher Donald Davidson's formulation, for example, "In doing x an agent acts [akratically] if and only if (a) the agent does x intentionally; (b) the agent believes there is an alternative action y open to him; and (c) the agent judges that, all things considered, it would be better to do y than to do x."[21] That is, knowing full well that another act is better, the agent chooses to do the worse. But to act intentionally, Davidson also says, just *is* to do what one deems better.[22] In some way, picking what one judges to be the better is the very essence of choice. So, we seem to be faced with a puzzle. The akratic choice is not really paradoxical, though, according to Davidson, because the two judgments involved are of different sorts – the judgment of intentionality involved in (a) is an unconditional judgment, while the judgment involved in (c) is a relative judgment, a judgment involving all things considered. Addictive thinking on this account amounts to judging indulgence to be the better choice in this case despite the fact that one's reasons, all things considered, argue for avoiding indulgence. According to Davidson, one ought to act on the basis of all available reasons; the akratic error is to fail to do so. On this version of akrasia, then, one acts irrationally, on the unconditional judgment of the goodness of just one option, rather than acting on a judgment made in light of all things considered.

The question that this analysis immediately raises, though, is what would make someone fail to take into account all available reasons. Clearly, the addict does fail in exactly this way. According to the DSM IV-TR criteria, that is in fact the essence of addiction: the addict continues to choose to use despite substance-related problems. Akrasia as an *explanation* of the irrational actions of an addict (or anyone), though, doesn't do any work, since it completely fails to address the question of *why* one might act irrationally. It simply says that this is what the akratic character does. What is going on, if the addict could choose differently, and should, but doesn't? Aristotle's understanding seems to be informed by an analogy with physical weakness, so if it is to be of any use here, we are going to have to work out how that analogy could be put into play. Some theorists have suggested that emotion could cause an agent to act intentionally against her better interests. This seems likely true, but in this case we will need an account of emotion if we are to complete the analysis, and here's why: if, as some philosophers suggest, emotions are judgments themselves, brought about by reasons ("I'm angry at you because you spilled my coffee on my lap"), then they would seem to be reasonable, and then one's action wouldn't be akratic. If, on the other hand, emotions are not judgments or reasons of any kind, then how can they enter into judgments? That is, how can one decide *on the basis of* an emotion to do something that is against one's better judgment if emotions aren't the kind of things that can enter into reasoning, or, by extension, into judgments? It would seem from this line of reasoning that the philosopher has produced a reductio ad absurdum against his own way of thinking (not that that's unusual). Notice, though, that these problems only arise if we assume that humans are rational beings motivated to action by judgments based on arguments. That assumption is clearly false, however appealing it might be. Humans are not philosophers, any more than we are Econs, the rational consumers that traditional economics assumes in its models. Psychological and biological considerations will have to enter into any viable analysis of choice, judgment, or, what concerns us here, addictive behavior.

Philosopher Neil Levy agrees that weakness of will isn't an established phenomenon in need of a philosophical account. He moreover agrees that the concept fails to explain anything regarding why people do what they, in their considered opinion, judge to be suboptimal. In his view, weakness of will isn't in itself a psychological kind at all.[23] Of the two kinds of analyses that we have just discussed – judgment-based and desire-based weakness of will – his view has more in common with the former than the latter. But for Levy, the judgment is influenced by what has come to be known as "ego depletion."[24] We will consider this idea in much greater depth later, but the general idea is that intellectual energy (which, as it turns out, is physical energy[25]) is a limited resource, and so if much is used by one set of tasks, there is less left for others. In the current case, when one has been exercising self-control in one area, or has otherwise used up energy doing the multitude of tasks required of us each day, one "takes the easy way out" when the urge to indulge arises. More specifically, the brain switches from using the more accurate but difficult sort of deliberative reasoning, which some have called intellection, or System 2 thinking, to the more primitive, but energy-efficient, quick, and inflexible kind of thinking, which some have called intuitive, or System 1 thinking.[26] In making this switch, one sets up an easier problem, or frames premises and conclusions in such a way that spurious arguments are accepted. One does not deliver an "all things considered" decision.

To return to the issue then – we say that the addict is one who either does not or cannot choose not to use. If we were not to accept either of the versions of weakness of will – that she either simply does not do what she judges best or that she changes her judgment – then what we would be left with is that she cannot choose otherwise, but is compelled to indulge in addictive behavior, despite significant negative consequences. This is what many addiction theorists believe. The true addict, many say, "can't help himself"; he is "overwhelmed" by his urges. Not only do we find this kind of language in current literature but we also see it as long ago as 1890, when philosopher William James characterized addiction in this way:

> The craving for a drink in real dipsomaniacs, or for opium or chloral in those subjugated, is of a strength of which normal persons can form no conception. "Were a keg of rum in one corner of a room and were a cannon constantly discharging balls between me and it, I could not refrain from passing before that cannon in order to get the rum"; "If a bottle of brandy stood at one hand and the pit of hell yawned at the other, and I were convinced that I should be pushed in as sure as I took one glass, I could not refrain": such statements abound in dipsomaniacs" mouths.[27]

On this depiction, an addict is one who is so overpowered by desire, or compulsion, that nothing conceivable could stop him from using, given the opportunity. In the scientific literature, as we shall see in detail in Chapter 2, accounts are given of this compulsion in terms of dysfunction of the dopamine-driven reward systems of the orbitofrontal cortex, in which judgments of salience and value, as well as inhibition and self-control are centered, respectively.[28] These kinds of accounts suggest that agency is compromised, if not obliterated, by a physiological condition. Thus, absent a medical intervention that can break these sensorimotor connections, the addict will, like an automaton, be doomed to repetition of the addictive behavior. But how can we make sense of a compulsion that comes from the inside? So what if someone's brain is flooded with this or that chemical? How does that fact translate into his being compelled, as one would be if another person grabbed one's hand, stuck a knife in it, and thrust the knife into a passerby's chest? Certainly the law does not accept that a probationer's return to drinking after being ordered to stop is excused on the ground that the probationer is addicted. So, what can be meant by "overpowering urge" or "compulsion" or "out of control"?

Philosopher Bennett Foddy suggests four things that might be meant when someone says that a person is compelled, and he rejects all of them as reasons for believing that no control exists in addiction.[29] Let us consider them one by one. First, someone might say that those who are addicted act compulsively because they "appear to be insensitive to the costs of their drug use." This is a criterion for addiction used in the DSM IV-TR. Second, one might characterize an addicted drug user's actions as compulsive because she regrets her drug use, and yet fails to curtail it. Third, one might say that people who are addicted are compelled on the grounds that they "report feeling strong desires which they feel unable to control." Finally, many neuroscientists would say that addicts act compulsively based on the fact that "their actions have identifiable neurological processes as their root cause."[30] Although Foddy is right that the factual basis of some of these claims is far from established, let us consider whether any of the reasons given would actually provide legitimate grounds for characterizing an act as compelled, were the facts to be as presumed.

First, note Foddy's claim that even if true, none of these reasons offers "uncontroversial proof" of compulsion, according to what philosophers mean by that term. Given that nothing stands as uncontroversial proof of anything in philosophical discourse, this point should not particularly move us, but the fact is, none of these reasons seems even good grounds for calling an act compelled. Returning to the list then, the first basis for saying that someone is compelled in her action (the one found in the DSM) seems to be beside the point. Many people are insensitive to the costs of the use of their credit cards, but we would not for that reason say that they are compelled to use them. There is no relevant difference between this case and the addictive case, and so this interpretation can be rejected. The second reason for calling an act compelled – that the individual regrets it, and yet does it again – certainly seems true of addicts; in fact, this is the characteristic that George Anslie finds central to addiction, as we saw earlier. However, just because someone regrets an act and nevertheless does it again, this does not even suggest, much less prove, that the act was compelled. Procrastinators provide us with a great example of people who repeatedly do something that they regret (some, not all, regret their procrastination) and yet do it again, admitting when queried that nothing compelled their behavior. This in fact adds to the remorse that they exhibit. A third reason for saying that someone is compelled is that the person feels compelled. Unless compulsion is like pain, though, and unmistakable, rather than like any of the variety of visual and cognitive illusions that we all experience, believing that we're seeing or feeling one thing when we're really seeing or feeling something else, the mere fact that someone's desires appear to be uncontrollable is no sure sign that they are.[31] What is more, those who struggle with addiction often in fact do control their desires when the context demands it. All we need to observe to convince ourselves of that fact are the multitude of nondrinking alcoholics awaiting a DUI trial. Finally, as for the fourth reason Foddy says one might give for saying that addictive behavior is compelled, we have already considered it above: the fact that addiction can be correlated with changes in the brain in no way proves that addictive behavior is compelled. In fact, this is precisely what is at issue in the debate between defenders of the disease model and those who uphold a choice model.

Source of the conflict

The problems and puzzles we have run into in attempting to define addiction all seem to derive from presuming some version of either a dualistic or a reductionistic metaphysics. On the one hand, if mind is a separate thing from body (dualism), then there would seemingly be no constraints on human freedom. What, after all, could constrain our freedom, other than thoughts, if the mind is not subject to physical laws? The fact that neural correlates of certain mental processes have been or may be discovered, as several contemporary philosophers have argued, does not mean that these neural processes are *identical* with the mind, or that they *determine* the mind. In fact, such determinism would be impossible on a dualist conception of reality. As René Descartes would have it, given the distinction between mind and body, judgments are mental processes and not physical ones, so addictive behaviors would have to be the result of choice, unless people are to be thought of as zombies, driven by mindless physical appetites, but they are not. For those who accept any version of dualism, humans are minded beings who make judgments and choices. Those who accept the choice model seem to be committed to something like this. The level at which addictive behaviors should be judged, given this kind of view, is the psychological, with the possible exception of those who think of addiction as a "disease of the spirit." In that (quite popular) case, more is involved in addiction than just psychological categories and consistently poor choices, but whatever is involved, it is something beyond physical determination. In this case, as well as in the cases of other choice models, the proper manner of address and treatment of addictive difficulties is through the addict's character, his motivations, his beliefs, and his psychological attitudes.

If, on the other hand, actions, ideas, beliefs, and emotions just are, or are causally determined by, constantly oscillating neurons shooting neurotransmitters at one another in a perpetual electric storm, then we have a very different story to tell. Everything, human and otherwise, this account suggests, is just part of the causal matrix that constitutes the natural world. Numerous philosophers and neuroscientists have reached this conclusion on the grounds that humans are not free, for example, in ethical matters, but merely enjoy (or suffer from) an illusion of free will.[32] Taking this approach, and simply leaving the story of addiction at the level of neurotransmitters and reward circuits, though, would, at its extreme, leave humans in the unenviable position of being something akin to confused zombies (that is, zombies under the illusion that they aren't). Addicts on this account would be helpless to do anything about their problem, because not only are they compelled by the brain changes that define their addiction; what is more, even the causes of any desire they might have to avoid indulgence would be determined by physical processes over which they have no control. This view, in other words, taken to its logical conclusion, requires that we just give up the idea that mentality is something real, with causal powers and other characteristics of its own. On this view, there is no role for the psychological per se, because psychological categories can always be reduced to physical ones.

Rather than either of these alternatives, I argue throughout this book that the body and the mind of the human being comprise one organic whole, and that even though "parts" of the person may seem to be in conflict with one another, particularly in addiction, the same can be said about the mind itself. The story that addicts have to tell is often one of deep conflict, but the conflict is between competing impulses in the whole being. It is not a conflict that can be helpfully resolved through accepting dualism. Neither will it be resolved, however, by trying to explain the phenomenal aspects of this specifically human experience through looking deeper and deeper into the "parts" of the organism. It is not the case that some ultimately precise understanding of the neurons, synapses, and neurotransmitters, or the molecules from which they are constituted, will finally tell us how addiction is born, or how it might go away. The relations between these elements are just as important as the elements themselves. Systems do not merely consist of sets of parts. In fact, the very language of parts and wholes ("mereology"), as we will see, fundamentally misdirects our thinking and thereby underlies at least some of the difficulties that consistently come up in attempting to help those suffering from addiction issues.

As philosophers James Ladyman and Don Ross have put it, the attempt to "domesticate" our conception of the ultimate nature of reality, conceiving it in terms of "homely images of little particles," is a forlorn project. [33] There just are, they say, "no little things and no microbangings."[34] Even more to the point, according to a naturalized metaphysics, that is, one that comes from and answers to science: "it is no longer helpful to conceive of either the world, or particular systems of the world that we study in partial isolation, as 'made of' anything at all."[35] The "things" we see and use every day are no more and no less real than the smaller parts that we use to describe them. But those smaller parts, which can themselves be understood in terms of even smaller parts, are no more fundamental than the things that they constitute. None of the parts is more fundamental than any of the others. In contrast to the typical conception of physical things as substances of either one or two (or more) kinds of "stuff," in this metaphysics, all entities are ultimately constituted of moving relations.

Humans, like all organisms, belong to an even more particularly specifiable type of system. Like stock markets and rain forests, humans are complex, dynamic, open systems, constituted of interconnected, interdependent agents that are in constant interaction with each other and their environments, adjusting to changes as they make changes to the world around them. These systems are marked by a number of characteristics. For one, they behave chaotically, so that small changes to inputs can make dramatic changes later in the whole system. Because of this, unlikely events, such as mass extinctions or market crashes, are not all that unlikely; they occur much more often than would be predicted by a normal bell curve. In an addicted person, small changes can have surprisingly large changes in a person's entire orientation toward her substance or activity of preference. Further, systems of this kind don't just act automatically, since their elements are not fixed, but rather are adaptive. They are constituted of entities that change their strategies as they accumulate experience, making these systems truly dynamic.[36] Finally, systems of this kind exhibit continually developing diversity and specialization in emergent hierarchies of organization. To understand the true nature of addiction, and to ameliorate the problems caused by it, we will have to completely reconceive of the nature of human beings and our relation to the world around us. We will have to purge ourselves of the prejudices that come with presumptions of mereology, reductionism, and linear causation, in favor of a conception of reality that allows for the real existence of many emergent levels of "things," each possessing its own types of behaviors, properties, and relations. Critically, the framework of our thought must be shifted from stuff to "goings-on."

A different way to think

Addiction on the current account is neither a set of choices nor a disease nor a psychological or social entity of any sort, although it concerns biological, psychological, and social systems alike. Addiction, rather, is a more or less stable *process* that both constrains and is constrained by the larger and smaller processes that constitute and constrain certain human lives. To begin to understand this, it is important to note that neither humans nor any other organisms are composed of parts, properly so called. The organs that we identify in human or other organic bodies wouldn't be those organs outside of the systems in which they are involved, and the cells that constitute those organs (and the molecules that constitute those cells) are both synthesized by and create the organisms and the lives to which they contribute. That is, the tissues and organs that we identify functionally in organisms are intrinsically tied to the organism from which they develop and to which they contribute. They are not independent things that together make up the living thing, in the way that parts of a mechanism are first manufactured and then put together to make the machine. And it's not even that the organism exists first, and then the organism "tells" cells which kinds of organs to form, as in so-called top-down causation. This can't be the case, because the organism doesn't exist until the cells that constitute it have developed, so there is no "top" to cause the smaller units to do anything until it has formed. For that reason, the term "self-organizing," often used with respect to such systems (and for other, inorganic ones, such as whirlpools and cyclones), is to some degree misleading. While certainly it is true that nothing *else* organizes such systems, the term suggests that there is a "self" that does the organizing. This, we have just said, is not the case. "In fact," as anthropologist Terrance Deacon says, "the coherent features by which the global wholeness of the system is identified are emergent consequences, not its prior cause."[37] That is, the organism that is the whole (the "self," or the "top" of which we are speaking) can't be the controller of the system, because it is itself emergent from that system.

Even with ordinary inanimate objects, according to the best that current science can tell us, there are no ultimate parts; rather, there are only processes.[38] As was suggested above, Ladyman and Ross hold that, contrary to standard views, "[p]recisely what physics has taught us is that matter in the sense of extended stuff is an emergent phenomenon that has no counterpart in fundamental ontology."[39] In every case, macrosized objects emerge from molecules in motion. These molecules themselves consist of atomic-level (and lower) processes, with the "whole," or higher-level processes, interacting with other processes in the environment, until the point when the object's processes disintegrate. It doesn't matter whether we're talking about mountains, skateboards, or solar systems. All physical things not only can be understood as processes but moreover *are* so understood by those at the forefront of our science. This idea is not new. In fact, one could say that it is as old as the ancient Greek philosopher Heraclitus, who said, in opposition to his Ionian contemporaries, that "it is impossible for a man to step into the same river twice." But the idea that processes are ultimate is one that human beings resist intuitively, and with good reason: things around us *seem* to be stable, substantive, and persisting. Thus, the process view of reality has been resisted philosophically at least since Aristotle asserted, contrary to Heraclitus, that all material objects consist of qualities inhering in a substrate. And the process view has been resisted in the modern world since Descartes unequivocally distinguished thinking substance from material substance. It is just easier, personally and scientifically, for us to think of the objects around us (and, by analogy, of the microentities of which they are constituted) as *things*. After all, that is what experience teaches us as children, and that is the level at which we usually interact with things. However, it is also easier for us to think that the sun rises and sets than it is to think that the earth rotates, but that doesn't make it true.

Even if it is true that all things are ultimately processes, the question remains why this fact could possibly help provide a fuller understanding of addiction, a phenomenon that clearly occurs at the macrolevel. One response is that if addiction is a process, then it is a temporal phenomenon, emerging and disappearing as conditions warrant, and not a permanent, or even semipermanent characteristic of a human being, part of her "character" or "nature." One *is* not an addict, despite the fact that people often speak in that way. We are human beings, which, as Deacon and cognitive scientist/philosopher Mark Bickhard, among numerous others, argue in accord with the present view, means that we are complex dynamic systems, more or less stable patterns of activity, constrained by and constraining other patterns. Emergent from complex systems of this type are psychological states, tendencies, and behaviors. In people with addictive problems, we find a *pattern* of internal and external interactions, a dynamic pattern, sometimes more and sometimes less stable, depending on conditions in the lower-level patterns from which the higher-level ones emerge, and dependent as well on the social conditions into which it emerges. By "stable" I mean not healthy and fine of mind, but rather entrenched, deeply habituated, statistically relatively unlikely to change.

The patterns that constitute both human beings and their addictions seem to be constrained, or kept from undergoing certain changes, from both below and above. For instance, as we will see in Chapter 3, the conditions necessary for developing an addictive pattern seem to run in families, with some part of that being attributable to genes, and some part to the environment shared with parents, but those patterns themselves are emergent from lower-level ones and dependent upon higher-level ones. Inherited properties are not all about genetics, and genetics is not deterministic. The influence that genes have on addiction is a function of any number of concurrently existing (or missing) epigenetic factors, and so destabilizing addictive patterns of behavior is from this perspective perfectly possible. Further up the macrolevel scale, we will see that in some cases the environment counters the tendency to develop an addictive pattern, because it affords no opportunity to use addictive substances, or even just because there is simply strong social discouragement against indulging in them. Given this mutuality of causal connections, language of directionality is misleading, and ultimately, incorrect. Nevertheless, in an effort to be consistent with common discourse, we might reasonably say that addictive patterns of action are shaped both from the "top down" and from the "bottom up."

But, one might ask, how could patterns possibly constrain patterns? It isn't the *patterns* that constrain other patterns, we're inclined to think, but what the patterns are *made of* – that is, our tendency toward substance thinking suggests that patterns couldn't themselves cause anything, or prevent anything (another type of causation), because patterns are only abstractions. Surely it is the things that are arranged into patterns that count. Quite the contrary is true, however, as the history of science shows. Mark Bickhard reminds us of example after example of Cartesian substance metaphysics being replaced with process models, as when the phlogiston theory, according to which a fire-like substance was released in processes such as burning and rusting (explaining why the things burning or rusting became lighter) was replaced with the oxidation theory. Similarly, with respect to heat, the caloric theory, according to which the presence or absence of a substance (caloric) was said to account for something's temperature, was ultimately replaced with the molecular motion analysis. What is more, those who are versed in quantum physics tell us that there are no ultimate particles, but only processes of quantum fields, in which what are more easily described for purely heuristic reasons as particles are instead actually "excitations" of parts of a quantum field. Again, we *think* in terms of particles, but that doesn't mean that they actually exist as we think of them, even within the theories of which they are constitutive. In all these cases, it is patterns of interactions rather than substantial things that ultimately came to be understood as comprising the events and objects around us, and the things that we call causes.[40]

It seems, then, that patterns of organization can and do have causal efficacy. As Deacon puts it, "[b]ecause there are no material entities that are not also processes, and because processes are defined by their organization, we must acknowledge the possibility that organization itself is a fundamental determinant of causation."[41] On this view, at least in one sense, the reductionistic physicalists are absolutely right: nothing is left out once we describe every bit of matter in a system, since what is left out is not a thing at all. What remain once material substances are rejected are the patterns of organization... and the constraints that those patterns create for others, at higher and lower levels of organization. Interestingly, it is precisely because of this structure that process ontology can't be defended empirically: there is nothing one could observe that could prove such an ontology to be the right one. Everything that can be observed is just the stuff that we ordinarily think is there. What is at issue in this case is whether the patterns themselves actually count as entities in themselves, exhibiting causal powers attributable to their own level of specificity. The patterns do count, and they have been overlooked for far too long, in favor of a mistaken emphasis on the things that are involved in patterns and that are caused by them. Substance metaphysics is unwarranted not because it has been proven false, which would be impossible, but because its implications for trying to do certain kinds of science make it untenable. Any assumption that renders impossible what we are already in fact doing successfully, can be taken as false. As we have seen, the assumption that substances underlie all properties and relations has had unacceptable consequences in a variety of areas of scientific study. The reasonable conclusion is not that we should keep the phlogiston hypothesis, for example, and continue to try to make sense of the fact that metals become denser when fired in light of that hypothesis. Rather, the reasonable conclusion is that we should abandon the ontology that includes phlogiston in favor of one that supposes the process of oxidation as its start. Mutatis mutandis, we should not continue to try to make sense of such things as mind/body relations in light of substance metaphysics; rather, we should abandon that ontology in favor of the more functional process metaphysics.

Why care about metaphysics?

As unlikely as it might seem to someone who doesn't normally think in philosophical terms, the ontology that one adopts turns out to be relevant to thinking about addiction. One reason that might be cited in favor of accepting process ontology, as we have said, is that understanding both humans and their addictions as processes, rather than as things, emphasizes their temporal nature. Humans are not in general addicted throughout their lives. Babies, if born addicted, are treated in their earliest days so that they are not addicted in the years to come (although having experienced the pattern could be a factor strengthening the probability that they will experience addiction again). Most people, happily, are not addicted at all in their earliest years. In fact, most people who develop addictive patterns experience this shift in their teens and twenties, and, on behavioral notions of addiction at least, there is significant research to show that most people do not remain addicted late into adulthood, even without treatment or groups.[42] Again, of those who enter treatment, many people recover from addiction, and live without that pattern in their lives for the remainder of their lives. Thinking of addiction in terms of processes allows us to think more freely about the possibility of disrupting it. One way that it does this is by allowing the addict to think of herself as an ever-changing being, with many open-ended possibilities. Particularly when we think of people in terms of complex systems, wherein small changes in one part of the system can result in large changes elsewhere, the process model is particularly hopeful.

The main value of a process ontology for this and other types of analyses, however, is that it allows for a consistent conception of the phenomenon of emergence, and hence for a way to conceive of mind as neither distinct from, nor as reducible to, but as on a continuum with body – one set of patterns essentially upheld by and integrated with others, operating in mutual causal loops. This shift in conception is vital to our having a proper understanding of the nature of organisms, and minded human organisms in particular, but most particularly for our purposes, it is important for our understanding the specific character of addicted humans. Organisms are natural beings, but they are not the same as nonliving natural beings, even when the latter are involved in complex dynamic systems. Organisms bring about an increase in order, or a decrease in entropy, as they self-maintain and develop, whereas it is the natural tendency of their nonliving molecular components to move toward a decrease in order, or an increase in entropy. The peculiar properties characteristic of living beings, as Deacon demonstrates in a meticulously worked-out model, are emergent from properties of nonliving beings.[43] That this must be so is clear from the fact that the first lifelike process "was not reproduced, it had no parent, and therefore it did not evolve. It emerged."[44] And mind similarly emerged out of organisms interacting with their environments. The mental and physical patterns particular to addiction are also processes that emerge in minded organisms when the conditions are just so.

As important as it is for properly understanding life itself, and, as we will see, value and even mind, the concept of emergence is not currently generally accepted in either philosophy or psychology, although in the physical sciences it is held in higher favor. In philosophy, the theory of emergence has a long and mottled history. In order to explain and defend the perspective of this book, which depends centrally on this concept, it will be necessary to see how emergence, as it is understood here, is distinct from the version that quite rightly fell out of favor. So what do we mean by "emergence"? Nothing mysterious, nothing inexplicable in terms of purely physical laws. In general, we shall begin by saying that the concept of emergence used here refers to a property or entity that exists as a function of two or more things that are themselves of a different character from the whole. Philosopher J. S. Mill defended this notion as long ago as 1843, although it was his student George Henry Lewes who coined the term "emergence." According to Mill, the principle of the Composition of Causes (causes that work together to create an outcome – such as bits of metal of a particular weight coming together to make a slab of metal whose weight is the sum of the bits) is sometimes contravened. This is the case, for example, in chemical reactions. Mill says that "[t]he chemical combination of two substances produces, as is well known, a third substance with properties different from those of either of the two substances separately, or of both of them taken together."[45] Consider for example, NaCl, or table salt. Sodium, a metal, and chlorine, a dangerous poison, when bonded together make one of the most widely used food seasonings. But nothing that one can say about the components, either taken separately or together, could explain this result. Numerous philosophers following Mill defended emergentism, including C. D. Broad, who argued for the emergence, or irreducibility, in the case of the mind.[46]

Many difficulties led to emergentism's falling into disrepute by the middle of the 20th century. Some of the main problems are evident, upon reflection. First was the challenge from the logical positivists, that emergentism is an explanatorily bankrupt mystery theory, similar to vitalism, the explanatorily empty belief that the reason that organisms live is that they are imbued with a "life force," an "élan vital."[47] The problem according to this challenge is that allegedly emergent properties are meaningless, in that they fail to answer the scientific question of *how* is it that two things, each with properties of their own, can together become a different thing with new and different properties. To say that the novel properties emerge (or that a new entity emerges) is on this view to say nothing more than that the object has the property (or that the entity exists) because it has the property (exists). If, for instance, sodium and chlorine are entities with their own intrinsic properties, then they are what they are, and whatever results from them must be traceable to those properties. If the theory of emergence is true, however, then something new, with new properties, emerges when the two elements are bonded together in a certain way, and those properties operate according to a set of principles that are not the ones that describe the behaviors of either of the constituents. But according to the "empty explanation" criticism, to say that these new properties emerge, and are not explicable in terms of those characterizing the original two substances, is simply to say that it is a brute fact that the new properties exist.

What is more, philosopher Jaegwon Kim argued that explanations in terms of emergence as so far described are subject to two further powerful criticisms[48]: first, if emergent entities and properties are dependent upon microlevel entities and properties, and if they are at the same time supposed to cause changes in the microlevel entities, then the concept of emergence would seem to involve a vicious kind of circularity. One class of things causes another class of things, which things in turn exert causal influence on the things that caused them. Second, emergent entities and their properties would seem to be causally redundant, for since they result from the microentities on which they rely, any causal efficacy that they exhibit can actually be traced down to those microlevel entities. So, if emergent entities and properties can be causes, it is only because of the lower-level entities and properties to which they can be traced. But in that case, only the lower-level things can be counted as real. As Kim notes, one way that the above problems can be avoided is to employ emergent properties conceptually, as levels of (mere) description that might be useful for gaining insight into various aspects of phenomena in which we are interested, but not to accept them as real. If emergent properties aren't taken to be real, with causal efficacy of their own, then the paradoxes and puzzles disappear. Unfortunately, however, so do the explanations that we seek.

Another way to avoid the flaws of traditional emergence theory, and the way that will be defended here, is to deny the foundational assumption of a substance-based world in favor of a process-based one. In particular, the kinds of processes with which we are concerned here are those that organize around maintaining far-from-equilibrium systems, that is, those that operate contrary to the general tendency toward increasing entropy. A simple example of a self-maintaining system is a candle flame:

> A candle flame maintains above combustion threshold temperature; it melts wax so that it percolates up the wick; it vaporizes wax in the wick into fuel; in standard atmospheric and gravitational conditions, it induces convection, which brings in fresh oxygen and gets rid of waste.[49]

This kind of process is, of course, dependent upon lower-level processes (molecules of oxygen and wax, for instance, in addition to higher-level processes such as combustion and convection). Life is another, much more complex instance of self-maintenance, emerging from nonliving processes. Organisms are constantly engaged in processes of organizing. They incessantly generate new "appropriately structured and appropriately fitted molecular structures," employing energy and materials from the outside to fuel their internal processes. These self-maintaining systems are thus essentially dynamic, persistently and successfully pressing back against "the ubiquitous, relentless, incessantly degrading tendency of the second law of thermodynamics."[50] And not only do individual organisms reverse entropy by maintaining themselves but they also reproduce themselves by replicating both the patterns that constitute them and the materials subserving those patterns. What is more, organisms decrease entropy globally through evolution by adapting to their environment, coordinating with the other elements in their ecosystems. Increasing complexity and increasing order is the natural dynamic of these systems, the pervasive exception to the second law of thermodynamics.

Seeing things this way requires a flip in what we see as the foreground and what we see as the background. In traditional substance metaphysics, things take the foreground, and their relations make up the background. This fundamental reversal of the direction of natural processes is a defining characteristic of emergent transitions. Such transitions arise naturally from two or more ordinary processes undoing each other's efforts, with each process constraining the other in a way that has the overall effect of causing a wholly new pattern to emerge.[51] This new dynamic pattern, constrained by the ordinary, entropy-producing patterns from which it emerges, as we have said, decreases entropy, as it utilizes its environment and changes to be able to use it even more effectively. With this emergence of a self-maintaining pattern comes the emergence of function, for the asymmetry of an organism's relations to other things in its environment extends to the internal processes contributing to that maintenance as well. An activity or process can only be a function in the context of a goal, just as relative value can only exist in the context of an aim. Contributing to the self-maintenance of a far-from-equilibrium system that would not continue to exist without self-maintenance activities is the essence of a function.

What is more, self-maintaining processes, particularly those that are also self-organizing, such as living processes, define a distinction between "self" and "not self." Some processes are essential to the self-maintenance, and others are not. Those that are essential to the processes of self-maintenance will count as "parts" of the "self," even if the self that we are talking about is no more than a "persistent and distinctive locus of dynamical organization that maintains self-similarity across time and changing conditions."[52] That is, even if the self isn't actually an entity, but more like an abstraction, there will nevertheless be a locus around which a dynamical pattern maintains something analogous to an identity over time and in an environment. And even without an identity in the strict sense, a dynamical system distinguishes between external things that contribute to the system's continued existence ("good") and those that threaten that existence ("bad"). The functioning of the system's own subprocesses, as well, can either contribute to (functioning "well") or detract from (functioning "badly") the system's continued self-similarity. Thus normative properties (value), including function, emerge naturally from nonnormative ones, according to this process-based view of emergence, but *only relative to the system(s) in question*. These are not objective properties in the world, but neither are they reducible to the subserving ordinary processes that obey the general principle of entropy. When lower-level processes are related in such a way that individual self-undermining processes counter one another, the system as a whole moves toward increased development and stability, and establishes relationships of value with respect to other processes

"Normative function," says Bickhard, "is just the bottom of a long hierarchy of normative emergences. All of mind and mental and social phenomena are fundamentally normative, and they all emerge in a hierarchy with biological functional normativity at its base."[53] Like function and value, mind on this kind of process ontology emerges from the asymmetries inherent in biological processes. Mind is not, however, directly reducible to biological organization or function, any more than value and function are reducible to the components of the systems to which those properties relate. The reason, in fact, that we have had such a hard time philosophically accounting for the existence of mind is that "we have stubbornly insisted on looking for it where it could not be, in the stuff of the world."[54] To see how mind relates to body, we need to look to what is *not* there; we need to look not to *stuff*, but to constraints created by opposing patterns of action.

Philosophers and cognitive scientists attempt to map living dynamics and cognitive processes directly to simpler physical processes, and thus to try to reduce the mental to mechanistic processes occurring between unchanging substances with no structure.[55] They try to trace one kind of phenomenon to a categorically different kind. It is no wonder that the "explanatory gap" is such a puzzle! Ordinary processes do not mechanically produce mental activity in any direct or additive manner, and if you try to understand the relation in that way, you will inevitably come face-to-face with a chasm. Microscopic work is necessary for macroscopic phenomena, but it is not sufficient. Mental processes arise, as do organisms themselves, from self-maintaining systems adjusting to changing conditions in the environment, and the mental processes that emerge in this way are patterns of activity irreducible to their constituents. Mentality is thus naturally describable as intentional, a set of higher-order processes involving the further processes of information reception, preparation for action, and many, many others, at various levels of organization. There is no limit, in principle, to the orders of organization that can emerge from the same basic system.

Here is where we return to addiction. Addictive mental dispositions to repeat behaviors, to find salience in particular objects and activities, and to undergo particular types of psychological experiences are simply higher orders of organization in complex dynamic systems based completely in natural processes. Addiction involves complex patterns of interaction from the molecular to the cellular to the systemic, from the organismic to the environmental. It involves physiological, psychological, and higher and lower orders of complexity. It even includes the social and the abstract. Addiction is an irreducible reality.

Once we move away from trying to understand its features as either the chemical-electrical functioning of neurons or as the intentional, experiential phenomena that only those who are addicted can know, we can escape both from radical reductionism and from brute, inexplicable dualism. "Mental states don't exist, any more than do flame states," says Bickhard, rather provocatively. His point is that neither mental states nor flame states are *things*; they don't have that sort of ontological status. Rather, they are both processes,[56] emergent from other processes and interacting with other processes to produce yet more encompassing processes. None of these are separable from the others, so "top-down" and "bottom-up" characterizations of change are the result of fundamentally wrong thinking. Every process serves as a constraint, or limitation on possibilities, on those with which it interacts. Thinking of mental states or biological states as *states* drives misconceptions all the way down the line, creating profound implications for how we understand addiction.

As we shall see, understanding human mental and physical life in terms of emergent patterns, rather than in the terms of either the dualist or the radical reductionist, will provide us with a different conception of addiction than has yet been available. This alternative to the false dichotomy so far presented to us will allow us to appreciate contributions from neuroanatomy and neurophysiology, as well as from biochemistry and psychology. In addition, there is room for contributions from genetics and sociology and cultural anthropology. Addiction is a multifaceted process emerging from both lower-scale and higher-scale interacting dynamic patterns, open ended and at most only relatively stable. Each of these levels of organization that contribute to addictive patterns in organisms, from the molecular to the cellular to the mental to the social, is a real system, with real causal powers of its own. Analyzing addiction in terms of each of these levels and their interactions will help us see how it is brought about by genetic and epigenetic influences, by attachment failures and traumas, by terrible mommies and driven, stressed-out societies. And it will provide us with a path forward for addressing this phenomenon without either reducing people to impotent chemical systems or thrusting on them blame for choices that lead to failed lives and social disarray.

3
Addiction and the Individual

Alcohol addiction has been referred to in print as a disease since the end of the 18th century.[1] By 1956, the American Medical Association (AMA) had endorsed the disease model, and the view has since received public and unequivocal endorsement by numerous influential medical organizations, including the World Health Organization.[2] Researchers commonly use a variety of methodologies that rely on the disease model to attempt to understand various aspects of addiction, and several methods that have been used to study addiction suggest that the disease model is a good one. For instance, twin studies and adoption studies have provided evidence that genetics plays some role in addiction. Moreover, molecular biology explains certain phenomena that occur in the brain with repeated exposure to addictive drugs. These findings seem to make sense of the compulsive element that is associated with many cases of addiction, at the very least suggesting that something other than simple choice is involved. Nevertheless, much care must be taken to situate the cart relative to the horse in this research, and to disentangle the many and diverse threads of addiction research, if we are to evaluate the contention that addiction is a disease.

Psychological accounts of the disease

Because of psychology's developmental path as a discipline, at least two fundamentally different paradigms have come to guide addiction research. One conceives of addiction in "folk psychological" terms, using such words as "craving" and "anxiety," while the other describes it in terms of neurobiology. Despite their completely different orientations, the two conceptual frameworks are used simultaneously by many researchers, as they endeavor to offer explanations of the psychological experience of addiction in neurobiological terms. Others seek interventions in terms of talking therapies for certain behaviors and biological symptoms. Mental structures and functions, though, are clearly not physiological structures and functions. The two sets of categories do not even overlap, and it is not clear how these two paradigms are supposed to relate. Some psychologists say that psychological experiences are "mediated" by neural activity, while others say that the neural activity provides a "substrate" or "subserves" psychological experiences. These are vague phrases that point to something that is wanted, but they do not explain anything. What it seems to come to, though, is that due to their differences in approach and research methods, some scientists assume that addiction is a physiological phenomenon, and that any psychological descriptions of it ultimately reduce to physical ones. Others see the psychological categories as fundamental, and want to preserve the independence and causal efficacy of those structures and functions. We will see as this discussion progresses that the emergent model of life, mind, and social groups that we discussed in Chapter 1 are helpful in reconciling these two elements of the disease model, without either having to reduce one to the other or being forced to assert yet another kind of dualism.

To begin at the most obvious place, let us consider that the "disease" of addiction is defined for clinical purposes in psychological terms. According to what has become a fairly standard formulation among disease model theorists,

> [d]rug addiction is a chronically relapsing disorder that has been characterized by (1) compulsion to seek and take the drug, (2) loss of control in limiting intake, and (3) emergence of a negative emotional state (e.g., dysphoria, anxiety, irritability) reflecting a motivational withdrawal syndrome when access to the drug is prevented.[3]

Addiction here is characterized by behavioral and emotional symptoms, in terms of feelings and states of mind. More specifically, it is marked by three distinct "stages," according to Nora Volkow, director of the National Institutes for Drug Addiction, and her highly respected coauthor George Koob. These stages, which collectively constitute what has come to be known as the "addictive cycle" include "'binge/intoxication,' 'withdrawal/negative affect,' and 'preoccupation/anticipation' (craving)."[4] These stages follow on one another with increasing regularity, according to the disease model, given chronic exposure to an addictive drug, with increasing intensity, until the addict "loses his ability to control" his actions. The DMS-IV-TR lists four classes of drug as capable of instituting this cycle: psychostimulants (methamphetamine, cocaine), opiates (heroin, morphine, oxycontin), alcohol, and nicotine. Gambling is the only activity currently listed among the addictive disorders, and even that is characterized as an impulse control disorder and not as an addiction per se. It is described, though, in terms nearly identical to those used with substance abuse and dependence, and the list is liable to grow. Shopping, playing video games, and preoccupation with sex are among the activities that are already being spoken of in terms of addiction, or something very close to it.

Hedonic theories

The thing that these substances and at least one activity have in common is that they produce rewarding experiences, and, for some people, much greater rewards than do ordinary pleasures, such as food, exercise, or sex. The notion of being "high" is truly significant here; the reward experienced is above and beyond the experience of reward achievable through those other means. What is more, the length of time that reward is experienced through substances and activities of addiction is far greater than it is for regular, nonaddictive pleasures. That is, the pleasure of sex may be intense, but it does not last long relative to the effects of alcohol, cigarettes, or opium. Given both of these facts, it is not surprising that someone would want to repeat the experience. Hedonic theories of addiction focus their attention on this feature. The pleasure, the elevated mood, the alertness or relaxation is brought about by the addictive substance is immediate, undeniable, and relatively long lasting, regardless of the negative experiences that may occur in conjunction with use. Repetition of the cycle continues, because what happens *in conjunction* with use does not eliminate the emotional associations of the satisfaction that use brings. As Joseph LeDoux discovered, memory is intimately connected with emotion; in fact, his research shows that the emotional element of any given memory seems to be pretty much permanent.[5] When the memory itself is completely forgotten, the emotional associations that our brains create with respect to persons, places, things, and experiences remain intact. Even when the emotion seems to have been extinguished, so that you no longer experience, say, fear in the presence of a snake, it can be resurrected by certain stimuli, such as returning to the place where you saw the snake. An addict may in the most visceral sense continue to make the connection, "do X for a good time," long after she no longer remembers particular experiences of use with pleasure, and even after she no longer remembers the particular feeling that is that experience of the "good time." Emotions are both older and quicker to move us than deliberative reason, hedonic theories emphasize, and so a person who has been stuck in an addictive pattern may well retain automatic positive reactions to a substance of abuse, even when she has been abstinent for a significant amount of time, and reason reminds her that the long-term outcomes of return to use will be wholly negative.

Others have argued that people who become addicted may start to indulge in the drug or activity because of the pleasure reward, but they continue to seek out and imbibe their preferred substance or activity because cessation results in painful withdrawal. On this theory, it is the contrast of pleasure that explains addictive behavior. The very same motivational system that allows highly or unexpectedly[6] positive experiences to condition the addict to seek repetition of a behavior can also operate to create an aversive response to the significant displeasure that occurs when the drug (or the "rush" from gambling) has left the system.[7] On this view, it is avoidance of the pain of withdrawal that motivates the addict. From the hedonic perspective, either the pleasure itself or the pleasure/pain opposition is what explains continued use of addictive substances and activities, as well as the return to them even after abstinence has been achieved.

Incentive sensitization

In many studies, subjective states of pleasure and persistence in drug taking have not been found to be highly correlated.[8] After repeated exposure to a drug, some people continue to "want," or be preoccupied with, a drug even when they no longer even "like" its effects.[9] This persistence of "wanting," or sensitization, to a drug is a significant component of the phenomenon of addiction, and one of the main factors that distinguishes it from drug dependence. Because of associative learning that takes place, long after exposure to the drug has ceased, an addicted individual can remain sensitized to cues relating to drugs and activities of addiction, as well as to the drug or activity itself. As a result, upon being exposed to images, places, or people associated with the drug of choice, not to mention the drug itself, the individual is strongly motivated to return to drug seeking and use. Only in some cases do addicts additionally display an ongoing positive attitude toward their substance or activity of choice. [10] Often, in the face of directly suffering its harms, addicts will have a consciously negative attitude toward the object of their addiction, but that doesn't stop the craving for it or the seeking it out. As with an unresolved "sensitive issue" between two people, once it has developed, it is difficult for any discussion or activities touching on that issue not to arouse those sensitive feelings again, and it is difficult to avoid thinking about it when anything reminds one of it. Because one of the things that dopamine does is motivate seeking generally, when this system becomes sensitized, anything that reminds an individual of the object of his addiction, whether it be feeling a particular way, or images of drugs or paraphernalia, or people or places associated with drug use or gambling, the response of seeking and use is thrown into operation. This happens even without any conscious consideration of a reward or aversive association being involved.[11] And because of the kind of automaticity that's involved, once action in the direction of use is launched, it is generally followed through to completion.[12]

What goes on in the brain for the most part, including the associative and emotional learning that drives our motivation,[13] operates largely behind the scenes. For this reason, what certain objects or activities signify to us or evoke in us is often not consciously recognized. Not just addicts but all of us can consciously and "officially" tell ourselves stories about what we're doing and what we believe and what we plan to do, while those stories may have little to do with what our biases or sensitivities actually are, and little or nothing to do with how we are likely to act. This shouldn't be surprising – most things that we do throughout the day are done more or less nonconsciously, from going through the routines associated with showering and dressing, to driving familiar routes, to clicking through the Internet news. Given this, it seems obvious how it can happen that an addict who can resist cravings and all sorts of obstacles as long as sobriety remains in the forefront of his mind, can surprise himself, and find himself smoking or stoned, or just craving doing so, upon being presented with an associated object, person, or place.

Habit

Some research has suggested, based on such observations, that the common phenomenon of habituation, with its attendant automaticity, could explain the phenomenon of relapse into addictive behaviors.[14] This explanation does not do as much work as the motivation salience sensitivity approach does, however, because most habits are not experienced in terms of "triggers" that seem to drive people into behaviors. While entering the freeway might, if I'm not paying attention, result in my arriving at my university rather than at the dentist's office, just the mere sight of the freeway does not set off a perseveration with respect to the university. Habits can generally be recognized and broken with a facility that seems contrary to the compulsivity that many believe to be characteristic of addiction. What is more, although habituation surely is a component of addiction, using it to explain the "loss of control" characteristic of addiction would not be consistent with the disease model that gives rise to the definition we are considering. We do not generally see habits as medical ailments for which insurance should pay to treat us.

Several different psychological accounts have thus been offered for explaining why addicts exhibit the behaviors that they do and experience the feelings that they describe. In attempting to determine which of these accounts provides the best explanation, psychologists began, as technology made it possible, to try and identify the physical processes that occur in addiction, and to use this knowledge to confirm some of these accounts and to develop others. In this way, the disease model became entrenched as the received view of addiction among the scientists who study it. If addiction is the result of observable biological factors, goes the reasoning, it cannot be a function simply of poor choices.

Neuropsychological accounts

The hedonic, habituation, and salience sensitization models of addiction, we should note, tell us nothing of why the addictive cycle ever starts or how it works. Specialists in the biological side of psychology have attempted to provide an answer to the second question. Through experimentation with animal models and through use of imaging techniques to study the human brain, scientists researching the physical aspect of addiction have developed theories of what happens at the molecular, neural, and neural systems levels when someone is addicted. It is said by many psychologists, as was mentioned above, that the psychological characteristics of addiction are "mediated" through the neurological systems described in these models. Thus, we find in biological psychology, correlative theories for each of the hedonic, salience sensitivity, and habitual accounts that we saw above.

In order to understand these theories, we first have to have a general picture of how the brain works and how drugs affect the brain. The brain is a vastly complex, dynamic system comprised of many different kinds of cells, the roles and importance of which are just beginning to be appreciated. The cells that are most relevant to this discussion are neurons, those vastly numerous (perhaps as many as 100 billion in a human brain) and complex cells whose communication with one another regulates everything that happens in the body and processes all of our experiences. Neurons are electrochemically charged cells that communicate with one another through chemical signaling. They receive inputs from receptors located on their many dendrites, or spikey extensions, and send outputs to other neurons through their axons. Once they receive sufficient excitatory inputs and reach a critical threshold of excitation, they "fire," or generate an action potential. The outputs of these firings are neurotransmitters, chemicals that in turn bind with receptors on the adjacent neuron, contributing either an excitatory or an inhibitory influence to that neuron. Neurons are vastly complex and dynamic in their own right, and are differentiated in millions of ways, as are the spaces between them, the synapses. Neurons release their specific neurotransmitters into these synapses, where they either bind onto the cell on the other side of the synapse or are reabsorbed into the releasing cell. These hundred billion neurons all fire in their own patterns, or oscillations, and in connection with other neurons, in incessantly shifting patterns that are constrained by interactions with larger patterns of this continuous electric activity. Not only new inputs, such as sensory perceptions and drugs delivered to the brain, but every single experience that we have, whether internal or external, changes the brain, because whatever it is, whether a calculation, a stomach churn, or the most fleeting emotion or thought, it involves the electrical discharge of neurons and all the complex changes that that entails.

Next, it is important to note that a neuron's firing does not influence the neuron across the synapse on just one occasion; rather, when a neuron's firing stimulates another to fire, it also causes a long-term potentiation (LTP), a disposition for those two neurons to be synchronized. This tendency of neurons to become sensitized to the firings of others with which they have connections is part of the mechanism thought to make learning and memory possible; it is what is meant by the commonly used phrase "neurons that fire together, wire together." This kind of synaptic strength adjustment is at the foundation of brain plasticity, a phenomenon that has become central in neuroscience research over the past two decades. Plasticity is important in the disease model of addiction because much, if not most, of the learning that we do happens unconsciously, particularly certain types of learning, such as associative and procedural learning.[15] Part of what happens in addiction is that people develop habits through synaptic strengthening, as well as making strong emotional, conceptual, and active associations to smells, sounds, people, and things associated with their addictions.[16] What is more, past experiences, by the way they shape our brains, shape our expectations (largely in terms of associations), and in turn, those expectations shape our perceptions and responses even more than new inputs do. This is because the networks of neurons in our brains are also *recurrent*. That is, there is feedback communication among neurons as much as there is feed-forward – in fact, inputs of the former kind may be ten times more numerous as those of the latter. This means that repeated similar experiences shape how we understand the world to be organized, and that in turn influences how we perceive new sensory and bodily inputs. In addiction this might mean, for instance, that the addict feels happy and sees a certain street corner as promising and positive in a way that others who have never bought drugs on that corner would. Another example is a smoker trying to kick the habit, who stops at a convenience store and walks out with a pack of cigarettes without ever really thinking about it. These points will all be relevant as we discuss the various ways in which the disease model of addiction has been elaborated on and defended.

Let us return, then, to the DSM-IV-TR's descriptions of substance abuse and dependence disorders. Four major classes of drugs, as we have said, are outlined in the volume: psychostimulants, opiates, alcohol, and nicotine. These drugs, and the four major brain systems on which they are thought to operate in addiction, including the opioid attachment-reward system, the dopamine-based incentive-motivation apparatus, the self-regulation areas of the prefrontal cortex, and the stress-response mechanism, provide the foundation for biological psychology's explanations of what addiction is, how it occurs, and why addicts remain vulnerable to relapse even after lengthy abstinence. The reward/learning network seems to have evolved to process natural rewards, motivating us to seek such things as food and sex, essential for species survival.[17] But just because a system evolved for one thing does not mean that that is the only thing that it can do. Fingertips, for instance, evolved for touch, and much later, they came to be used for reading Braille. Addictive drugs and some activities not only take advantage of the naturally occurring reward/learning systems in the same way that Braille reading does the sensitivity of fingertips but these drugs and activities also engage the relevant systems much more powerfully than do any natural rewards. What's more, use of these drugs can also change the structure and function of these systems.

On the received view, then, addictive drugs and activities take advantage of, or "hijack," the neural circuitry that is normally involved in experiencing pleasure, in learning, and in incentive motivation.[18] According to a vast research literature, reward processing depends on dopamine-using systems in the so-called mesocorticolimbic system. Dopamine is the neurotransmitter associated with feelings of reward or the anticipation of reward when it is found in this particular part of the brain, although it plays other roles in other brain areas. The mesocorticolimbic system is the emotional processing area of the brain, constituted of the prefrontal cortex, the thin sheath that wraps around the outside the cerebrum, together with certain nuclei of neurons that lie beneath the cortex. Specifically, the reward circuit has been shown to include centrally the ventral tegmental area, which projects to the nucleus accumbens, the amygdala, and the prefrontal cortex. Each of the four classes of addictive drugs works in a specific way, but the relevant effect in each case is that it increases synaptic dopamine in this particular system, either directly or indirectly. Since neurotransmitters work something like locks and keys, any given neurotransmitter can only bind with a specific kind of receptor on adjacent neurons, the one that "fits." If no receptor is available, the chemical remains in the synaptic space. Opiates, for instance, operate by mimicking endogenous opiates, or endorphins, locking onto opioid receptors. Psychostimulants, however, block dopamine removal from the synapse by locking onto the dopamine transporters, thereby leaving an overabundance of dopamine in the synaptic cleft. Alcohol works by blocking GABA receptors, preventing this inhibitory neurotransmitter from doing its job of slowing dopamine production, and also onto NMDA glutamate receptors, resulting in the overstimulation of neurons. Nicotine, by contrast, blocks the receptor for acetylcholine, thereby promoting continual firing of the neuron and prolonging the production of dopamine. In all these cases, what ultimately happens with addictive drugs is that they increase dopamine in the emotion-generating areas of the brain, bringing about a powerful sensation of reward, along with influencing the motivation, the valuing, and the choice-processing areas of the brain.

Neuroscience of hedonic theories

So much about the operation of specific neurotransmitters in the brain's reward/learning circuits is generally accepted as conventional wisdom.[19] But exactly what the role of the dopamine system is in the phenomenon of addiction is much less clear. According to hedonic hypotheses, for example, administration of the drug results in highly positive reinforcement, since drugs of addiction (and the excitement of gambling, etc.) result in the production of significantly more dopamine than natural rewards do, for more extended periods. According to Koob and Volkow, administration of addictive drugs increases dopamine levels in the striatum, including the nucleus accumbens area.[20] Increases of dopamine in this area, and particularly when those increases come quickly, are associated with heightened pleasure, euphoria, and so on. According to the "opponent process theory," every overly high dopamine event is attended by an opponent lowering of dopamine, which serves to restore homeostasis.[21] The counterbalancing process, however, because it is slower and lasts longer than the original reward experience, is unpleasant. Ultimately, with chronic exposure, the body adapts to the infusion of excess dopamine by losing some dopamine receptors and making other changes in the neurons in the reward circuit areas.[22] The upshot is that the down-regulation part of the opposition increases over time. As that happens, more of the drug is required to achieve the same level of reward, and the cessation of reward is met with yet further lowered dopamine and serotonin levels.[23] Serotonin is another neurotransmitter associated with mood. Lack of it in certain areas of the brain is associated with depression. Moreover, since the reward system is less sensitive after the down-regulation that comes with persistent drug taking, the pleasurable effect of natural rewards is lowered overall. In psychological terms, as we saw in the section above, on this "opponent processes" or "positive-negative" model, people initially take drugs to achieve pleasure, and then after the brain adapts, transitioning them into addiction, they take drugs to avoid symptoms of withdrawal.

The problem with this kind of theory is that it does not account for the relapse phenomenon, which often occurs after extended periods of abstinence. After such abstinence, the brain will have up-regulated back to its natural condition, and so avoiding withdrawal wouldn't seem to be a motivation for using. Another hypothesis, though, might address this issue. Not only the reward system but motivation and learning pathways as well are co-opted by addictive drugs on the standard view. According to some versions of what might be called the overlearning theory of addiction, the sum total of dopamine available in the critical brain areas isn't the only thing inciting addiction. Because there is a constant feedback loop between expectations and experiences, and because the brain is constantly adjusting in order to deal with its environment, the reward that one experiences is also influenced by one's expectations. Learning depends on prediction, and learning that results in the tendency to approach one's substance or activity of choice approaching behavior depends on reward (although learning that depends on aversive consequences certainly does not). Brain-imaging experiments have shown that when one receives a greater reward than expected, as happens with substances associated with addiction, or when one wins a bet, or nearly wins, more dopamine reaches the target area, the anterior cingulate part of the cortex, in which novelty detection, reward values, and error signaling are processed. When one receives the amount of reward expected, the anterior cingulate remains unchanged, and when one expects a reward and does not get it, or gets less reward than expected, or even just gets it later than expected, less dopamine reaches that area of the cortex.[24] So, the theory goes, since drugs and activities of addiction produce much more dopaminergic activity than do natural rewards, people repeat them until they become automatic. At this point they behave like lab rats: when the stimulus (stress, discomfort, or whatever) is encountered, they hit the reward button.

Neuroscience of habit

Actions that are at one point considered and chosen become overlearned. That is, certain stimuli come to habitually evoke certain responses,[25] such as reaching for your toothbrush evokes the action of reaching for the toothpaste, much more powerfully than anything else can evoke toothpaste reaching. Addiction on this kind of theory is just a strong kind of habituation, since it involves the brain areas involved in all habituation.[26] Since habits are characterized by insensitivity to consequences (they aren't goal directed; rather, they're just what we do given a certain stimulus), some say that habitual learning could account for the transition from conscious choice to automatic action that occurs in drug taking. This definition certainly fits the language sometimes employed with respect to addicts and their "drug habit." However, although these strong implicit memory associations would explain a lab rat's repeatedly pushing a lever to self-administer drugs, it is insufficient to explain human addiction, the service of which, as we have said, often requires significant planning far down the road from actual use.[27] For this reason, it seems that addiction cannot be just a matter of habituated responses, although that element certainly does appear to be present.

Neuroscience of incentive sensitization

The final psychological theory that we considered above, which seemed to offer the best explanation for the aspects of addiction involving perseveration, craving, and relapse in the face of "triggers," was the incentive salience sensitivity hypothesis. This hypothesis focuses on how certain cues come to evoke excessive motivation for drug taking, which we saw earlier referred to as "wanting," as opposed to "liking."[28] Incentive salience sensitivity is a function of the orbitofrontal cortex, according to neuroimaging studies. The orbitofrontal cortex provides internal representations of the salience of external objects and events, assigning each of them a particular value. This is an essential system when operating normally, for it is what allows organisms to choose between different goals. As we said earlier, when a neuron fires, it not only stimulates the firing of neurons to which it is connected but it also creates an LTP for those neurons to fire together as well. With at least some drugs of addiction, LTP in the nucleus accumbens seems to be enhanced, perhaps increasing activity of glutamatergic ("go!") neurons.[29] According to some researchers, then, the fast-working and large increases in the amount of dopamine in this area categorize the drug experience "as one that is highly salient, an experiential outcome that commands attention and promotes arousal, conditioned learning and motivation."[30] It is this incentive sensitization process that is thought to subserve the motivated seeking that we have seen to be characteristic of addiction, while learning systems provide the associations determining what one seeks and how. How prone an individual is to sensitization can be a function of a number of factors, including genes, hormones, past trauma, stress, patterns and amount of drug exposure, and even age, with teens being more susceptible to these changes than adults. We have reason to believe, then, that this kind of change, as well as those associated with pleasure and habit, is very individual, and is a function of far more than the mechanisms that neuroscience alone can describe.

Some caveats concerning research methods and the disease model

All theories have a backstory. The development of the addiction model is no exception. The fact that the AMA spent so much time in the 1980s establishing its position that addiction is a disease had much to do with practical matters, such as getting insurance companies to pay for treatment. That was surely not the AMA's only motivation, but the medicalization of many conditions previously considered to be just normal parts of human life was happening at the time, both extending the medical field's purview and making it more profitable. But there were scientific reasons for the development of the disease model as well. As research techniques improved over the mid- and late 20th century, it became possible to understand much more about how the brain functions, and about how various drugs affect that functioning, and this seemed to offer promise for developing interventions. This is important because some of the studies that we have considered seem to suggest that addiction amounts to a phenomenon that can be seen in the brain, and that can be fixed by changing either the way that particular cells, usually neurons, or subneural structures (such as receptor sites), or certain chemicals, interact. Moreover, the disease model presumes that just a few brain systems are implicated in addictive patterns, so that if sufficient focus is placed on these isolated locales, we will understand addiction and be able to treat it. Much of the evidence for this view is grounded in the imaging techniques that have become so popular in the past couple of decades, and that indeed have created a remarkable ability to see structures and certain functions in the brain in a mercifully noninvasive manner. There are a number of problems with the assumptions of the standard view, however.

First, we must consider the assumption that there is a causal relation, or an identity, between the brain changes that advanced technology now allows researchers to track and the phenomenal experiences that take place as a person becomes addicted. It may very well be true that nicotine blocks GABA cells and so stimulates dopamine cells to keep firing (or prevents them from ceasing to fire), and it may be true that nicotine users experience pleasure at ingesting nicotine. It may further be true that chronic nicotine users as a group show a diminished sensitivity in nicotinic receptors relative to nonnicotine users. And it may be the case that after chronic use, nicotine users experience a diminished sense of pleasure in smoking. The claim, though, that it is the increased dopamine available in the synapse between cells that causes nicotine users to experience pleasure after using, and the attendant claim that they experience a diminished sense of pleasure after some time of chronically using, makes too quick a leap between the neurophysiology and neurochemistry, which are objectively measurable, and the mental phenomenon of pleasure, which is not. The "how" here would need to be shown before we could exchange physical terms for mental terms. This issue, in fact, is behind one of the main questions motivating this book: how should we understand the addict's mind relative to her biology and environment? Figuring out this relationship is at the root of our efforts to resolve the false dichotomy inherent in the dispute over whether addiction is a matter of disease or of choice.

This dichotomy at one level is basically the question of whether the physical markers that have come to define addiction for one set of researchers are *necessarily* connected to those psychological markers that define addiction for another set. That is, neurobiological researchers, using imaging techniques and animal models, have identified physical changes that on average, or in some statistically significant number of cases, accompany symptoms that fit the DSM IV-TR's categories of substance disorders. But do the brain changes characteristic of addiction ever happen without someone's being addicted? And can someone ever be addicted without his or her brain undergoing these changes? Every individual, as we have seen, is a self-organizing system, unique in the macrolevel patterns that it displays, with a unique history of development and unique interaction with its environment. Hard science may provide us with good information that is helpful for understanding addicted individuals' behavior and other symptoms, and about their brains, but we would do well to understand the statistical nature of any claims made – causal or correlative or otherwise – as we consider the conclusions arrived at through this model of addiction.

A second assumption made all too often by neurobiological researchers is that the meaning of the brain-scanning images used in research is self-evident.[31] This assumption is made much more broadly with vastly less information in the lay population. Although an abundance of brain-imaging work has been done on addiction, as well as on a variety of other kinds of functions and changes in the brain, exactly what all of these images actually show requires interpretation. The by now "common knowledge," for instance, that addiction involves, among other things, the "reward circuit" in the brain, as well as memory and learning systems, together with motivation and salience evaluation areas of the brain, as well as the cognitive control areas, is only common given some pretty significant assumptions. Researchers focus on these areas, including the nucleus accumbens and ventral pallidum, the amygdala, hypothalamus and anterior cingulate, and so forth, because this is where imaging studies show the brain "light up" when the associated processes are taking place. But brains don't light up, and individual areas of the brain never work alone. Computers make pictures of brains just as they do of far-away galaxies; they take some information that is not an image, and create an image from it. In the case of functional magnetic resonance imaging (fMRI), for instance, the images that we see in the pages of our magazines are highly manipulated representations of the results of detecting changes in the magnetic properties of blood. Right after an increase in neural activity, there is increased demand for oxygen. As this oxygen arrives in the hemoglobin, there is a small change in its magnetic resonance, which is what is detected. The computers involved in representing fMRI results process the myriad images taken by the fMRI machine over a particular time span and average them together. Then they show, by subtracting the overall activity of the brain from the activity of the brain in a particular area, that the specified area is more active during that time span than other areas.

All the measuring and representing of activity through these means is indirect; fMRI does not work by detecting the electrical activity happening as a neuron fires, or by detecting the rapid increase or decrease in local metabolism. Rather, it works by measuring the increase in regional cerebral blood flow in response to the increased metabolism that happens when a particular part of the brain is operating. These scans measure activity in the millimeters-large size range, which means that they are measuring the activity of several million neurons. But a relatively large-scale picture like that, as we saw in Chapter 1 with the movement from microlevel patterns to movement at the macrolevel, might well be (and in fact we will say that it is) the outcome of perhaps many lower-level patterns working against one another. So, the changes in metabolic activity recorded are always averages, hiding the particulars of what is happening at greater levels of specificity. Moreover, the images are always superimposed on background activity, so that the difference in activity that we attend to obliterates the context in which this activity is happening. Scientists have no way to distinguish between the real increase in a particular brain area's activity and apparent activity that may be due to some other task being done in that area at the same time, and random activity that may be a side effect of something else. Finally, imaging studies never speak to individual brains, but always to "representative" brains, or statistically significant correlations between individuals imaged. That is, these studies assume that all brains are doing the same thing when the same parts are activated, which results in the conclusion that the particular activity being observed must be responsible for the experience or change correlated with it. Given what we have said about the uniqueness of organisms, though, we ought to be extremely conservative in reaching any conclusions about individuals based on the imaging techniques used in the science that studies addiction at the neural level.

An even more fundamental assumption made in imaging studies, but subject to increasing resistance, is the idea that mental processes can be localized to operations in specific parts of the brain. Connected to the problem of the interpretation of images, but not identical to it, this concern addresses the "modularity" assumption popularly adopted by cognitive neuroscientists. It has long been assumed that particular tasks are accomplished by, and particular experiences result from, activity in a specified area of the brain. We saw this assumption operating in the accounts of addiction given above. A number of neuroscientists, however, have begun to object to this view, noting that responses of almost any kind are distributed over many, if not most, regions of the brain.[32] William Uttal, for instance, a highly respected researcher who uses imaging studies extensively in his own work, is one of the most strident critics of the localization thesis. His concern is not that imaging tools are not useful, but rather that scientists, in their enthusiasm for them, have failed to remain critical of the assumptions involved in using them. He compares the kind of modularity popularly presumed to characterize mental processing to a kind of contemporary phrenology – the 19th-century practice of predicting a person's mental characteristics based on lumps in the skull.[33] More careful attention to exactly how computerized images are created, and the hypotheses employed in interpreting their results, would render the science using them much more reliable.

A related problem is determining exactly what it is that a brain area is doing when it "lights up" in an fRMI test. Some areas, for example the anterior insula and the anterior cingulate, both cited as important in some addiction imaging research literature, appear to be activated in as many as 25% of the results recorded in all imaging research, according to Russell Poldrack, director of the Imaging Research Center at the University of Texas at Austin.[34] This means that the information available, at least so far, with regard to how the brain gives rise to mental experience, is vague. There is evidence that certain brain areas *are* involved in certain processing tasks, but *how* they contribute to this processing is unknown. So, although it might be possible to record structural and functional changes that attend symptoms and behaviors of addiction, our assessment of the true nature of addictive patterns must be understood in light of significant qualifications and caveats.

Other criticisms of the disease model

Critics of the disease model object to it on a number of grounds independent of those connected to the limitations of research methods. For one thing, some critics charge that the disease model fails at the first task of any scientific model: to account for the phenomenon. In particular, it fails to account for the timing of addicts' relapses and for the planning and organizing of use episodes that happen often at significant temporal distance from the indulgence itself. Others maintain that addiction does not itself fit into the logical space of disease. For example, Donald Douglas argues[35] that considering alcoholism in particular to be a disease is a function of reversing the concepts of cause and effect.[36]

Although it can cause diseases, it is not itself a disease. "What kind of disease," he asks "can coexist with the best of health?"[37] Many people who are believed by others to be addicts and who see themselves as addicted are in terrific health. To say that they are not "real" addicts in this case is just to argue in a circle. Other logical mismatches between addiction and disease concern when the individual has it: is it reasonable to say that he has the disease when he is abstinent? If so, what is it that makes it a disease? If not, Douglas asks, then why do so many alcoholics drink after achieving significant periods of abstinence? Finally, and most importantly, to say that choosing to drink is the cause of alcoholism, while simultaneously saying that having the disease of alcoholism restricts one's ability to choose violates the laws of logic, and prevents any noncircular definition of either the disease or the choice.

Coming from another perspective, other critics say that treating addiction as a disease is pragmatically unsound. While the original idea behind framing addiction in terms of disease was at least in part to rid it of its stigma and to encourage addicts to seek assistance, the move to the medical model had a hidden side. For one thing, it put the responsibility for transitioning out of addiction on treatment professionals, rather than on people with problems. This has proved to have dangerous results: by thinking of addiction in this way people who have problems with addiction have an excuse for not trying to control their behavior. Particularly when someone relapses into use, if he presumes the truth of the disease model, then he has no motivation to try to minimize it. In fact, he believes that he can't.[38] For another, it creates a disease for which there has been until recently no logically connected treatment. Those who declare addiction a disease most often cite 12-step programs as the best or the only viable approach to treating it, despite the fact that the central focus of these programs, if you count the number of steps that include a concept as an indication of its importance, is a "higher power." This approach is essentially spiritual in nature, which seems to be an ill-fitting response to a disease as defined in the contemporary medical world.

However, some approaches to treatment do seem to take the physiological conception of disease seriously. But even here, the disease model encourages fallacious thinking, this time of oversimplification. A flight of hubris was expressed August 15, 2011, for instance, in the headline "Scientists Can Now Block Heroin, Morphine Addiction." The press release, accompanied by video, makes dramatic claims. "Our studies have shown conclusively that we can block addiction via the immune system of the brain, without targeting the brain's wiring," said lead author Dr. Mark Hutchinson.[39] Perhaps it has been "shown conclusively" that administration of (+)naloxone, a nonopioid mirror-image drug, prevents the immune system's usual amplification effect on opiates, which should allow drugs such as morphine to be used for pain management without the additional addiction-forming euphoric effects occurring. At least in laboratory tests, use of this drug appreciably reduced opioid self-administration in rats (we have already discussed the problems with extrapolation from animal models to humans). But, although this may stop some people who must use opioids for significant periods from becoming dependent, what has been achieved is actually a far cry from what Dr. Hutchinson claims: "The drug (+)naloxone automatically shuts down the addiction. It shuts down the need to take opioids, it cuts out behaviors associated with addiction."[40] Thinking of addiction as an induced disease prompts the misleading conclusion that it can be obliterated with chemical tricks, just as smallpox can be prevented with a vaccine. Although such drugs can be extremely useful tools for avoiding and managing addiction, to think of them as cure-alls is to miss many of the interlinking levels at which addiction operates.

In addition to logical, practical, and oversimplification problems, the conception of addiction as a disease faces some factual challenges as well. As we saw in Chapter 1, psychologist Gene Heyman opposes the disease model on the grounds that it defies psychological and sociological research results. He points out that the vast majority of people who ever met the criteria for drug abuse and drug dependency stopped using drugs by midlife without treatment. This, he says, does not support the received view of addiction as a chronic disease. The studies show that addicts who go to clinics continue to use drugs, while those who do not receive treatment stop. But, the people who end up in studies about addiction are mostly people who go through treatment clinics. This gives a skewed picture of remission rates. Also, the evidence that Heyman produces suggests that "remission" isn't even the proper word, for the people who stop taking drugs seem to stay stopped, as though it were over, rather than simply being held at bay. Finally, people who go through clinics are much more likely to have other psychiatric or physical problems than those who do not, and so the proper conclusion to draw, Heyman says, is that when addiction persists, it is because people don't have access to other meaningful options. Their lives involve barriers that other lives do not. This, though, is not a picture of a disease, although it may be a picture of a phenomenon that accompanies other diseases.

Yet another kind of criticism comes from Stanton Peele, psychotherapist and long-time writer on addiction. He believes that there are reasons to think that the disease model, or the "alcoholism movement," as he first called it, has political roots.[41] This movement is politically powerful, he says, with a significant capacity to suppress discordant views and skew the direction of research, something with which Heyman could agree. Heyman notes that, although the four studies he cites in support of the choice model were high-caliber research done by respected researchers and funded by national health institutes, they never found their way into mainstream paradigm-building outlets such as textbooks, nor were they cited in important journal articles. According to Peele, the portrayal of addiction as a growing epidemic is a self-serving view promoted by the large and growing addiction treatment industry.[42] He argues that rather than medicalizing addiction, we should look to the social factors that foster addictive behaviors and start making changes there. These considerations will occupy us in later chapters. For now, it is enough to note that there are significant reasons of various kinds for resisting the received view that addiction is a medical disease.

Behavioral theories

Picoeconomics

The issues that we have just discussed, together with some others that we will outline below, may make us skeptical of the medical model. An alternative approach to understanding addiction focuses on behavior. Behavioral psychological approaches, for instance, maintain that, while addicts may not win the struggle against their urges, ultimately no humans are, as the disease model would have it, "out of control." People are always moved by their own choices. However, some people sometimes cannot motivate themselves to choose in a particular case what they in general want to do. We considered this in Chapter 1 under the philosophical framework of weakness of will. On George Ainslie's picoeconomic approach, addicts' capitulation to temptation is a result of two internal motivational forces competing, with one winning out over the other as a result of proximity in time of the potential reward.[43] This theory plays a touch-and-go game with free will, given some of its assumptions, but at the end of the day, it suggests that although addicts (and others) capitulate in the face of immediate rewards, they do have the power to choose otherwise. To see how this theory works, it is first necessary to agree that any agent is constrained to choose whatever option before him promises the greatest reward. This is not to be taken as the most rational reward, because behavioral economists, unlike classical economists, include emotions among the factors that figure in our assessment of value. This may seem like a rather deterministic assumption, but as we observed in Chapter 1, it is difficult to see why anyone would choose what she does *not* think promises the greatest reward. The way to explain repeated capitulation to relapse, Ainslie suggests, is not to presume that the person as an integrated agent makes no decision at all, and so is compelled, as though from the outside (whether by her brain or something else), and is in that sense without control. Nor is the correct view that the addict chooses freely, from the privileged point of view of a rational observer. Rather, on Ainslie's view, the individual is actually understood to be, or at least to act as, two separate agents, or, perhaps better, in terms of "one person's successive motivational states," each vying to determine the agent's choice.[44]

Ainslie and his colleague John Monterosso found that the fairly ubiquitous phenomenon of judging immediately available goods, even if of lesser value, as preferable to greater goods available only in the future, exhibits itself even more sharply in substance-dependent people than it does in the rest of us. In a series of experiments performed by a host of behavioral economists, psychologists, and neuroscientists over the past thirty years, it has been repeatedly shown that smokers, cocaine and methamphetamine users, and opiate users and heavy social and problem drinkers all discounted the future much more steeply relative to the present than did control groups.[45] Although the reward might be shunned, or at least be less valued compared to the longer-term good (say, of a life free of addiction), when considered from a distance, when receiving the reward was at hand, preferences suddenly flipped. While that is true for most of us, the difference in preferences for rewards nearer rather than further was more pronounced among substance users. For whatever reason, drug users and drug-dependent subjects discounted larger but delayed rewards, even when those rewards were monetary, something presumably having little to do with their addiction, and even when the delays were very short, these subjects discounted rewards much more steeply than did nonusers.

Correlation, however, as Monterosso and Ainslie are aware, is not causation, and even if there is a causal connection, the studies conducted say nothing about which way the connection goes. Addiction could be either the cause or the effect of the steeper discounting of future goods characteristic of addicts. Still, this particular type of discounting, with preference for long-term goods remaining relatively stable as long as the shortly available good is still at some distance, but suddenly and sharply reversing as soon as the shortly available good becomes imminent, does say something about substance users' impulsivity, and perhaps suggests something about their capacity for self-control. These unanticipated but sharp shifts in preference, Ainslie and Monterosso argue, are best explained by positing a conflict between two "selves" within the person, or at least two differentially defined motivational states. The model that Ainslie proposes presumes, first, that "mental processes are learned to the extent that they are rewarded,"[46] so people do what brings them reward. Complicating this point, though, is that people don't simply prefer one reward over another, plain and simple; rather, their preferences interact with each other over time. Hyperbolic preference curves, Ainslie says, in this clearly economically influenced model, show that contradictory processes compete with each other for the agent's behavior. The self at one moment is, he says, "helpless against what future selves may momentarily prefer," and has no one to call upon to control those future selves.[47] Thus, although in the time subsequent to indulgence the addict may truly value a sober future, the self is not unified temporally, and thus the possibility exists (and the likelihood, if something is not put in place to prevent it) that when temptation once again presents itself, the addict's preferences will suddenly flip, and he will find himself once again in an addictive pattern of behavior.

Ego depletion

Another behavioral theory of addiction, introduced in Chapter 1, is the ego-depletion hypothesis. On this hypothesis, self-control is a finite commodity. Thus, the argument goes, if people experience too much stress or have too many demands requiring self-control, they will have diminished resources available for resisting temptations. A number of experiments have been performed in this area. In one, a group of experimental subjects were instructed to eat only healthy foods such as radishes and celery from a buffet, while avoiding available rich desserts. This group later persisted for a shorter time at a difficult cognitive task than the control group, which was allowed to eat freely.[48] The relevant exercise of self-control isn't just of a momentary nature, either, as other studies have shown. People who have made long-term commitments to self-control, as do dieters, for example, regularly display more depleted levels of self-control after having to exercise significant amounts of it in a particular situation than do those who have not made such commitments. In a series of experiments that show this, chronic dieters and nondieters were exposed to either tempting situations or nontempting situations (an overflowing bowl of snacks was either readily available or at a distance), and subsequently were challenged to determine their available level of self-control in another situation. In one version of the experiment, both dieters and nondieters were offered ice cream, in an ostensible flavor-ranking task, and in another version, dieters were put to a difficult cognitive task. In the ice cream experiment, those dieters who had been exposed to temptation ate more than those who had not, but the nondieters did not show such a divergence. In the cognitive task experiment, exposure to food temptations resulted in subjects giving up sooner on the problems presented. In all these cases, subjects who had exerted self-control in one area subsequently seem to have had a depleted store of it available for later challenges.[49]

Addicted individuals, like chronic dieters, must exercise ongoing self-control. As a result, when they are faced with temptation, particularly when it is unexpected, they often give up quickly on cognitive tasks. Individuals who have been stressed in this way are often less discerning than they might be, for example, in the face of their own poor arguments in favor of using. Since people in this situation lack the extra cognitive resources required to think through the speciousness of their arguments, they experience a judgment shift away from their "rational" arguments for abstinence in favor of the case for use.[50] According to Neil Levy, the relevant dissociation is not between "wanting" and "liking," as was presented above, but between motivation and "*any* phenomenal state at all."[51] His idea is that if self-control is an exhaustible resource, it can be depleted by any temptation that lasts long enough, regardless of the strength of its appeal.[52] This hypothesis provides an explanation of the otherwise seemingly inexplicable fact that addicts can abstain for significant lengths of time, and then, in the face of something that no one would consider a major challenge, capitulate to temptation. Maintaining abstinence for a significant time requires significant reserves of "will power," which in the face of repeated temptations, makes relapse increasingly likely. On this hypothesis, it's not a matter of which *event* precipitates a relapse, but rather one of how long and in the face of how many temptations an addict controlled her urges before some random event or emotion was too much for the depleted ego to overcome. This hypothesis, Levy says, also offers an explanation of the power of "triggers." Since every temptation requires some of the addict's stores of self-control, each one encountered increases an addict's chances of relapse. Finally, according to Levy, this theory provides the best explanation currently on offer for distal addictive behaviors, the sometimes elaborate set of behaviors necessary to accomplish a use episode that is anything but automatic. Unlike the disease model, which has to see such activity as automated in some sense, the ego-depletion model, seeing relapse in terms of a shift in judgment brought on by exhausted stores of energy for self-control, can explain distal activity of addiction as ends-means reasoning of the usual kind, engaged in once the decision to use is made.

While both the picoeconomic and the ego-depletion theories do help illuminate certain elements of addiction, they are no more complete on their own than is the disease model, since they merely push the central questions back a step. For instance, with respect to hyperbolic discounting of the future, it is not clear whether it is this tendency that brings about addiction or whether addiction brings about short-term thinking. Some researchers have suggested a cyclical effect, in which those who tend to become addicted more deeply discount future goods to begin with, but then as they move into addictive patterns of behavior, do so to an even greater degree.[53] Ego depletion, it should be noted, is a well-known phenomenon affecting everybody's choices, and so by itself it cannot provide an adequate account of addiction. Like the picoeconomic theory, it offers reasons for why people might make the choices that they do with respect to addictive drugs and activities. Neither, however, explains what causes only some people to make choices in what would be recognized as a particularly addictive pattern. Empirical theories are good as far as they go, but they do not tell us what drives the distinction between those who would be characterized as addicted and those who wouldn't.

So, where does it start?

Neither of the broad classes of theories of addiction offered can provide a complete account of the phenomenon. Indeed, the opposition of the two kinds of theories is artificial, for humans are biological organisms that respond to changes in their internal and external environments – and one way that they respond is by acting, making choices. Some of those choices involve continued capitulation to indulgence in substances or activities of certain sorts. An analysis of these patterns of behavior, whether in terms of brain chemistry or anything else, is only the beginning of an understanding of addiction. We also need an account of who becomes addicted, and why some people seem to become addicted easily, whereas others can use the same amount of the same substances without becoming addicted. We also want to know why many people have demonstrated the ability to transition out of addictive patterns, whereas for others such a transition seems impossible, no matter what their level of motivation. Any effort to answer these kinds of questions requires an appreciation of the human addict as a complex and essentially dynamic process, historical in nature and necessarily embedded in an evolving physical and social environment.

Many researchers supporting the disease model of addiction cite statistics suggestive of a genetic component to addiction. Adoption and twin studies, for instance, like some others that we will discuss in Chapter 3, have indicated that at least part of some individuals' predisposition to addiction is to some degree a function of genetics. This is one reason for supporting the disease model, if the conclusions drawn from these studies are correct. The received wisdom, cited in virtually all of the addiction literature, is that perhaps half of a person's "risk" for addiction is a function of genetics. Exactly what this "risk" means, however, is an important question, since DNA does not determine how people's lives turn out. DNA contains instructions for making proteins. It is not a set of instructions for creating a human being. Far less, then, could DNA be specific a set of instructions that it could determine behavior patterns. While someone might well have a genetic predisposition to undergo the brain changes characteristic of addiction once drugs are chronically ingested, if she never experiments with addictive drugs, she will certainly not become an addict. What is more, as we will discuss in Chapter 3, the expression of one's genome is as much a function of epigenetic factors as it is of genetic ones. There is no disconnect between nature and nurture on our hypothesis, and so no such simplistic analysis as that one becomes an addict because of a genetic predisposition, will do. On the contrary, all the circumstances and events in a child's environment, positive and negative, have consequences for the processes of both physiological and psychological development, and hence for her vulnerability to addiction.[54]

The picture of the individual as a complex dynamic process emerging from the interactions between numerous other interacting highly complex dynamic processes seems to accommodate the richness of the results that research on addiction has provided to date. Neither genetics nor molecular biology nor neurophysiology nor psychology alone can provide an adequate explanation of this complex phenomenon. Stress, trauma, and social factors all play roles in the development of addictive patterns. And while research at each of these scales of analysis is helpful for pursuing partial treatments, no one level of explanation can hope to provide a path to treatment for all. If one researcher on his own finds at least two very different types of alcoholics, based on two different neural circuits, and if addiction occupies a spectrum on the control axis from something very much like a habit that can be unhabituated, to a screaming compulsion so strong that, as one addict put it, "the only thing that would make me stop once I started drinking was handcuffs," why should we think that addiction is specifiable as either a disease or as a particular manner of making decisions? And why should we think that our analysis should stop at the individual? As we will see, things are much more complicated than that.

4
The Ecology of Addiction

People don't become addicts in isolation. This is not news. In addition to the well-cited research showing that social connection is essential for the very survival, much less for the flourishing, of children, much work on addiction over the past two decades has focused on the importance of childhood influences on later substance use and abuse, and of social influences on transitioning into and out of addiction. For our purposes, this raises a problem: how can the results of this huge body of research showing the power of social relationships with respect to addiction be squared with either of the classes of theory that we have discussed? The role that other people play in increasing or decreasing an individual's risk of addiction and hope for living free of it seems to deny both sides of the dichotomy.

Gregory Bateson, in contrast to the competing paradigms that we have considered, characterizes addiction to alcohol in his "Cybernetics of Self: A Theory of Alcoholism," as a disorganization in relationships between the alcoholic and his world.[1] On Bateson's view, alcoholism, and addiction more generally, isn't merely a question either of dopamine levels in the brain's reward circuits, or of associative learning, or even of mental wrestling with temptations and arguments. Instead, it involves the individual's being "out of sync" with the world of which he is a part. According to Bateson, individuals who have problems with addiction can only be understood within the context of a whole system. He says that the addict's behavior and beliefs, and thus the world as it exists for him, are intertwined in an irreducible matrix. The addict's

> (commonly unconscious) beliefs about what sort of world it is will determine how he sees it and acts within it, and his ways of perceiving and acting will determine his beliefs about its nature.

> The living man is thus bound within a net of epistemological and ontological premises which – regardless of ultimate truth or falsity – become partially self-validating for him.[2]

The addicted individual, according to Bateson "has a take" on the world that determines how he behaves and feels within it, and those beliefs and feelings in turn will determine how he understands the world. Bateson's analysis of the addict's predicament thus relies on framing the human being as an essentially embedded organism whose environment influences both who and what he is, and is influenced by him, in an ongoing dynamic circle of causation. Bateson is thus in accord with our own hypothesis that addiction is a phenomenon emerging from a complex, hierarchically organized system. Indeed he asserts a version of it.[3] As he puts it, "[t]he pattern of addiction occurs within a system of continual oscillation at many interacting levels. The behavior of the 'self' is dynamic and is linked to the continual oscillations that such a system displays." [4] All organisms, as we have discussed, are complex dynamic systems, ever-changing interacting patterns that give rise in some cases to experience from points of view, or "selves." These selves are emergent dynamic patterns of action, always in interaction with their environments. Based on this framework, Bateson conceives of the addicted individual in terms of ecology. Addiction in this sense is a pattern embedded in a person's thinking and feeling that emerges from the rhythms of her biological organism interacting with those of her external environments, both physical and social.

This kind of approach is a person-centered, as opposed to a drug-centered, analysis of addiction, although of course no one could ever suffer from addiction problems without drugs or powerfully rewarding activities entering into the causal matrix. Focusing on the person, though, let us consider how those who become addicted can be distinguished from those who do not, in terms of their relationships with their environments. To begin, we might reflect on the questions that we left off with in the previous chapter: who becomes addicted, and why? Drug-centered theorists say that it is the drug that is responsible for addiction. Environmental availability of drugs and addictive activities create addicts. In that case, those who live in drug-infested neighborhoods, who grow up in drug-using families, or who go to high school should become addicted. Since drugs have become so readily available in public schools, colleges, and universities, not to mention bars and coffee shops, this theory does not seem to account for the persistent fact that only about 10% of the population will become addicted, although many more than that will use and even abuse drugs. Mere exposure, it seems, does not provide a satisfactory explanation of who becomes addicted, or why. Person-centered considerations are important as well, and an ecological approach that includes both promises even more.

If there is an answer to the question of who becomes addicted, other than the genetically doomed, which we will show will also not suffice as an explanation, the short answer would be "the stressed." When an organism is out of sync with its environment, as when the environment is unpredictable, or denies goods required for survival, such as early nurturing, food, or water, or threatens the loss of those goods, or when the organism faces persistent aggression and/or social defeat, it adapts by producing chemicals that prepare it for emergency. These chemicals, although essential for dealing with momentary stress, create an unstable internal milieu when present chronically. In short, when things do not go smoothly between an organism and its environment, the organism is stressed. Long-term stress wreaks havoc on the body/mind. An extensive literature provides evidence that emotional stress (and particularly interpersonal or social stress for humans) is a theme running throughout addicts' lives, from the gestational period through childhood and adolescence, in the transition from casual use into addiction, to relapse in adults after periods of abstinence.[5] Since stress seems to be part of nearly everyone's life, it alone cannot be identified as the cause of addiction, yet it exerts a powerful influence on those prone to addiction. Let us then consider the specific types and timing of the stress that is associated with vulnerability to addiction and relapse.

Stress and development

Developing brains are most sensitive to their environments, and this period is most influential since the ways in which a brain develops early on will create constraints on the patterns of activity, including further development, that happen later. From the embryonic stage through late adolescence, developing brains are highly susceptible to stress. Given that human brains continue to develop long after birth, doubling in size in the first two years and continuing to grow and organize into young adulthood, the impact of the immediate environment in which this growth takes place cannot be overstated. "The vast majority of the development of axons, dendrites, and synaptic connections that underlie all behavior is known to take place in early and late human infancy," asserts neuropsychology researcher Allan Shore, although he notes that critical periods in the development of certain systems, such as the prefrontal cortex, last much longer.[6] Since these kinds of development do not just happen automatically, but must be stimulated by internal and external environments, the types and amounts of interaction that babies and children engage in will affect how the emotional systems as well as other systems in their brains develop. This development in turn influences how and with respect to which people and things they experience pleasure and pain, attachment, and value later in life. Early on, babies' mental and emotional development literally is a function of their caregiver's rhythms. Rushes of dopamine and endogenous opiates hit the synapses every time a baby's regular caregiver returns to soothe her, or reacts in an engaged way with her. Consistent interactions of this nature stimulate the development of the neurons that release these bonding- and pleasure-associated chemicals, and the receptors that allow neurons to use them. Stress, though, such as that brought on by separation from a caregiver, or by interaction with a highly stressed or an unresponsive caregiver, reduces the amount of the relevant neurotransmitters that is released. This in turn reduces the development of both dopamine and opioid receptors. These two conditions together imply that less of these pleasure- and attachment chemicals can be used by postsynaptic neurons.[7] Such truncated development has serious consequences for the kinds of attachments and pleasures that a person can enjoy, and ultimately for a person's ability to regulate her emotions and behaviors.

A substantial body of epidemiological research demonstrates that a child's environment in her early years strongly influences her later social and emotional functioning. With respect to addiction in particular, children who live through adverse life experiences have an increased statistical likelihood of using illicit and prescribed drugs later, and of using them at a younger age than do people who do not have such experiences as children. In the highly recognized *Adverse Childhood Experiences (ACE) Study* of 2003, retrospective research was done on four different age cohorts with respect to ten categories of adverse childhood experiences (called ACEs, these include such things as physical abuse, sexual abuse, neglect, substance abuse or mental illness in the household, etc.). For each ACE a person experienced, the likelihood that she would engage in early substance use was two to four times greater than for those who didn't have such experiences.[8] Compared to people with no such events in their childhoods, individuals with more than five of the listed life events were seven to ten times more likely to report drug use or addiction. What is more, this study showed that there was a graded relationship between the total number of ACEs and the age of drinking onset across all four age cohorts, dating back to 1900. What this means is that the relative number of adolescents who had used alcohol increased in proportion to the number of adverse events they had experienced in childhood (although the absolute numbers were different in each of the different cohorts), regardless of the generation of which they were members. The fact that this graded number was consistent across all the age groups shows that the effect seems to be independent of cultural attitudes toward alcohol use, at least within the United States and within the past century.[9] From this research, it seems apparent that adverse events experienced in childhood correlate with both likelihood of drug use and abuse, and with earlier use of alcohol, proportional to the number and degree of such events.

We can talk about the developmental effects that were just discussed in another way. Consider what happens to children's brains in terms of memory and automated responses when they are exposed to stressful situations, especially traumatically stressful ones. They lay down memories of those visual, auditory, tactile, olfactory, and perhaps gustatory perceptions *together* with the emotional inputs that are their own brains' reactions to those situations. The experience of father striking mother, for example, is thus informed by the responses of the child's amygdala and other "limbic," or "emotional brain center" inputs, as much as it is by the response of the perceptual processing apparatuses in operation at the time. These children's memories thus inform their expectations, so that at the sight or sound of a similar situation, the child's limbic system response will charge into action, ready for another trauma. Children who are exposed to traumatic stressors, for this reason, according to one researcher, "exhibit profound sensitization of the neural response patterns associated with their traumatic experiences. The result is that full-blown response patterns (e.g., hyperarousal or dissociation) can be elicited by apparently minor stressors."[10] Like ex-soldiers who flinch when a FedEx helicopter shows up on the horizon, children who are hypersensitized through trauma cannot regulate their emotional responses to certain stimuli encountered later in life. Hyperstressed kids experience, in addition to the ordinary effects of drugs, the additional powerful effect of relief that such substances provide from their uncomfortable "normal" condition. As a result, temptation to indulge in such escapes would be difficult for them to avoid, once they have been exposed to them, and, given the social environments of most teens, they will be exposed to them by early adolescence.[11] It is no surprise, then that these are the children most likely to use and abuse addictive substances and activities.

As always, however, we must ask about the direction of the causal influence. Do these deleterious events cause early drug use and higher rates of addiction, or are the subjects of this study prone to experience both adverse life events and drug and alcohol use for some other reason? Further research by the authors of the "Adverse Childhood Experiences Study" and others suggests that the first hypothesis fits the data better. In later work, ACES's authors suggest biochemical reasons for the behavior patterns that follow stress during brain development. According to one follow-up study, neurodevelopment may be affected by trauma because stress prompts increased production of the stress hormones cortisol and epinephrine, as well as such neurotransmitters as dopamine, serotonin, and norepinephrine, some of which prepare an organism to be on high alert, and others which try to return it to homeostasis.[12] Dysregulation of what is known as the hypothalamic-pituitary-adrenal (HPA-axis) function – the system that controls the production of stress chemicals, in particular the glucocorticoid hormones – results from repeated or ongoing stress. The brain adapts, to put it simply, to always be ready for an emergency. Such adaptation, we should not be shocked to learn, impedes children's ability to regulate their emotions and behavior, which may in turn lead to the use of drugs and/or alcohol to try to cope.[13] This means that the stresses a child experiences not only change her brain chemistry in the moment, but, as with infants, such stresses affect her brain's development and later functioning as well. The dopamine and opioid systems in the brain, as we discussed, react to the presence or absence of stable caregivers. In dynamic terms, interaction with a self-organized, stable pattern of behavior is essential to a developing brain's ability to gain self-regulating properties. A baby whose distress is never or irregularly responded to by a reliable caregiver will not develop the self-regulation patterns necessary for a healthy life. The ability to cope with stress comes from interactions with predictable patterns in its caregiver. At first, the caregiver provides the comfort that down-regulates stress hormones when stressors arise. Gradually, the ability to affect its own biology is learned by the infant. Left in isolation, though, or in the presence of an agitated or otherwise disorganized behavior pattern in the caregiver, a baby's ability to develop stress-regulating mechanisms is seriously compromised.

This theory has received support from experiments using animal models. Stress responsivity in rat pups mirrors the responsivity levels of their mothers, as the mother's stronger patterns of activity entrain the offspring's, and just a little difference matters a great deal.[14] Being separated just briefly from their mothers results in heightened stress responses in offspring, as well as in other deleterious health effects. As we have said, these changes needn't be life threatening, or even dramatic. Small variations in maternal behavior, such as licking the pups less, or nursing in a suboptimal position, makes a difference to the offspring's endocrine responses and attachment behavior. These changes in turn correlate directly, as we have seen, to greater vulnerability to using drugs of addiction, in addition to a wide variety of other biological and psychological effects.[15] However, when baby rats were shown more maternal attention, in terms of licking and grooming, the offspring expressed less fear and anxiety, and less reactivity to stress.[16] Moreover, they exhibited an enhanced ability to self-regulate their emotional states. In addition, when pups were handled by the experimenters in the first days of their lives, resulting in increased licking by the mother rat once she returned to the nest, they again showed lowered reactivity to stress, as well as decreased memory neuron loss later in their lives.[17]

Perhaps even more interesting, these behaviors are transmitted over generations. The method is not genetic inheritance, but culture. The transmission is the result of behavioral (and specifically tactile) rather than genetic influences, as can be seen from the fact that female pups that suffered the same isolation, but were handled early in life, became more attentive and calming mothers than did their isolated but not handled counterparts.[18] Similarly with rhesus monkeys, daughters that were rejected by their mothers were found to have mothers that had been rejected by their own mothers, suggesting again that it is the maternal *behavior* and its attendant effects that are transmitted over generations.[19] And, most relevantly for our purposes, similar correlations are found between generations of human mothers and daughters.[20] This does not fit well with the genetically deterministic worldview that has been bestowed on us by some researchers. Psychiatrist Stuart Greenspan and philosopher Stuart Shanker comment in this regard that

> [f]or a generation raised on determinist principles, the idea that the evolution of the human mind and of human societies was the result of formative cultural practices that guide caregiver-infant interactions during the formative periods of development, and that these critical cultural practices were not genetically determined, but, rather, were passed down and thus learned anew by each generation in the evolutionary history of humans, may come as something of a shock.[21]

Nevertheless, the evidence supports the notion that culture is the manner of transmission of these practices. Neglectful or harsh mothers beget neglectful or harsh mothers, and that has an effect on each subsequent generation's ability to manage stress, and on the likelihood that affected generations will self-soothe with substances. With regard to human subjects as well, Greenspan and Shanker affirm the view that early brain development is dependent in large part on the quality of a child's interactions with her caregiver. They say that, regardless of how much potential a child's brain has, unless she "undergoes very specific types of interactive affective experiences that involve the successive transformations of emotional experience and that are the product of cultural practices forming the very core of our evolutionary history, that potential will not be realized in a traditional sense."[22] The reason, on their view, is that the potential that a child may have "does not reside in the physical structure of the brain, but is defined only in the types of complex interactions between biology and experience" that we have been talking about.[23] A child's cognitive and emotional development, and thus her vulnerability to addiction, is never a matter of her individual brain's genetic structure unfolding alone. Appeal to the emergent level of personalities is essential for explaining the development of the brain that is susceptible to addiction.

The story encompasses even more than offspring and caregiver, however. As Paul Plotsky discussed at the Culture, Mind, and Brain Conference held at the University of California, Los Angeles, in 2012, it was not only the stress of separation, or even the mother's resulting agitated behavior that ultimately made the difference in pups' ability to regulate their stress responses. Plotsky had shown in earlier experiments results similar to the ones we just discussed – that pups that suffered separation or loss of their mothers early on consistently showed later increased responsiveness to both stress and amphetamine. The neurochemical explanation for this was that the separation resulted in changes in dopamine transporter expression and, in turn, in significantly increased dopamine responses to stress.[24] But this change was hypothesized to be a function not simply of the distress of the pups at being left alone but also of the disordered behavior of the mother, which had also suffered from the separation, upon being returned to the cage with the pups. So far, this seems like simply another example of stressed mothers' effects on offspring. When the mothers in Plotsky's experiment were brought back into a two-room cage, however, rather than into a standard single-space cage, so that they were able to build new nests and move their pups, they returned to natural mothering, and the effects of the pups' "adverse event" were reversed.[25] These results suggest two things: first, that normal psychological development is not merely a function of avoiding stress, or of having a reliable social relationship, but also of having an environment in which social relationships can be allowed to operate normally. The environment in which an organism develops is not an external element, a space in which genetic information simply unfolds. Rather, the environment has been shown to be a significant player in brain development, exhibiting the power at both first- and secondhand to either enhance organisms' ability to respond to later stressors in their environments or to seriously disable it. Further, Plotsky's results suggest remarkable plasticity in the mammalian brain, for a change in the environment can change the direction of development already under way. This is evidence of both the dynamic nature of organisms and of their personalities, which provides reason for addicts to have hope. All too often people with addictive difficulties believe that they are "biologically determined" to be addicts, or that once they have suffered trauma they cannot overcome it, and that once addicted, they're always addicted.

The continuing influence of stress

Stress is essentially an imbalance between stimulating and tranquilizing chemicals, and imbalance is uncomfortable. So we should expect that stress in adult life, as well as during development, has repeatedly been found to be implicated in drug use, abuse, addiction, and relapse.[26] In numerous studies with nonhuman primates, particularly rhesus monkeys, which are, like humans, a highly complex, socially oriented species, social context and social stress have been shown to play critical roles in alcohol consumption, both among adolescents and among adults.[27] "Social separation," researchers in this area say, "engages a deficit-triggered motivational system" in primates so potent that it that outweighs other deficits, including food and water deficits. That is, social separation for these animals has serious repercussions – so serious, in fact, that the monkeys won't eat or drink water when their social bonds are disrupted. In one study, rhesus monkeys reared without parents, in peer-only settings, showed increased physiological responses to stress, which we would expect, given our considerations so far. Additionally, during times of stress, these monkeys drank significantly more alcohol and were more likely to drink to intoxication than were their peers that were reared in nonstressed conditions, with maternal care. But the stress affected even the less reactive individuals. When social stress was introduced to the even better adapted mother-reared monkeys, their alcohol consumption increased to match that of the peer-reared group.[28] So, even those that enjoyed a nurturing environment during early development drank heavily when faced with social stress.

An often-cited series of nonprimate experiments performed by researchers at Simon Fraser University corroborated the importance of environmental stress on the development and persistence of addiction.[29] Bruce Alexander, lead author of the studies that resulted from these experiments, described his team's method for discerning the cause of self-administration of drugs by laboratory rats. Their question was whether the self-administration so often observed in addiction studies might not be better described as a self-medication device than as a function of previous exposure to the drugs. In order to answer it, these researchers sought to discover whether seeking relief from a stressful environment, rather than the effects of the drugs themselves, could better explain compulsive drug self-administering behavior exhibited by rats that were "raised in isolated metal cages and subjected to surgical implantations in the hands of an eager (but seldom skillful) graduate student followed by being tethered in a self-injection apparatus."[30] Their idea was, in other words, that animals raised in physically and socially impoverished environments, with none of the stimuli or nurturing necessary for the development of normal responses to daily challenges, which are then attached uncomfortably to a self-injection device, might continuously self-administer drugs not because the drugs in themselves were addictive (the drug-centered approach), but instead because the drugs provided relief from environmental stress.

To test their individual-centered hypothesis, these researchers built "the most natural environment for rats" that they could come up with in a laboratory. For rats, it was scenic, spacious, and rich. They called this construction "Rat Park." Rat Park eliminated the standard stresses that lab rats typically endure, of cramped, isolated, boring, and painful or at least uncomfortable living conditions. As it turned out, the rats living in Rat Park had little taste for the morphine-laced water according to which their "addiction" was measured, even when they had been forced to consume significant amounts of morphine for weeks prior to the experiment, to ensure that they would experience withdrawal symptoms if they did not take it. This was in contrast to rats raised and tested in traditional cages. The difference between the behaviors of the respective groups of rats was significant. Under some conditions, the animals in cages consumed nineteen times as much morphine as did the rats in Rat Park.

To understand the extent and power of the results of the Rat Park experiment, we should consider some of its details. The experiment set involved four groups of rats reared and tested in different environmental conditions: one group was reared and tested in cages; one group was reared and tested in Rat Park; one group was reared in cages, but moved to Rat Park shortly before testing began; and one group was reared in Rat Park, but moved into cages shortly before testing began. The researchers, in short, tested rats exposed to every combination of cage/park rearing and testing. The rats were tested continually on their choice to drink either water or a bittersweet morphine solution, with the solution being switched out every five days for a more bitter-tasting and less potent version. At each level of morphine solution tried, the caged rats, whether reared in cages or in Rat Park, drank much more morphine than did those that lived in Rat Park during the time of the testing. This suggests that the present state of distress is more indicative of drug use than earlier stress later compensated for, and that even an absence of developmental stress didn't matter when present conditions deprived the animals of stimulation and company.

Alexander concluded from these experiments that the drug-centered view is mistaken: addiction is not caused by drugs themselves. If it were, living in Rat Park should make no difference in how much rats already dependent on morphine would drink. The conclusion that Alexander arrived at was that typical experiments test something other than what they are intended to test. What they actually test is the effects of laboratory settings on animals, rather than the animal's natural responses to drugs. He says that "the intense appetite of isolated experimental animals for heroin and cocaine in self-injection experiments tells us nothing about the responsiveness of normal animals and people to these drugs." Drugs themselves do not trap mammals (including people) into addiction, according to this research. This view, as we have said, is corroborated by the fact that most people who take drugs do not become addicted to them. For most who imbibe in drugs or alcohol (or gambling), the stimulation remains just an occasional recreational pleasure. If Alexander's team is right, the key to understanding addiction is much more complex than mere molecular interactions – although again, it is true that no other *thing* exists – only other *patterns* exist, but those patterns are themselves highly efficacious. Based on these experiments, the drug-centered view is too simplistic.

An adequate account of addiction requires thinking much more broadly than just about the individual, or about the individual together with a drug. We must think of the organism, as we saw in the cases of the development of children, as operating within an environment that includes other organisms and patterns of activity that interact in

traits, including vulnerability to addictive patterns, they do suggest that the relative influences of environment and genetic contributions to a disposition to addiction have not yet been clearly disentangled. And recall that even in the Stockholm studies, the stronger genetic effect was found in only one pattern of alcohol abuse.

The other kind of study often used to attempt to disentangle genetics from environmental factors involves twins, both identical and fraternal. Twin studies are presumed to be the best way to test for genetic similarities. This is because both kinds of twins ought to have the same environment, but only identical twins have the same DNA, and so the genetic factors ought to be isolable from the environmental ones. And research does show that identical twins are about twice as likely to share addictive patterns as fraternal ones. But the conclusion that this match must be the result of DNA, Gabor Maté has argued at length, is just false.[44] The rate of concordance between identical twins as contrasted with fraternal twins, he maintains, is equally consistent with environmental factors being the relevant influence. First of all, the argument goes, fraternal twins don't share the same internal environment as identical twins do. They are just as physiologically different as any other siblings, and so their interactions with the world will not be biochemically any more similar than any other siblings' interactions. Their experiences of their environment throughout gestation and development will for that reason be different in ways that identical twins' experiences of their environment will not be. Second, says Maté, because fraternal twins are as physically and temperamentally different as any other siblings are from each other, parents will, however unconsciously, respond to them differently, as will everyone else. This means that their social environments will be just as distinct as are any siblings' environments. By contrast, identical twins are alike in these ways, which will prompt the same responses from others in their environments. For this reason, says Maté, identical twins' environments won't really be that different, even if they are raised separately. This is a strong claim, though, warranting something stronger than mere speculation as support. What does "really that different" mean? If it means significantly different in the relevant ways, then the argument is pure presumption. If it is extrapolation from the sameness of DNA to the sameness of the children who share it, then it is grossly oversimplifying, presuming the children to be more mechanical than human.

In another line of reasoning, Maté argues, perhaps more convincingly, that identical twins, unlike fraternal twins, do share the same uterine environment for nine months, and so are exposed to the same epigenetic factors and the same kinds of experiences in the world before adoption. So, he argues, even those identical twins separated at birth and raised in different familial environments do not prove the genetic hypothesis. Nurture has already had a chance to have its effect by the time of birth and separation, so the genetic factor is not isolable even in this case. What is more, all twins experience separation trauma when they leave their mothers, when they leave each other, and when they leave whatever caregivers they may have in the time between birth and adoption. So it would seem that both groups of twins would be equally set up for vulnerability to addiction on that account (on this reasoning, though, note that it would seem that all adoptive children are so set up). In the case of twin studies, as in the case of the adoption studies, the implication seems to be not that genetics has a clear and strong influence on the disposition to addiction, nor that it doesn't; rather, the implication is that addiction in human beings cannot be reduced to a single level of analysis, either physiological or psychological. It is a higher-order pattern that can only result from the complex and dynamic interaction of an indefinite number of factors, including genetic inheritance, physical environment, and psychological environment.

Other factors

A couple of further considerations must be addressed before we extend our discussion to include the influence of culture on addiction. First, remember that when we discussed Heyman's criticism of the disease model of addiction in Chapter 1, we noted that most people included in research studies are those who sought clinical treatment. These individuals also suffered from other health conditions in addition to their addictive problems, such as anxiety, HIV/AIDS, or ADHD. The influence of some of these conditions on addiction's trajectory is well established. Maté points out that ADHD "is a major predisposing factor for addiction."[45] It shows up in a disproportionate number of substance abusers of all types, and, according to Maté, "is no more inherited genetically than addiction is."[46] The same arguments are relevant in both cases. Generalized anxiety disorder as well is disproportionally represented among addicts. In one study, for example, which was designed to circumvent the obvious fact that anyone undergoing treatment for alcohol dependence would be experiencing anxiety, the comorbidity rate for generalized anxiety disorder among alcohol-dependent patients was nearly half. In this study, the disorder was shown to have existed prior to the onset of alcohol problems 67% of the time.[47] Another, much larger study showed that having social anxiety disorder increased the chances of someone's having an alcohol disorder by a factor of four.[48]

Likewise, bipolar disorder is highly correlated with alcohol and other drug use disorders, but in this case the relationships between the psychological and use disorders are very hard to disentangle. Researchers do not seem to have uncovered a single causal order between them. With respect to marijuana, for instance, it sometimes appears to increase bipolar symptoms, and sometimes to decrease them.[49] If this result argues for anything, it is that bipolar symptoms may have different causes in different people. Finally, in the case of major depression, which is also highly correlated with alcohol problems, the causal arrow seems to go in the opposite direction from that characteristic of anxiety and ADHD disorders.[50] Whereas researchers conjecture that alcohol is used as a method of self-medicating ADHD and anxiety disorders, and in particular social anxiety disorder, depression instead seems to be the result of alcohol abuse. Much work has been done specifying these relationships for gender, race, economic status, and a variety of other variables, but for our purposes the main point is that addiction does not arise in isolation. It arises in specific contexts, in relation to physical and/or social environments at various levels of proximity, and it shows up as both cause and effect.

Another thing to consider prior to an examination of cultural influences on addiction is that the social world in which we are embedded is different at different times in our lives, regardless of gender, race, or economic status. This fact is important to understanding the patterns of addiction. When children are quite young, as we have seen, their parents are experienced as virtual extensions of themselves. Everything that their parents do or do not do affects the child's own stress and reactivity levels. When they become adolescents, their peers become more influential elements of their environments. Even the popular press has made it known how much they conform to the behavior of their friends, even more than do adults. *Scientific American*'s *60-Minute Mind* podcast, for instance, reports on research that suggests that adolescents' weight is correlated with that of their friends, and not just because they choose friends who are like them in body type but also because others' behavior influences their own, to the extent that they gain and lose weight based on the behaviors of those around them.[51] While generally there is no reason to correlate something such as the influence of friends on specific behaviors to something as serious as DMS-IV-TR-defined dependence, since most people who try smoking or drinking or other drugs will not become addicted, absent any independent evidence for that correlation, in this population there is reason to attribute a correlation. The fact that adolescents are influenced by their peers to begin smoking, drinking, or taking other drugs is relevant because early onset of the use of alcohol and drugs of addiction has been shown to increase the frequency of dependence in adult life by four to six times.[52] Even the age of onset of smoking, which seems a popular vice for adolescents but not directly related to other drug dependence, has been found to be a significant predictor of alcohol use and dependence.[53] Rather than the much-maligned marijuana, if there is a "gateway drug," it would seem to be tobacco.

We can with reason, then, seek contributing causes and correlations to addiction from the molecular level to the organismic level to interactive levels with parents and social groups. The one thing that we cannot find is a single cause, or even a single state, that is called "addiction." What we find is a process, which mainstream researchers characterize in terms of three stages, but which others characterize in terms of the ongoing processes that may be limited to the level of individual choices, or that may be traced to epigenetic effects on the unfolding of our DNA. I suspect that this latter analysis won't make sense unless we at least postulate the existence of the DNA that unfolds, but that DNA is essentially best understood as itself a process that comes into existence and changes at many points over the span of an organism's life. Each of these complex patterns of ever-changing action is involved in what we know as addiction, but none of them alone constitutes it.

5
The Culture of Addiction

The solution is the problem, and the problem is the solution

Individuals are both created by and give rise to their cultures. Not only does no one become an addict in a vacuum, but also, in addition to one's physical environment and immediate social interactions, human addiction takes place within a larger culture. As sociologist James Barber puts it, "[w]e learn to drink, smoke, and take drugs because others show us not only how to do it but also how to enjoy it."[1] The relation of addiction to culture is, like all the other levels of analysis that we have considered, dynamic and complex, and different in every case. In many of these cases, specifically within the past few hundred years, psychoactive substances and addicted populations have been, and continue to be, both the cause of and the cure for many of society's problems. Without addicted laborers, some of whom were paid in kind for producing the very substance to which they were addicted, the global markets in tobacco and caffeine products, such as coffee and tea, could not have arisen, not to mention the smaller but significant opium, cannabis, and coca markets.[2] The use of these substances played a large role in keeping laborers laboring, and markets growing. Today, given the DSM-V's inclusion of food addiction among its listed disorders, we might add the fast-food market to the list. Low wage-earning fast-food workers often take advantage of readily available cheap and fast food, saturated with fat and salt, because it suits both their schedules and their incomes. The discounts or free food that they often receive at such jobs suggest that the corporations for which they work find the arrangement mutually convenient.

It is difficult to overstate the role that these substances played in the development of world markets and political power. Chinese colonizers, for instance, depended on the incessant opium smoking of their "coolies" for their profits and power. Colonial leaders allowed monopolies to be created and protected for the sale of opium, sometimes keeping half or more of the workers' wages as proceeds. China's colony Singapore received as much as half its revenue from opium in the 19th century.[3] In Europe and the United States, the relevant products were alcohol and tobacco. In Eastern Europe prior to mechanical agriculture, peasants were notorious for being drunk for days on end, and the same was true of poor Europeans who came to America to work. But even alcohol consumption was no competition for tobacco. Beginning in the 17th century, tobacco production occupied all the European colonizing countries, with the slaves who produced it receiving daily rations of the crop. Every demographic engaged in some form of tobacco use, from diplomats to tourists to laborers, and, most prominently of all, soldiers. By 1670, the English were using about a pound of tobacco per capita annually, while the Dutch were using about one and a half times that much.[4] Tobacco was used in various forms throughout the 18th century, but by the middle of the 19th century, smoking was the clearly favored manner of consumption. First pipes and cigars, and then, by the early part of the 20th century, cigarettes became the preferred manner of indulgence. In the late 1950s, Americans were buying some 15,000 cigarettes a second, and by the mid-1990s, a third of the world's population over the age of fifteen was smoking cigarettes.[5] But those numbers, staggering though they may seem, are small in comparison to the quantities of caffeinated products consumed, particularly coffee. According to historian David Courtwright, "by the late twentieth century it [coffee] consistently trailed only oil as the world's most widely traded commodity."[6] It is no wonder that coffee and cigarette breaks came to shape the very structure of the workday in the middle of the 20th century for white- and pink-collar workers in the West.

One account of why these substances became so ubiquitous, in addition to their unparalleled ability to create profit and tax revenue for the wealthy and the powerful, through keeping the money earned by workers in the hands of their employers, is that these substances also served and continue to serve to control indigenous peoples and other impoverished workers. For centuries, stimulants and pain- and grief-soothing substances have kept people working long hours at grueling, repetitive, mind-numbing jobs, through heat, hunger, and disease. In the 17th century, when Europe was afflicted with every misery imaginable, substances such as tobacco, coffee, and tea, according to Courtright, served a "dire utility" in "helping peasants and workers cope with lives lived on the verge of the unlivable."[7] At the very least, it seems that preoccupation with seeking and consuming drugs results in such apathy that workers are unlikely to try to do anything to change their circumstances. Like religion according to Karl Marx, these substances, are the opiates of the people, keeping them distracted from their miserable situations.

In the 20th and 21st centuries, coffee breaks, happy hours, and drive-through fast-food restaurants, as well as cocaine and, increasingly, prescription drugs, serve to keep spirits up and people working. It is also true, however, that some of the substances that have been tolerated and even encouraged for centuries can all too easily render workers useless. Years of cigarette breaks – we, as a society, have gradually learned – turn into massive expenditures in healthcare down the road, and the same was discovered about the three-martini lunch. With respect to the weaker varieties and smaller quantities in which the palliative substances were used by peasants and slaves, the price for allowing or even encouraging use was small. But as the dynamics of society changed, as well as the means of production, so did attitudes toward the use of specific substances. In an agricultural setting, no one seemed to mind if hemp harvesters were ingesting cannabis all day long, or if serfs were swilling stale beer. But as soon as spirits were distilled, trouble arose. This much stronger variety of beverage resulted in complaints from government officials and employers alike.[8] Cheap gin in particular, which became widely available in Europe in the early 18th century, was so obnoxious to productivity that a contemporary author complained that "the lowest class of people could afford to indulge themselves in one continued state of intoxication, to the destruction of all morals, industry, and order."[9] Before the 17th century, distilled alcohol was considered a medicine, sold only in apothecaries, and at a prohibitive price for commoners. But by the early 18th century, distilling technology and increased production made it possible for it to be sold even more cheaply than beer, making heavy drinking a possibility for people of all economic ranks and statuses. But that democratizing carried a price in terms of the destruction of the moral status quo (obedience to law and church), industry (hard work), and order (compliance). Much like cannabis and psychedelics in the 1970s, the use of spirits in the 18th century was cited as the direct cause of crime and disorderliness. Threatened and real disruptions among working class individuals who failed to show the proper fear of authority and shame for their actions created significant apprehension among respectable citizens and political leaders, particularly as workers became increasingly concentrated in cities. With industrialization and globalization expanding, the number of variables potentially threatening the established order rose. Ultimately, when the substances responsible for creating such huge profits and tax revenues resulted in disorder and threats to the national economy, not only the U.S., but one country after another opted to impose restrictions or even ban the very items that had helped their economies to expand and flourish. At the same time, the individuals who had developed habits of using those substances came to be denounced as moral reprobates, and later, as addicts. When the solution to the problem of how to provide labor for industrialization and products for the rise of the global economy began to take on a life of its own, that solution itself became a problem, with the owner of the problem no longer being identified as the economy or political unit. Now the problem belonged to the individual, who emerged as the "addict."

This observation suggests two questions. First, to what extent and in what ways is the concept of addiction a social construct? If it turns out that a large part of what we call addiction is the use of substances and/or engagement in activities that disturb the order and productivity of a society, then the conception of it in terms of a brain disease seems to be constructed, at least in part, for control. Those who act inconveniently can be "treated." Alternatively, if construing the use of certain substances and activities as a disease creates an economic boon to society, then the conception of it in this way seems to be fortuitously profitable. A new disease that creates a new treatment industry can be very valuable to an economy. Second, to what extent is addiction brought about by social circumstances themselves – whether the phenomenon is then analyzed in terms of changes in the brain or not? If industrialization and the development of a consumerist, competitive world economy, for instance, actually encourage the development of patterns of behavior that we call addictive, then attempts to resolve individuals' suffering with "treatment" aimed at fixing them rather than addressing their circumstances just reinforces the social circumstances that give rise to the problem. Individuals are sent for treatment, taking the blame upon themselves for their misery. Meanwhile, the socioeconomic structure that is at least in part responsible for creating the construct of the "addict" continues to be supported by a burgeoning medical industry that benefits from that construction. No doubt these issues are deeply intertwined with one another and with the physical phenomena associated with addiction. The social construct of addiction is emergent from the economic, political, and cultural environment that gives rise to both the need and the ability to escape from stressful conditions in the first place.

A cultural construct

The very notion of addiction only became popular as the medical and insurance industries grew and prospered, and consumerism rose to the greatest heights it had ever seen. Sociologist Gerda Reith argues that "[t]owards the end of the nineteenth century, a convergence of interests between the industrial nation-state and the medical profession coalesced into a (fragmentary) discourse that postulated a state of 'addiction' as a 'disease of the will,' and created a new type of individual – and 'addict' – as a distinct identity."[10] As American culture became ever more industrialized, she says, "[t]he bourgeois emphasis on industrial productivity and labour discipline elevated the properties of self-regulation and control to personal as well as political virtues, and also gave rise to an increasing intolerance of behavior regarded as potentially disruptive."[11] In order for productivity to continually grow, it became increasingly important for workers to self-regulate their consumption of certain products. Whatever else they did, workers would have to be reliably functional in increasingly complex social environments. The implication of this seems to be that it is the potential for disruption of socioeconomic flow, rather than the quantity of consumption itself, that establishes a substance's or activity's character as addictive, or the agent as an addict. In fact, increased quantity of consumption of all types of goods has consistently been pressed, and has surged radically over the past one hundred years. Identity itself has come to be created through one's patterns of consumption: who one is, is a fluid construct rather than an essence, a matter of choices rather than of nature.[12] An identity based on choice, though, although it is apparently an identity created through freedom, is nevertheless based on a freedom of a very particular, and a very peculiar, sort.

In Daniel Bell's language from forty years ago, we see in the "cultural contradictions of capitalism" a "fundamental conflict between the ascetic values of the protestant work ethic" on the one hand, and "the hedonistic values of instant gratification that come with capitalist consumerism" on the other.[13] As has become commonly recognized, Americans, like members of many affluent nations, are bombarded regularly with advertisements encouraging indulgence in everything from chocolate to vacations to automobiles and jewelry ("every kiss begins with Kay"). Meanwhile, and sometimes within fifteen seconds, the message is sent that one ought to be prudent, to develop self-control, through consuming yet more: services from the most responsible investment firm, or Weight Watchers, or Special K. This schizophrenic approach to consumerism is essential to consumer capitalism, and the message is clear: more is better; consumption is good. Consumption of additional products, whether diet products, consumer counseling, or medical treatment for addiction, is the answer to the "disease of the will" of out-of-control consumption. Most notable of all about this situation is that the responsibility for all of this consuming, overconsuming, and counterconsuming rests squarely with the individual. The system of hyperconsumption itself in which the concept of "addict" arises is never examined.

Before alcoholism came to be understood as a disease, regular drunkenness was simply regarded as a behavior, undertaken in the name of pleasure. But as this drunkenness came into conflict with social control and developing forms of productivity, several groups began to petition to eliminate it. As wide support around the world for prohibition illuminated, alcohol itself, not the user, was understood as being to blame for its excessive use. After the policy of prohibition in the United States became increasingly clearly unworkable, a conceptual revolution with respect to alcohol and its abuse was required to justify repeal of the constitutional amendment that had implemented the policy. The notion of an "allergy" to alcohol spread. As it happened, in the same year that the 21st Amendment was passed repealing prohibition, Alcoholics Anonymous (AA) was founded by Bill Wilson, along with his doctor, Robert Holbrook ("Dr. Bob"), who told him about a new disease theory of alcoholism. According to this theory, certain people are just born with a predisposition to alcoholism (later referred to as "addictive personalities"). Framing addiction in terms of disease allowed the medical industry to get into the business of treating it. As the disease model blossomed, so did the number of "addicts" found to be in need of professional treatment. One California study found that between 1942 and 1976, the number of citizens in treatment increased at least twentyfold (2000%).[14] With the AMA's official declaration in 1987 characterizing addiction as a disease, whose treatment "is a legitimate part of medical practice," third-party reimbursement (insurance payments) became possible for the treatment of addiction, bringing yet another segment of the economy into the game. Addiction treatment became very big business. Between 1978 and 1984, the number of for-profit residential addiction treatment centers increased by 350%, and their caseloads increased by 400%.[15] Today, the Substance Abuse and

Mental Health Services Administration estimates that spending at the over 11,000 addiction-treatment centers in the United States will reach $35 billion in 2014. It has become a major public line-item expense. Federal programs such as Medicaid and Medicare, as well as state and local programs, funded about three-fourths of that expense as of 2003 and will continue to carry the heaviest burden, although the percentage paid by private insurers is growing.[16]

The disease conception of addiction is so thoroughly entrenched in American culture that it is difficult to find any psychiatric, medical, educational, or even criminal justice policy that doesn't embrace it as a fundamental assumption. This is true despite the fact that the preferred method of treatment in some 90%+ of treatment centers is based on 12-step spiritual models, rather than on medicine. The deeply entrenched assumption of the disease model might be thought to result from the simple fact that this approach results in the best treatment outcomes, were it not for the fact that the model carries with it political power and authority, which means control over certain people's freedom by certain privileged others. As substance use or any other addictive behavior comes to threaten productivity, social order, or economic power, those individuals who engage in that use or behavior are rendered appropriate targets for diagnosis, "intervention," and treatment. As author Elaine Rapping argues, the view that not only does addiction as a biologically determined disease obviate any need to look elsewhere for other, perhaps social sources of the problem, but it also provides a properly concerned way to deal with people and behaviors that appear threatening. Those individuals and behaviors that might disrupt the status quo can be dealt with apparently compassionately and objectively by being understood and treated in terms of biological dysfunction. The facts that they are locked away, stigmatized, and otherwise disempowered, however, cannot be missed. "The biologically determined explanation," she says, "comes and goes, predictably, as society comes to find *certain kinds* of indulgence, favored by *certain kinds* of population segments, anxiety provoking."[17] In considering the social development of the "disease of the will" conception of addiction, we must not forget to reflect on who among us is deemed addicted, and where they stand in the socioeconomic machine.

Consider, for example, the attitudes expressed toward the various "addictive" substances by our legal system. Illegal drug use and sales accounted for two-thirds of the rise in the federally incarcerated population and half of the rise in state-incarcerated populations between 1985 and 2000, according to Michelle Alexander in her much-acclaimed book, *The New Jim Crow: Mass Incarceration in the Age of Colorblindness.* Arrests for marijuana possession, despite its relative innocuousness (particularly in comparison to prescription drugs), accounted for nearly 80% of the growth in drug arrests in the 1990s.[18] Alexander's point here is that it isn't just anybody who is getting arrested. In the vast majority, those who comprise these incarcerated populations are people of color. A commonly cited statistic is that, while African American males constitute about 6% of the general population, they constitute about 35% of the prison population. And that is just one subgroup of the disproportionally incarcerated. These populations with high incarceration rates exhibit less stable and fewer permanent relationships, a situation created by the incarceration itself. This is not to mention associated phenomena such as less available stable work and inferior jobs for those who have been incarcerated, as well as increased exposure to violence and poor nutrition. These circumstances result in living situations marked by high levels of stress for everyone involved, which, as we saw in Chapter 3, render not only adults but also children in such environments more vulnerable to drug use and abuse.

Further exacerbating the problem is the prevalence of the drugs themselves and their attendant dangers in lower socioeconomic neighborhoods. Although individuals in middle and upper socioeconomic classes enjoy the use of drugs, they do not wish to have them widely available in their own neighborhoods. It has been argued for decades now that drug use, drug sales, and addiction have affected poor and minority communities more harshly than they have white and more affluent communities, despite the fact that middle-class whites are significantly more likely than blacks to use illegal drugs and alcohol.[19] Reasons for this include the same race and class discrimination that have resulted in certain groups being blamed for other social ills, including welfare and food stamp abuse, and child neglect and abuse, despite available statistics to the contrary. In the case of addiction, we can agree with William Kornblum that some of the reasons that poor and minority populations are perceived to have worse addiction problems than others is that the sale of drugs has typically been located in poorer, more densely populated areas. Why? For one thing, when individuals are crowded tightly together, any one person's activities are less likely to be noticed, When this crowding reflects a difference in wealth, rather than simple geographic limitations, people in such situations are also, due to their poverty, likely to be less valued than their richer counterparts, and therefore less likely to receive resources dedicated to improving health and safety. Another reason that drug activity and addiction have affected poor areas more harshly than rich ones is the lack of opportunity for job training and education for those already poor in resources and respect. As the United States has transitioned into an information-based economy, changes in production methods have often "deprived low-income minority individuals of better-paying, more secure industrial employment," leaving them with little hope and little to do.[20] Drug distribution was one of the few ways in which many people could provide for themselves and their families, and the option of moving away from such "vice districts" remained unavailable to most inhabitants. By the 1980s, the ghettos and immigrant neighborhoods of New York City, Los Angeles, Washington, DC, and Miami had become loci of the cocaine and crack trades, which brought with them high levels of homicide and addiction. "The disproportionate involvement of minority and recent immigrant groups in the illegal drug industry," Kornblum explains as inextricably linked to "historical patterns of vice market concentration in stigmatized, segregated communities."[21]

It has been argued widely for at least forty years that police forces were created and continue to exist for the purpose of controlling people of lower classes.[22] While law enforcement often turns a blind eye to infractions committed by members of the middle and especially the privileged class, it responds to the socially unacceptable behavior of the poor and disempowered by "cracking down," which results in more incarceration and the perpetuation of the cycle that creates the need for illegal drug use and distribution and other vice markets. Such tightening of enforcement and increasing of penalties does nothing to alleviate the variables that produce the value and even perceived need for drug use. The stresses, trauma, and hopelessness of living in poverty and discrimination remain just as they were. In fact, "cracking down" makes all of these things worse. According to Alexander, the massive incarceration of largely people of color in connection with drug use operates together with "a web of laws, regulations, and informal rules, all of which are powerfully reinforced by social stigma"[23] to confine certain people to the margins of mainstream society and to deny them access to the mainstream economy. Drug enforcement policy creates a subclass, which further defines the concepts both of addiction and of whole swathes of the population. This approach of isolating people of color (and people of lower socioeconomic classes in general, we can extrapolate), Alexander charges, operates as a "stunningly comprehensive and well-disguised system of racialized social control."[24]

It's not just control of recognized marginalized groups that the construct of addiction achieves, however. The social control extends much further, although in decidedly different ways in different parts of the population. Whereas the original disease model, as conceived by the founders of AA, assumed that the addict herself would have to voluntarily seek help, perhaps after "hitting bottom," the notions of "tough love" and "denial" became popular through the later part of the 20th century, culminating in the practice of "intervention," or forcible commitment into treatment. The very idea of an addict in denial suggests in a rather insidious, self-justifying, nontestable way, that the addict himself is not capable of acting as an autonomous individual, that he is unable to determine for himself whether or not he is addicted. In a bizarre twist, then, a person can not only prove by his denial that he is an addict but also in some sense can *become* one through the act of objecting to the characterization. Addiction thus becomes a disease that one can "develop" instantly at the attribution of someone else. If an individual decides to attribute all of his problems to a substance or behavior, rather than to social structures and stresses, physical or sexual abuse, or anything else, or, more importantly, if someone else attributes his problems to his "addiction," then he becomes an addict. The ascription of someone's problems to addiction can change his whole life: how everyone around him views him, how employable he is, how welcome he is at various kinds of social and volunteer events, how trusted he is around children, and even whether he is accepted as a citizen in his community.

Who gets to decide who is an addict is thus a matter of no small import. It is not analogous to having tests run to determine whether someone has diabetes or heart disease. If a person uses an activity or substance more than certain other individuals deem reasonable, regardless of whether the "addict" in question maintains a job, pays her bills, or perhaps even reaches high levels of success in many areas of her life, she can still find herself facing intervention for her addiction. This means that any troublesome relative (or any person with a particularly meddlesome family) can be coerced into treatment, on the grounds that her denial itself is a primary symptom of her disease. This is most problematic with the increasingly pervasive practice of hospitalizing difficult youth, which becomes a legitimate way for parents to allow them to become somebody else's problem, by bringing to bear institutional control. Experts can take the place of parents in dealing with children's addictions, legitimizing parental abandonment and alienation, even though this approach has the attendant effect of further dividing and disempowering families. And this is not true simply in the case of drug addiction. Unwelcome behaviors ranging from gambling to video gaming to eating to sex to viewing porn can now land you in treatment if you're sufficiently rich. For the poor, the "treatment" is often jail.

In the event that the argument from the ever-expanding types of culturally specific addiction is not persuasive that addiction is at least in part a social construct, consider another sort of case. That the astounding increase in levels of addiction in the West is the result of social attitudes as much as it is the result of expanding medical insights seems plain from looking at the contrast between the American response to heavy indulgence (in this case, in alcohol) and the South Korean response. In South Korea, heavy drinking by men is "encouraged, even demanded, in certain social contexts."[25] While social norms and mores discourage drinking by women and solitary drinking by men, South Korean culture supports regular drinking contests in bars after work, after which many contenders have to be carried home. Men who indulge in this manner are not considered addicted, and drinking in this manner is not considered a problem. As it happens, even with this high level of consumption, due to the social structures that constrain the time and circumstances of a man's drinking, statistics show that the dependence-to-abuse ratio is reversed in South Korea relative to the West. That is, although a larger number of men abuse alcohol in South Korea than in the West, a smaller percentage of them become physiologically dependent on it than do their Western counterparts. This suggests that not only do cultures construct the concept of addiction differently but, moreover, some would not use the concept of addiction at all, or develop any of the practices or institutions that accompany its recognition as an individual problem requiring treatment. Different cultural conceptions of the place of excessive indulgence within the overall system of customs and practices determine in large part where there even exists such a thing as addiction. Moreover, those very social conceptions, norms, and traditions themselves seem to have a significant influence on the degree to which the population of users becomes dependent on substances.

Martin Levine and Richard Troiden argue that some addictions have been completely culturally constructed.[26] Consider, for example, the idea of the sex addict. Levine and Troiden argue that the concepts of sexual addiction and sexual compulsion are based in cultural beliefs regarding extrarelational sex that became more openly widespread in the late 1970s and '80s. Because those who came of sexual maturity in the sexual liberation movement of the '60s and '70s were seen as a threat to social cohesion, the sexual behaviors developed during that period and shortly thereafter were construed as deviant by those adhering to traditional standards. Levine and Troiden say that, rather than being varieties of medical conditions, "[s]exual addiction and compulsion refer to learned patterns of behavior that are stigmatized by dominant institutions."[27] On their view, it is political and social agendas that created the possibility for this kind of addiction to enter the ontology and linguistic conventions as disorders in need of treatment. Whether this behavior is portrayed as an addiction or a compulsion, or an impulse control disorder (these are described slightly differently), Levine and Troiden argue that the diagnosis rests on "culturally induced perceptions of what constitutes sexual impulse control."[28] Broad differences characterize the attitudes and practices of different cultures and different ages. In "sex-positive" cultures, such as Mangaia, for instance, casual sex with many different partners is normal. It is the religious emphasis on low sexual desire and activity that would be seen as abnormal. "There is nothing intrinsically pathological in the conduct that is presently labeled as sexually compulsive or addictive," assert Levine and Troiden. "[T]hese behaviors have assumed pathological status only because powerful groups ... define them as such."[29] Characterization of "excessive" sexual behavior as a disease has its utility as well, though, as we have seen in the popular press, in exculpating wandering partners of moral wrong. When politicians and celebrities have found their careers jeopardized by sexual infidelity, they have in recent years found it convenient to blame their behavior on an addiction to sex.

The implications of portraying certain types of activities or substance use in terms of an addictive disease, though, are double-sided. On the one hand, characterizing people as addicts doubtless creates the potential for an autonomy-robbing power differential between addicted people and nonaddicted ones. On the other hand, though, because of this very diminution in autonomy, the attribution of addiction also provides an excuse, an escape from responsibility. Being "diagnosed" is used both as a way of demonizing some individuals, a way of separating them from the "healthy" folk, and as a way of releasing them from responsibility for certain behaviors. The flexibility of the term serves to make every kind of problem potentially an "addiction," which allows the legal system to construe treatment as either or both punitive and/or rehabilitative, depending on the case. As Gene Heyman points out, this dual implication of characterizing addiction as a disease existed before either the legislation governing addictive drugs or the science behind the medical model existed: "from the start, addiction invited both legal prohibitions and the impulse to cure it."[30] The very meaning of admitting to or being accused of being an "addict" carries import that could be either a condemnation of an individual's life, as when an employer or partner uses it as the basis for dissolution of a relationship, or exculpatory, as it has come to be in a growing number of legal cases. Gambling addiction has made a double transition in the eyes of the law over the past 200 years, according to I. Nelson Rose. Rose says that, while gambling prior to the 19th century was judged a sin, not to be spoken of, with its wins assumed to ensure eternal damnation, it gradually came to be seen instead as a vice, the fault and responsibility of the gambler.[31] This view, still the mainstream, implies that legal gambling debts, for example, are unenforceable, since the purveyor of gambling, like the purveyor of prostitution, is seen as exploiting the gambler's vices, and acts at his own risk. With "pathological gambling" becoming a recognized disorder in the 3rd edition of the DSM, the view that gambling is a choice totally within the control of the gambler began to fade. Like sexual addiction, addiction to shoplifting, and alcohol and drug addiction, the disease model has been used successfully by many defendants in cases involving excessive gambling. Some attorneys even advertise on their websites that they can assist clients by showing that the defendant's actions are the result of addiction. At the very least, they claim to be able to undermine the charge of specific intent to undertake criminal activity, thereby minimizing penalties. Of course, if this line of defense is employed in order to receive a "not guilty by reason of insanity" verdict, then the addict faces a dubious future within the labyrinth of mental health institutions

Social inequities and other ecological factors

As any addiction researcher or therapist would agree, drugs and other addictive behaviors serve a function in the addict's life, at least in the early phases of use; otherwise, the inclination to excessive imbibing would never develop. As we have seen, various stimulants have kept workers in a variety of developing economies working steadily to bring about fortunes for the producers of the substances to which the workers were addicted. Moreover, many returning soldiers and other post-traumatic stress disorder (PTSD) sufferers use drugs or alcohol to mask overwhelming feelings, as do individuals with depression, bipolar disorder, and anxiety disorders. Over and above that, we are obligated to look at the stymying social inequities that have continually developed alongside world markets over the past century, but particularly dramatically in the past 15 years, and the changes that these inequities have brought to the quality of life for huge masses of people. According to Credit

Suisse Research Institute's 2014 report, for instance, "[a]ggregate household wealth has more than doubled since the start of the millennium from USC 117 trillion in 2000 to USC 263 trillion in mid-2014," with the number of millionaires rising 164% during that period.[32] At the same time, an Oxfam report calculated in early 2014 that the eighty-five richest individuals on the planet owned as much of the world's resources as the poorest half of humanity combined. Since the beginning of the worldwide financial crisis in 2008, the number of billionaires worldwide has grown to 1,645, while homelessness around the globe has increased steeply. From July-November 2007 to the same period in 2008, for instance, the number of families entering New York City shelters rose by 40%.[33] In another powerful example, a survey by the National Alliance to End Homelessness found that 10% of clients being assisted between 2008 and 2009, at the height of the mortgage lending crisis, were experiencing homelessness as a result of foreclosure.[34] The majority of these individuals were renters whose landlords could not afford their mortgage payments, leaving the renters with no recourse and no deposits to recover. While many of us think about the huge differences between rich and poor as occurring between wealthy, developed countries and traditionally impoverished countries, the numbers of impoverished and homeless people in the United States belies that claim. "Around the world, inequality is making a mockery of the hopes and ambitions of billions of the poorest people," the Credit Suisse report announces.[35] This sort of disparity in income and security brings with it a kind of despair that prevents people from finding sources of meaning and value in many aspects of life.

Neuroscientist Carl Hart, a distinguished professor tenured in two departments at Columbia University, member of the National Advisory Council on Drug Abuse, and research scientist in the Division of Substance Abuse at the New York State Psychiatric Institute, grew up a poor boy in Miami who both used and dealt drugs. He argues that drugs are not the problem. He says that for him, while growing up the "problem was poverty, drug policy, lack of jobs – a wide range of things. And drugs were just one sort of component" that wasn't as important as researchers have suggested."[36] In a 2011 review of numerous kinds of neuroimaging and neuropsychological studies, Hart's research group showed that claims regarding the effects of methamphetamine on cognitive performance and changes in the brain were flawed, not replicated, and exaggerated. Not only are the media to blame for spreading misperceptions about drug use and its dangers, Hart says, but so is the scientific establishment, because scientists rarely speak up to correct misrepresentations by their peers. Why? Because the value for scientists is to avoid being wrong. Making claims outside the orthodoxy might expose them. But the price for adhering to orthodoxy in these cases is high. According to Hart, punishments for possession in the United States have been "inconsistent with the scientific evidence and ... exaggerated the harms associated with crack cocaine use. The monetary and human costs of this misunderstanding are incalculable."[37] The social milieu in which they are taken, rather than the drugs themselves, have the most dramatic impact on whether individuals become addicted. For many of those whom we would call addicted, Hart's lab found, when worthwhile alternative life choices were available, drug addiction was not a widespread issue. Bruce Alexander's group, as we saw previously, discovered a similar pattern with respect to the rats in Rat Park – social environment played a significant role in whether rats chose to self-administer drugs. In fact, as Heyman, asserts, "every major epidemiological study conducted over the past 30 years" reports the same thing – when viable alternatives for a valued life are available, they will be eventually be chosen over drugs.[38] Such options all too often, however, aren't available. According to the US Bureau of Justice Statistics, personal income from all sources for 83% of jail inmates interviewed in 2004 was less than $2000/monthly, and less than $1000 for 59%, although over half were employed full time in the month prior to arrest. Add to this that over half of the jail inmates interviewed had grown up either with a single parent or under the care of a guardian, as well as that only 50% of them had earned a high school diploma, and the picture emerges of a population with little hope for viable alternatives for a good life. It is no surprise, given these numbers, that 66% and 69% of inmates interviewed reported regular alcohol or drug use, respectively. Meanwhile, the National Institute of Justice and the National Center on Addiction and Substance Abuse at Columbia both estimate that the actual number is closer to 80%.

Corroborating this wider view of the factors contributing to addiction, one researcher on causes of drug addiction in Pakistan found that social and cultural beliefs, in combination with socioeconomic conditions, play an important part in the explanation of why some people are more likely to become addicts than others.[39] Over 23% of those responding to the "World Opium Survey 1972" cited the attempt to escape from personal or economic problems, difficult, laborious jobs, or "sexual reasons" as their impetus for using drugs. While nearly 34% of the addicted individuals surveyed claimed that they began taking drugs as a cure for physical illness, disease, or injury, 74% of them were addicted to opium, which is never prescribed by physicians. The implication of this survey, according to Karamat Ali, is that "social disorganization and deprivation of legitimate means for achieving socially accepted goals" leads to addiction.[40] The "sexual reasons" response is interesting, given social facts in Pakistan: there, sex for any reason other than procreation in marriage is frowned upon (and in many cases is illegal or impossible, because of constant sex segregation). In this case, drugs are often taken for the purpose of making sex last longer with prostitutes, since interactions with these women are infrequent, as well as to deal with the stresses of prohibited homosexuality, or simply to overcome the anxiety and guilt associated with sex in order to enjoy it. Again, social circumstances here prevent individuals from obtaining generally desirable human goods. Crushing poverty has the same effect. "Hard jobs with low nutrition, poor health condition [sic] and no recreation compel poor people to use drugs," Ali concludes.[41] Similarly, in a study of impoverished Colombian adolescents, Daniel Lende found that teens often used drugs to shift their attention from "worrisome, stressful or painful things."[42] Drugs were cited as a way of alleviating the stress associated with family, poverty, and prevalent armed violence. Other researchers had previously found that intrapersonal distress was related to drug use for boys and girls in Colombia to a greater degree than it is in the United States, as were violence and drug availability. This difference, the researchers speculated, could be because the drug trade and violence are more endemic to Colombia than to the United States.[43] However, Gilbert Quintero and Sally Davis found in 2002 that Hispanic and Native American teens smoked cigarettes for reasons similar to those cited by Colombian youth, for example, to alleviate mood issues arising from family life, school, and the stresses that attend poverty and social inequality.[44] This finding, Quintero and Davis argue, should interest medical anthropologists, given the otherwise "highly charged, health-focused atmosphere" in the United States at the turn of the millennium. Although these Hispanic and Native American youths cited other reasons for smoking typical among US teenagers in general, such as image maintenance and the influence of peers, one of the most pervasive reasons for smoking given by this group (including 33% Hispanic youth and 24% Native American youth) was "to relax, calm down, and relieve stress in order to treat various emotional and bodily states of being, including 'nerves, anger, frustration, depression, and 'boredom.'"[45] Once again, we see that lack of alternative means for achieving high-quality human lives pervades the list of reasons provided for opting for addictive substances.

The other side of the money

The sort of passive endorsement that we find for locating relief in mind-altering substances in many cultures sounds not so different from the "happy hour" created in the 1960s in the United States that became "binge weekends" for working adults who entered into competitive, faceless positions in giant corporations. It seems that after-work and weekend binge drinking and eating, officially loudly bemoaned, serve to maintain social order, largely by promoting apathy in the face of alienation, income inequity, and unfulfilling work. When people are either escaping through indulgence or are hung over and remorseful as a result of it, serious attention and meaningful change is unlikely to be brought to bear on the oppressive religious, social and/or economic inequities. On this view, in which everyone is left on their own to navigate a path of providing themselves with housing, food, transportation, health- and childcare, in uncertain circumstances, it is easier to blame those who cope with the stresses of everyday life by numbing themselves in some way than it is to take a hard look at the structural and political arrangements that create the need to self-soothe. In such an environment, it is much easier to "treat" those who falter in the productivity cycle by putting them into treatment or jail than it is to take seriously the circumstances that make life so difficult. As we have noted, appeal to the disease model, to the power of the drug, and to the "addictive personality" shifts attention away from any questions that might be raised about social contributions to people's misery and self-medication and distraction, allowing instead everything from drugs to gambling to video games to shopping to just about anything that one might do or ingest, to become an object of certain "defective" people's obsession. This approach, however, has little to offer toward improving the lot of the addicted. As noted by Paul Hayes, professor of Drug Policy at the London School of Hygiene and Tropical Medicine, despite the cultural narrative to the contrary, "the experience of the overwhelming majority of addicts" is that "social isolation, economic exclusion, criminality and fragile mental health preceded their drug use rather than being caused by it," and, he argues, until this is understood, we "are doomed to misdirect our energy and resources toward blaming the outcasts and the vulnerable for their plight rather than recasting our economic and social structures to give them access to the sources of resilience that protect the rest of us."[46]

But there's something even more sinister than institutionalized racism and classism behind the shifting nature of addiction in the worldwide market. As is often the case in seeking causes of crimes and social ills, it is illuminating to follow the money. In following the money, we find that, for instance, keeping marijuana illegal has been a priority of certain organizations that benefit from the financial success of certain prescription drug companies. While the general tide of public opinion over the past several years has turned in favor of relaxing marijuana laws, the Community Anti-Drug Coalition of America (CADCA), for example, a vocal opponent of the legalization of marijuana, and other groups at the forefront of opposition to relaxing marijuana laws, tellingly "derive a significant portion of their budget from opioid manufacturers and other pharmaceutical companies."[47] According to a confidential financial disclosure from the Partnership for Drug-Free Kids, the organization's largest donors include "Purdue Pharma, the manufacturer of OxyContin, and Abbott Laboratories, maker of the opioid Vicodin. Perhaps worse, Alkermes, a major supporter of the CADCA, makes an opioid, Zohydrol, which is reportedly ten times as strong as Oxycontin."[48] When forty-two drug-prevention groups protested approval of Zohydrol, neither CADCA nor the Partnership for Drug-Free Kids joined the protest. So it seems that the political urgency of keeping marijuana illegal may derive from something other than concern for the health and well-being of the populace.

A good place to look for the source of that urgency might be the multibillion-dollar pharmaceutical industry. America constitutes only 5% of the world's population, but consumes 50% of the world's pharmaceuticals, and 80% of the world's narcotics. In 2000, 290 people per day (106,000 per year) died as a result of their prescription drugs.[49] According to the Centers for Disease Control and Prevention (CDC), 44 people die in America every day from prescription opioid overdose, three times as many as die from heroin, meth, and cocaine combined. Although this rate is rising steadily (the CDC reports a 117% increase from 1999 to 2012), addiction to these drugs does not have the same meaning in our culture as addiction to alcohol or other drugs does. Against these perceptions, however, consider that in 2012, drug overdose was the leading cause of accidental death, and 53% of these deaths were caused by pharmaceuticals. Of those deaths, 72% involved prescription painkillers. These are not the drug overdoses that we see in mainstream media, and drug overdose has not yet been publicly discussed as a serious public health problem. At least there has been no lessening in the prescribing and selling of these drugs.[50] The most plausible explanation for the continuing proliferation of these drugs, and the addiction and deaths that come with them, is that they mean big money, and big money means power. In 2010, Novo Nordisk, Inc., for example, saw $2.67B in sales, while by 2009 Bristol-Myers Squibb's revenues had a reached $18.8B. But it is the astronomical *rate of rise* in these companies' revenues that is most striking: Eli Lily's profits, for instance, rose from $875M in 2003 to $23B in 2010. As a result of the Medicare Prescription Drug Plan of 2003, the campaign that was led by a group of legislators, each of whom received hundreds of thousands of dollars in campaign dollars from pharmaceutical companies, "the pharmaceutical industry realized an eight billion dollar increase in profit."[51] While it would be going too far to say that our government and the pharmaceutical industry operate in a conspiratorial way to foster addiction and then blame the addicts for it, it surely would be reasonable to assert that when an industry has the capacity to influence major policy decisions, the role of that industry in the social phenomenon of increasingly endemic addiction cannot be ignored.

Meanings and addiction

In 2011, 6.9 million people were under corrective control in the United States. As we have seen, as many as 80% of those incarcerated were considered problem users or addicts of alcohol or other drugs. Not all addictions, though, are equally likely to land a person in prison, or cause him to be blamed or ostracized. Addiction to cigarettes is not significantly correlated with incarceration, nor is video gaming addiction, food addiction, or gambling addiction. For many of these "diagnosable" addictions, there is not even much social stigma attached, particularly, and tellingly, with respect to addiction to work. In many cases, it is the social meanings of particular drugs and activities that determine whether engagement with them is associated with blame, shame, and confrontations with the law. The primary drugs being used by the adolescents in the Lend study in Colombia, for example, were marijuana, followed by *basuco*, which is similar to crack, as well as cocaine, inhalants, and street-supplied pills, in short, the drugs of the poor and the young.[52] The drug that to which the Pakistanis were overwhelmingly addicted was opium, a drug about which Ali says that if you "[v]isit any shop, you will see beggars, domestic servants, truck drivers and stray children queuing to purchase this pernicious narcotic," whereas better-off young people tend instead to use LSD, marijuana, and morphia.[53] In the United States, marijuana and heroin are cheaper to access than cocaine and prescription drugs. In general, the "addiction problem," and the incarceration that attends it, seems disproportionately associated with those drugs and activities indulged in by the young and the poor. To some degree, it appears to be the meanings of these substances, as well as of the activities of gambling and certain kinds of sexual activity, that seem to drive policy, rather than hard scientific evidence about their relative dangers.

In a 2013 study, obesity accounted for 18% of deaths among adults between 40 and 85 in America, but since unhealthy weights have become the norm, it goes virtually unmentioned in public policy, except for requiring suppliers of unhealthy foods to inform consumers.[54] No public policy regulates the behavior of the consumers of food. At the same time in the United States, where marijuana has been legalized in several states, and decriminalized in others, or legalized for medical use, official US policy nevertheless keeps it on Schedule 1, among the most dangerous drugs available. But surely this discrepancy cannot be accounted for by scientific research. In fact, the research argues the other way, as we can see from the obesity case alone. Policy seems to be driven by some other force. And there are consequences. Kornblum argues that categorizing marijuana in this way "helped prepare the way for far more troublesome drug epidemics in minority communities like Harlem."[55] His argument is that portraying drugs such as marijuana as on a par with other Schedule 1 substances, since marijuana and some others of these drugs seem to have few ill effects, leads to the impression that the government's cataloging system should be ignored. Other drugs deemed sufficiently dangerous to be categorized as Schedule 1 drugs, many will reason, might be just as safe to use. At the same time, categorizing large numbers of substances as among the most dangerous brings about the incarceration of large populations for possession of drugs that could be legalized, decriminalized, taxed, and regulated. As Kornblum says, "the public at large has supported prohibitions it knows are not effective because to do so gives people assurance of a moral order however symbolic," and however contributory to "the stigma born by racially distinct people in America."[56] The problem here is that whether drugs or activities are considered addictive, and therefore are outlawed, is often much more influenced by social and political leanings and dogmas than by research findings, or what sociologist Howard Becker once called "politically inconvenient scientific knowledge."

Now consider the purported addiction popularly discussed in the United States in the 1980s and '90s, but which seems to have lost momentum recently in the addiction literature: the addiction to work. This one seems not to fit the mold of other "addictions," with respect to social and political attitudes, at least not in highly competitive societies. Certainly we don't find workaholics at the forefront of the incarcerated population or of those in treatment centers. In fact, workaholism is often claimed with an attitude of pride. What does this tell us about this form of "addiction"? It is not the case that overwork does not cause harm. Stress, distractedness, and lack of sleep wreak havoc on everything from cardiac health to personal relationships to driving safety. But these disruptions occur only at the individual level. More generally, "workaholism" contributes to the maintenance of the economy and social order. Whether for these reasons or others, it has not found its way into the DSM. Here we find a social construct modeled on addiction, but one that carries an even less negative connotation than food addiction. So, what seems perhaps most important in determining whether an activity engaged in beyond typical levels is considered normal or pathological has everything to do with the place that that activity has in upholding or threatening certain kinds of order and social structure. It has everything to do, that is, with the meanings that that activity carries within a particular society.

Not only are meanings important with respect to social aspects of addiction but they are also central to the experience of addiction from the subjective side, as well. As long ago as 1938, sociologist Alfred Lindesmith argued against the then-prevailing view that addicts were madmen, rapists, and killers.[57] Vigorously opposing the positivistic, quantitative methodology that became popular in the social sciences in his day, Lindesmith's attention was concentrated on qualitative research, comprising mostly open-ended, unstructured interviews with heroin addicts. As opposed to psychoanalytic and medical models that attempted to isolate the essence of addiction, Lindesmith was much more concerned with examining the *process* of becoming addicted. In this regard, he argued that "the symbolic meanings [that] drug users communicated to one another regarding the effects were essential to the transformation of a non-addicted heroin user into a heroin addict."[58] Lindesmith's unique contribution here was that, in contrast to both the behavioristic and the disease models coming into vogue at the time, he outspokenly distinguished the phenomena of tolerance and physical dependence from the phenomenon of addiction per se. In this sociologist's view, neither the behaviorist nor the disease model could explain the subjective experience central to correctly characterizing addiction.[59] In pointing to the irreducible subjective experience involved in addiction, Lindesmith was adducing an aspect of addiction that none of the reductionistic physical theories had the tools to address. The response to Lindesmith, however, as epistemology and philosophy of mind developed, was to focus attention on the rejection of mental/physical dualism, and on developing one of two alternatives: either reductionism of one sort or another, or what came in the American tradition of sociology to be called a "praxeological approach." On this latter view, with respect to addiction in particular, addicts not only learn symbolically, or linguistically, to attach meanings to drug use or addictive activities and their accoutrements but also "to use drugs as resources in given fields of practical action."[60] The focus in this case is on the context – specifically, the context of practical action. On the process ontology that we have adopted throughout this book, this central involvement of meanings in the development of both the vulnerability to, and the addictive uses of, substances and activities requires no new conceptual equipment and no special account. Certainly context is important, but it is not, any more than any other single thing is, "the answer" to explaining what addiction is. Addiction, like all human activities and psychological experiences, is the natural consequence of the progress of a highly complex, self-organizing system organism that develops in and interacts with its physical and social environments in particular ways. Addiction is a multilevel emergent phenomenon that cannot be fully understood at any one of those levels of analysis. In the next chapter we turn specifically to the role that meaning plays in the assembly of the set of phenomena that we call addiction.

6 Addiction and Meaning

Addictive processes emerge from hierarchies of interacting complex adaptive processes both internal and external to an individual. These processes include and emerge from cells and cell systems, and also from psychological phenomena, as well as from higher-level emergent processes operating at both the physical and social levels. From the beginning, the world outside the individual is dynamically involved in the development of his or her physical and psychological traits and dispositions. As we saw in Chapter 4, the influence of social conceptions on one's experience of diverse aspects of life, such as family, property, work, discomfort, and gratification, are profound and have a significant impact on whether, how, and to what extent individuals may become addicted. Patterns of activity at this level interact with personal and subpersonal patterns of action to create meaning. Meaning operates at the core of addiction for the addict and her close social circle, as well as for researchers, treatment professionals, and policy makers. When an individual becomes addicted to some substance or activity, what that thing means to her shifts fundamentally, as does her conception of herself and the rest of the world. The meaning of that substance or activity to her spouse, friends, children, or parents, although completely different from what it is for the addicted person, is a driving force in their lives. To understand how this works, we need a theory of meaning.

First, though, let us consider some common observations. Interactions between addicts and their nonaddicted friends and family often leave the impression that the two groups live in vastly different worlds. Nonaddicts try to understand addicts' actions in terms that make sense of what seems to be obviously self-undermining and otherwise irrational behavior. Addicts often feel that they aren't understood, and, as a result, that they are being judged or threatened or dismissed. It should come as no surprise, then, that people who interact with addicted individuals often interpret the addicted person's thinking in ways that fail utterly to correspond with the addict's own experiences. The two groups of people use similar sentences, but seem to talk past one another. Everyone, including the person struggling with addiction, agrees that the addictive behavior is destructive and pointless. However, nonaddicts tend to attribute the addict's repeated relapses to a failure to care about others, or about the addict himself. They may even attribute the behavior to the addict's trying to punish others or end relationships. These are considerations that perhaps never occur to the person struggling with an addictive pattern. Meanwhile, in one commonly cited model, the addicted person himself may be struggling with a cycle of firm-minded intention to abstain, followed by return to use, which is in turn followed by remorse and a return to firm-minded repudiation of use. He agrees with all the reasons why he should stop his use, shows clear understanding of the consequences of failing to do so, and wants to follow the path that he and those who care about him envision. He sees a happy freedom from the substance or activity that has plagued him, along with productivity and a positive future. Then suddenly something happens and the world shifts. Everything in a moment seems different, and use seems essential, even inevitable. But what has changed? Family and friends are stunned, disappointed, angered, and mystified. They had believed that everyone was on the same page. Was the addict lying the entire time? The only phenomenon common to the two groups seems to be the observed behavior itself. Their respective understandings of reasons, causes, and explanations seem to exist in separate, perhaps internally coherent, but unconnected systems.

We have two things to explain here: the systematic failure of communication between addicts and their friends and family, and the sudden and concrete world shifts that can take place within an addict's own experience. The latter is a well-known phenomenon in recovery circles. Moving in the direction from use to abstinence, this gestalt shift is expressed in terms of various metaphors, such as "seeing the light" or "experiencing a spiritual conversion." It is worth noting that both of the phenomena that we seek to explain are generalizable. Both the systematic failure of communication and the gestalt shift characteristic of transition out of addiction not only seem to concern addicts and the nonaddicts with whom they interact but also enter into communication breakdowns between any two groups with different worldviews in the one case, as well as into the sudden shifts experienced within individuals when they experience religious or scientific conversions. The theory of meaning offered here is thus general in nature. It is not intended to apply only to addicts or to dealing with addiction – although it is the only theory available that can account for certain phenomena central to addiction and recovery. As we saw in the previous chapter, addiction is at least in part a social construct. Without the meanings ascribed to certain objects, feelings, and events in particular contexts, no substance use or repetitive activity would ever amount to a psychological, much less a social, *problem*. There would only be cause and effect. But humans experience the world fundamentally as meaningful, and so it becomes critical that we see how meanings arise and how apparently identical objects, actions, and events can have such different meanings for different people, and for the same person at different times.

Concepts

To begin, let us inquire into what drives the systematic misunderstandings and failures to communicate that seem to occur between addicted individuals and their friends and families. Nonaddicts believe that what they see is simply what the world presents: someone they care about is acting selfishly and irrationally. Supporting this conclusion is the assumption that the way the nonaddict sees the world is the way it is. This conclusion presupposes a sort of theory of meaning. The theory tacitly assumed seems to be that meaning comes from the world's impressing itself on experiencers. Numerous philosophers, from ancient times to the present, have defended this sort of view. Historically, John Locke and David Hume, for example, believed that the way we understand the world is through experience imprinting itself on our minds, then being copied. Concepts, or "ideas," as these thinkers called them, are either the copies themselves of original experiences, either internal or external, or they are derived from these copies through such mental operations as abstraction of some parts from the details, the rearranging of parts, and so forth. Once copied or created from copied components, these concepts are taken to be representative of the way the world is.

However, some thinkers have been taken with the notion that concepts, at least the most important ones, must be "innate" or inborn in the mind or soul. This is because, according to this group of philosophers, which includes Plato, René Descartes, Immanuel Kant, and some contemporary thinkers, it is impossible to acquire certain concepts through sense experience. There are two reasons for thinking this. One reason offered is that certain ideas are necessary prerequisites for making sense of our sense experience. If we have no concepts at all to start with, these thinkers ask, then how would we ever recognize anything, or see how things can be related? How can you tell that what someone is pointing at is a dog (rather than the color of it, or the way it moves) when that person is first teaching you the word, unless you already know what a dog is? It is the age-old dilemma of learning, first posed by Plato: how can anyone ever learn anything new? If he doesn't know what it is, he won't recognize it when he sees it, and if he does, then he has no need to look. If not the concept itself, later thinkers conclude, at least the principles of individuation or something like that must be innate to the mind. Another reason given for belief in innate ideas is that certain kinds of concepts seemingly cannot be acquired through experience. Historically, those have included modal concepts such as necessity and impossibility. We learn from experience that things are in fact some way or other, but we cannot learn through this method that things could be no other way. Neither do we ever encounter the impossible, by definition. These kinds of concepts, the argument goes, must then be already "in the mind," regardless of whether we are ever conscious of them, and regardless of whether they were learned in another life, bestowed by God, or derived through evolution.

There are problems with both kinds of theories of meaning. On the one hand, innate ideas would seemingly require some kind of appeal either to the supernatural – to Plato's realm of Forms, or to God's creations of minds – or to evolution. The first option defies the naturalism that the current theory embraces. But the second option will not work, either, since it would mean that certain concepts, or at least certain mental mechanisms responsible for concepts, are the result of genetic determination. This seems incredibly unlikely, however, given that concepts emerge from the disposition of sets of neurons to fire together, which is in turn determined by constant adjustment of the strength of the synapses that connect them (firing together, thus "wiring together," via LTP). While the mechanism of synaptic strength adjustment is certainly determined by genes, DNA cannot be responsible for specific concepts. Genes would have to be capable of setting individual synaptic weight values for the approximately 100 trillion synapses that connect our neurons, using their approximately 10 billion functional base pairs. Since every brain is uniquely wired, unlike other body parts (one heart, comprising two atria, two ventricles, one pulmonary valve, etc.), it is impossible to see how genes could accomplish this.[1] However, if we understand ideas or concepts to be copies of the external world, we have no reason to expect that the conceptual frameworks could differ as much as they apparently do among different people, and within the same person over time.

A theory of meaning that better accounts for the two problems that we are considering has its grounding in pragmatism, the psychology of child development, and neuroscience more broadly. To make the case for it, we begin again from the presumption that living organisms are complex, dynamic systems that are constantly adapting to stay organized against the natural tendency toward increasing entropy. They are constantly evolving moving patterns, doing things to keep themselves alive in an environment. This means that certain things are going to have direct implications for their survival, and those things will be relevant to them. In other words, the fact of being a living organism by its very nature involves the capacity for meaning making in some sense. As human babies' extremely complex brains are developing, their attention is drawn to, for instance, their own internal discomforts – early on, generally signals from the gut. And they are just as aware of signals received from caregivers. Meanings, on this view, are essentially involved with action and purpose – on what one needs and wants to pick out from the environment, which, as we have discussed, is constantly changing us (feeding us, heating or cooling us, comforting us), and being changed by us. At the neural level, we have seen that the ways in which babies' brains develop are constrained by the environments in which they live. Now we can add to that the fact that even before we are born, associations between experiences are already being made, and the resulting meanings are beginning to be constructed. Below we discuss the specifics of how this meaning making operates, and how the meanings that we construct play into addiction and recovery.

First, though, it is important to see two things: 1) that the view we are exploring is not the received view of meaning, and 2) the implications that the more commonly accepted views have for the two problems we have outlined. In general, concepts are understood today by the preponderance of contemporary linguists and philosophers not so differently from the way that they were by classical thinkers. Certainly current theories vary in many details, but the majority of them generally regard concepts as mental representations that are to be understood as something like copies of the external world, caused in us by inputs from the world. Some lines of contemporary argumentation, such as that put forth by philosopher Jerry Fodor, in addition to this structure, maintain a tight link to nativists' views, retaining a central position for innateness in the theory of concepts.[2] Fodor's theory, which he characterizes as "informational atomism," includes two basic claims: first, that the content of our concepts "is constituted by some sort of nomic, (rule-governed) mind-world relation," in other words, that our concepts represent the world in some systematic way, and second, that concepts are simple and fundamental – the atoms of our mental representations. In this system, primitive concepts are undefined. This seems to be corroborated by experience: perceptual experiences, for example, such as the taste of licorice, the smell of a rose, or the way that a cocaine high feels, cannot be defined, although perhaps they can be described in some way (based on other sense experiences, which are useless if the person to whom we are doing the describing doesn't have *those* primitive concepts). The contents of these primitive concepts, according to informational atomism, are acquired through information encoded by our various sensory receptors. Then these primitive concepts are put together "by the application of a finite number of combinatorial principles" to create representations of things that we encounter in the world.[3] Just as we use the rules of grammar to construct sentences, Fodor's language of thought theory says, so do we build mental representations of the world out of fundamental concepts using a limited set of rules of combination. We can create an unlimited number of thoughts (or sentences, on our above analogy), using just these primitive concepts and combinatorial principles, because, as Fodor says, "the application of these constructive principles can iterate without bound."[4]

Why is this important? It is important because some version of it is the most widely accepted view of what meaning is, and one that explains how most people assume that their conceptions and beliefs work. It also reveals something telling regarding how individuals who think of concepts in this way often view people who do not see things as they do. If our concepts represent the world in the way that Fodor's computational view suggests, via information transduced and relayed over and over again from our sensory receptors to ever-higher levels of processing in our central nervous system, and if the *meanings* of our concepts are the things in the world that cause those concepts, then what you see is what you get. The way that you see the world is the way that it is: your concept of DOG is caused by dogs (caps are used here to distinguish concepts from the use or mention of words).[5] What your concept of DOG means is dogs, the things that cause the concept. So, the concept of ADDICT held by the addiction researchers in the various fields that we have considered, as well as by therapists and families of addicts, is caused by addicts. Unless someone is defective, she must *mean* the same thing that every other normally operating person does when she conceives of a substance as DANGEROUS, or when she conceives of an individual as an ADDICT. Fodor calls this feature of his view *asymmetric dependence* of error on correctness.[6] The way to understand error on this view is as a malfunction in a normally reliable process. Since the addicted individuals are by all accounts the defective members of a population, whenever there is a disconnection between their concepts and those of and nonaddicts, the addicts must be the ones who are wrong. They must be wrong (or lying) when they say, "I love you. My behavior has nothing to do with that." While there are caveats here to consider with respect to whether the meaning of concepts is natural or nonnatural, theory laden or not, the important point is that if the atomic informational approach is right, then people with normally operating senses and brains are in a position to tell the people with defective systems how the world really is. And that is a scary and unwelcome thought for people struggling with addiction, although it does seem to be how the medical model works. Truth and power accrue to those who would treat the defective addict's problem, while compliance and surrender to being "fixed" is the addict's lot.

Despite the widespread acceptance of this view of how the mind generates meanings, there are good theoretical reasons for thinking that it is wrong. For one thing, according to Walter J. Freeman, who heads the Freeman Laboratory for Nonlinear Neurodynamics at the University of California at Berkeley, it all rests on "a mistaken view of how neurons work."[7] Just how they work is exquisitely complex, but the main point to note here is that, rather than acting like the ones and zeros of binary code, the electrical signals in neurons act in a number of intricately complex ways that are best understood at the population level rather than at the level of individual neurons. Meanings operate, as we have said, in living, dynamic organisms, which are complex systems of systems, even down to the particles that make up the living cells and beyond. The neuronal level of activity attracted attention in the 1940s as the computing machine was being conceived. As we know, neurons at any instant are either firing or at rest. This conception of neurons led to the analogy to binary code, and the world was off and running with the metaphor of mind as computer. But the metaphor does not fit. Neuronal activity is actually measured in a number of different ways at the same time, at different parts of the neuron. For example, it is measured both in terms of its pulse rate (at one end) and in terms of the intensity of its wave amplitude (at the other). And every living neuron is always, always active.[8] With perhaps a hundred billion neurons undergoing thousands of simultaneous interactions in thousandths of a second, the effects of an individual neuron on the system are vanishingly slight.

It is the interactions among groups of neurons rather than the actions of individuals that are central. Moreover, it is ill conceived to understand concepts or representations of the world as symbols that are stored somewhere in the brain; instead, they are ever-changing, pulsing, activities. What is more, the affective systems in the brain cannot be left out of the calculation. Although it has no place in the atomistic informational account, emotion has everything to do with how our concepts are created and used. Neither an addict's nor his spouse's concept of the drug or activity affecting their family seems anything like a symbolic representation of something outside. It seems rather to be a viscerally loaded constituent of his world.

For this reason and others, it is reasonable to conclude that symbolic encoding of information from sense receptors does not amount to meaning, however much that information is manipulated. Interpretation is necessary before information can be said to *represent* anything; information is only information *to* someone or something.[9] Without positing a homunculus (a "little man" in our brains) somewhere along the line to interpret the information received, it seems that a system like the one Fodor supposes would never generate *meaning*. It would just exchange symbols for symbols. The obvious trick of proposing a "self" or "mind" that could do the interpretation would just push the question back – where and how does that "self" arise in the electrical storm of firing neurons that is all that seems to be inside brains – the very same brain that is supposed to be generating meanings? Another way of looking at the question is this: why does a person's idea of a baggie of heroin carry so much import for her as well as for the authorities? It is surely not because the retinas involved have absorbed certain photons, allowing them to detect the edges, the sides, and the color of the baggie, and so forth, transducing and sending that information forward for binding at ever-higher levels of processing. As we will see later, an understanding of what that baggie *is* requires that it be perceived in the first place in a situation within a whole world in which it plays a role.

Finally, the language of thought approach provides no explanation for why anyone should want to say that information detection and transduction of signals results in anything particularly *mental*. The sort of causation that atomic informationalism sees as the source of mental representations happens in all kinds of systems, such as those involving light switches and thermostats, to which no one would ever attribute mentality. Even if information detection and transduction happen in a brain, as Levine and Mark Bickhard note, as happens for instance when neurons respond to various neurotransmitters, that doesn't mean that there exists any *mental* content.[10] Neurons clearly do detect certain chemicals, and send signals in response, as we have seen. When a particular threshold of activation has been crossed in an individual dopaminergic neuron, for instance, the neuron fires, releasing dopamine into the synaptic gap. Information is detected and transduced, and a signal is sent (in fact, lots of signals are sent), and it all happens in the brain. But nothing in that process suggests anything of a specifically mental character.

Naturalism and prototypes

On the view that we have been elaborating, meanings for biological entities are a function of experience, and experience is always a matter of interactions between the particular internal and external environments of organisms. In our pursuit of an understanding of meaning making and its role in addiction, we are seeking an account that accords with all that we have come to understand about how human organisms, and in particular, addicted humans and those who care about them, understand the objects, places, and words involved in the experience of an addictive pattern. In seeking a theory of meaning that accounts for the phenomena observed in addiction, it seems important to consider not just conceptual issues but also the empirical data regarding how our concepts are built and what that says about their structure and function. First, since minds are not separate from the world, but are emergent from it, our conception cannot be that meanings are copies in the mind of things in the world. The term "copies" implies separation between the representation and the represented – and two different media in which those two things exist. That is just what does not exist on the present account. Second, because of the whole-brain massively recurrent and dynamic processing from which meanings emerge, they are necessarily always emotion- and history infused and peculiar to each individual. Moreover, meanings are not static things, but rather are constantly evolving processes. The same object or place (or word) can come to have different meanings to the same person over the course of a day or a year, and does, as she transitions into or out of addiction. This happens without the implication that anything correspondingly changes in the world, or in her perceptual apparatus, although it is true on another level that everything in the world, including individuals' perceptual apparatuses, is always changing. Such change needs an explanation.

In developing our understanding of how addicts conceive of the world, and how those conceptions can shift, we would do well to keep an eye on the findings of the best science associated with these questions. In addition to Freeman, numerous other neuroscientists have remarked on the fact that the general public, and many philosophers and psychologists as well, misunderstand the nature of the mind's representation of the world. The first thing to note is that, as we have shown, we do not "take in the world" by being passively imprinted with its forms. Although what information we do get from the world may be close to how it is, from our extremely limited perspective, as organisms with the perceptual and processing setups that we have, we in no way encounter the world "as it is." Neuroscientist Antonio Damasio, for example, puts it this way:

> [w]hatever the fidelity may be, neural patterns and the corresponding images are as much creations of the brain as they are products of the external reality that prompts their creation. When you and I look at an object outside ourselves, we form comparable images in our respective brains. We know this well because you and I can describe the object in very similar ways, down to fine details. But that does not mean that the image we see is the copy of whatever the object outside is like. Whatever it is like, in absolute terms, we do not know. The image we see is based on changes which occurred in our organisms – including the part of the organism called brain – when the physical structure of the object interacts with the body. The signaling devices located throughout our body – in the skin, in the muscles, in the retina, and so on – help construct neural patterns which map the organism's interaction with the object. The neural patterns are constructed according to the brain's own conventions, and are achieved transiently in the multiple sensory and motor regions of the brain that are suitable to process signals coming from particular body sites.[11]

So there is no sense in thinking that meaning, rather than lying in our concept of a thing, how it feels and looks to us, and the import that it has for us, emotionally and otherwise, resides instead in the objective thing itself, because there is no access to the thing outside of us, period. Every concept of every kind that finds its way into the virtual reality that is our experience of the world is emotion laden, spun out of interconnected neural systems including various limbic structures activated by and activating other parts of the brain's perceptual and processing apparatuses. Moreover, it is personal, depending as it does on the unique connections previously established in a particular brain. This does not mean that the world of our experience is not caused by interactions with the world; rather, it just means that our concepts, and the world that they constitute, are not things external to us. As philosopher Paul Churchland describes it, "the *content* of a concept is its highly peculiar *portrayal* of some aspect of the world, a portrayal that is often quite inaccurate, a portrayal that enjoys no automatic referential connection to the external world."[12] From this perspective, the denotative element, or reference, of any concept, rather than being the thing in the world that causes our perceptions, is just a conventional abstraction from these very personal, very perspectival portrayals that are developed over time by individuals. This is not the concept's meaning. The meaning of any concept is rather the place that that concept's content occupies relative to everything else in the individual's world, as carved out by her particular experience. This is not to say that there isn't a world outside us, or any such nonsensical thing; rather, it is merely to say that *our concepts* aren't merely the causal result of interacting with that world. Our concepts are our own internal portrayals of those things, brought about from internal as well as external elements. The smoker's concept of a cigarette, except in its most abstract outlines, is not the nonsmoker's; the details of a particular smoker's concept of "cigarette" are meted out entirely in emotional and physical connections to cigarettes and everything else in the world, derived from her specific history, body, and environment.

As Damasio notes, we are similar enough biologically that the representations that are built in individuals' minds are close enough that we "can accept without protest that we have formed *the* picture of some particular thing."[13] But the fact that we can accept it does not make it the case. Every idea and concept that we form is essentially tied to our own unique experiences and our whole body's neural and chemical structure and function. This was recognized in a crude form in the 18th century by British philosopher David Hume, who noted that even the most abstract ideas, such as the idea of God, "which seem the most wide of this origin [personal experience], are found, upon a nearer scrutiny, to be derived from it."[14] That mental representations, or *ideas*, as Hume calls them, are essentially private and experiential seems clear from his examples concerning emotion: "A man of mild manners can form no idea of inveterate revenge or cruelty; nor can a selfish heart easily conceive the heights of friendship and generosity." And of the experiences of external objects he says the same: one who has never had the opportunity to taste it, "has no notion of the relish of wine."[15] We could add that if it has never been experienced, a person could have no clear concept of a "high."' Hume was a simple imprint theorist, however, who could not have known about the active input and movement required for perception, or the involvement of feedback loops from parts of the brain shaped by previous experience, or by extension, the way in which our brains derive our concepts only over long experience. He does seem to recognize, though, that different individuals will have different representations of the world, and, until some confrontation occurs, won't know that they do.

Prototypes, unlike Humean ideas, are built slowly over time, and so, contrary to what the imprint theorists seem to have supposed, no one instance of a sense experience can therefore be the cause of a concept. As Churchland says, our semantic connections to the world are earned, by "strenuous cognitive activity expended over years of learning." This process of continual learning results in a portrayal of a fairly stable set of categories and their relations."[16] We experience sets of inputs that go together, over and over again, and learn to recognize regular groupings and to expect to find them. This means that the prototypes that are our concepts inherently carry with them relations to everything else in the world. We delineate individual things from the noisy background of the world, more and more precisely as we gain more experience, and so each concept has from the beginning an internal structure relating it to everything else, and it is the whole world together that constitutes the meaning of any and every thing. Our concepts themselves, on this understanding, inherently provide the possibility of the complex syntax that humans employ, of the limitless variety of things that we can say and think. They do this by providing within their own structure, which includes their relations to the rest of the world, implicit rules about the set of inferential roles that they can and cannot play. From the concept BROTHER, for example, because of its place within the whole semantic system, we see that we cannot directly infer anything about $A = \pi r^2$, the area of a circle, although we can infer things from that concept about maleness, familial relations, and so forth.

This variety of a holistic, prototype-based system of meanings can help us understand how people so radically misunderstand the experience of others. In fact, Churchland says in this regard that while for atomistic information theorists "it is a minor mystery why anyone ever misunderstands anyone else," on the holistic prototypical worldview, "it is a minor marvel that anyone ever understands anyone else."[17] This latter worldview has the ring of truth, when we think of how human interactions actually operate and, in particular, when we think of how addicts' interactions with "outsiders" differ from their interactions with other addicts. Although even individual addicts' experiences are all slightly different, and each person develops his own pattern with his substances or addictive activities, when they want to be understood, addicts often trust for understanding to others who have similar experiences, and, as a result, conceptual maps similar to their own, rather than to nonaddicts, who "just don't understand." A person with no experience of addictive patterns simply does not have a place in her map of the world, for example, for the urgency and compelling call associated with what she just sees as overpriced beer being hawked at a stadium, nor does she have a conceptual space for the map of a neighborhood that operates in the addict's mind, keyed to locations of liquor stores or pushers' corners, rather than to streets or subway stations or jogging paths.

Early development of concepts

The reason that the person with no experience of addiction completely lacks the sense of the compelling value of things such as beer in a stadium or cigarettes being puffed outside a restaurant door is because everyone's world results from her own particular constitution, activities, and interactions. The construction starts, as we have said, with intrinsically emotionally imbued concepts, which are developed through personal, emotion-laden experience, carved out from the world of "noise" with which we all begin – we have originally plenty of brain cells for processing inputs, but no organization with which to make sense of them. For example, a newborn experiences mainly undifferentiated noise, but the smells, sounds, and feelings in its own body of pressures here and there, and alarm or pain exchanged for pleasure and comfort, as well as the visual inputs that all come together when it encounters its mother or caregiver, become recognizable as a group, or a package, standing out from all the rest of the goings-on in the world. The first concepts developed in this way, distinguished from the rest of the world, are certainly not symbolic, but are nevertheless meaningful and complex, and without doubt affect laden. The milk that the baby tastes, with its accompanying feel in the mouth and its pleasurable accompaniment of cessation of discomfort in the body, may not yet be separated from the caregiver that provides it, but it will be at some point, and particularly early if the baby is bottle fed, and by more than one caregiver. The point is that every concept is hard earned, through much experience, and the more the baby learns, the more the baby is able to learn, since he has increasingly more points of reference for distinguishing one thing from another.

To make all this organizing and meaning making work, babies have to be motivated to interact with the world, given the significant effort and overcoming of fear that the task requires, and they are so motivated – through the same reward system that is activated when drugs of addiction are ingested. They begin to want to interact with the world because they get positive reinforcement from doing so. "Right from the beginning," note psychiatrist Stanley Greenspan and philosopher Stuart Shanker, in language very well suited to our dynamic complex systems analysis, "caregivers and infants are engaged in rhythmic, co-regulated patterns that enable the infant to begin attending to the outside world."[18] Positive and calming feedback provides rewarding experiences for the child, who otherwise, as we saw in Chapter 3, becomes stressed by the demands of a highly stimulating and unregulated environment. And rewarding feedback, as has by now become our mantra, evokes repetition of the rewarding activity. Such feedback loops become internalized in the development of concepts as expectations develop and operate in the activities of perception and response.

Initially, infants experience not the world of things, activities, and sensations that adults are accustomed to, but rather "a limited number of global states, for example, calmness, excitement, and distress."[19] Eventually, through soothing interactions in ordinary cases – and this will show how disruptive the stress we discussed in Chapter 3 can be – these global states become increasingly differentiated and elaborated. According to Greenspan and Shanker, there is at first in an infant's experience just discomfort and distress, then comfort and calm. Later, there is experience of a discomfort of a particular kind, followed by comfort of a particular kind. The infant, if responded to reliably, comes to recognize the caregiver as associated with relief and comfort, as something *good*. She develops expectations and emotional responses based on the caregiver's responses and emotional state. As we have seen, the very development of infants' nervous systems is shaped by the character of their interactions with a caregiver. The patterns that form the child's mind are constrained by the larger ones that form her emotional environment. As a result, people who experience heightened stress or trauma in their family relations as children live in a very different world from those who experience calm and pleasant nurturing. And, of course, everyone's sensory apparatuses and emotional processing systems develop uniquely, with differing degrees of sensitivity. This means that the tenor of experiences will be different in different individuals. The same physical encounters carry different meanings: "a hug feels tight and *secure* or tight and *frightening*; a surface feels cold and *aversive* or cold and *pleasant*; and a mobile looks colorful and *interesting* or colorful and *frightening*."[20]

The world that each of us inhabits is, then, fundamentally subjective and emotional, as well as physical and full of potential; it is a function of mobile, invested, interested, and emotionally experiencing organisms, as well as of its own physical features. Concepts of the meaningful things in our world are carved out of regular co-occurring sense experiences and their accompanying emotional responses. In physical terms, repeated encounters with individual objects result in similar neural firing patterns. But these firing patterns do not include merely informational inputs from perceptual receptors. "Wired together" with perceptual information are signals coming from "upstream," from the emotional centers in the brain, and from patterns already established. So, the world that begins by being experienced as undifferentiated global emotional states comes, as a baby gains more experience, to be differentiated into things and people and activities to which emotional responses are also associated.[21] The more a given set of inputs and responses fire together, the more they are inclined to do so, and the more "this type of thing" comes to be carved out from and related to all the other things included in the child's world. As more things come to be distinguished in the world, one's concepts become more precise. What is more, as we have seen, the character of any individual's responses to the things that he comes to distinguish in the world is also influenced by others' responses, particularly the responses of caregivers in early life, but, as for example with teenagers, the responses of peers as well. Meaning making, then, turns out to be essentially social, as well as emotional and perceptual, rather than syntactical and symbolic, although we can make and meaningfully use symbols as well. The social and physical environments thus become integrated into an individual's world, and shape her attitudes, beliefs, and behaviors with respect to any specific stimulus. The important thing is that meanings are not merely the result of or for the purpose of processing information; instead, they result from and perform profoundly important roles in living and acting in a world with others.

Prototypes and meanings in addiction

As people move into addictive patterns, they learn the special meanings of their substance(s) or activity of choice in the same way that anybody learns meanings: through the emotion-laden experiences that they have with it. At least at first, the cycle of heightened pleasure, elevated beyond what any natural reward could bring, tells the addict that the drug or activity is a *good* thing, as are its associated sounds, tastes, sights. Remember that, since meanings are portrayals of the world, rather than information received from the world, they will be limited and perspectival, and in some instances starkly incorrect. The *good* that comes to be included in the concept of the drug or activity reinforces the *importance* connected with it, and thus reinforces the seeking behavior that all natural goods instigate in humans and other animals, but more so, since this *good* is experienced as more powerful than any natural one. As we have seen, at the physical level, activities and substances that result in a greater than expected availability of dopamine in the relevant brain areas are associated with the perception of large rewards, while other activities and substances, such as food, sex, or solving a puzzle, which result in relatively less dopamine availability, are perceived to carry smaller rewards. And these reward experiences and expectations contribute to the formation of the concepts of their associated activities and substances. The "special" substances and activities therefore come to have a different meaning for those who experience them as especially satisfying relative to other activities or substances. Those substances and activities that arouse a greater reward response will be conceived as *better* than others, even if one "knows" through previous learning, perhaps less viscerally powerful learning experiences, that they are *bad* in other respects. Further, not only do some substances and activities operate to create an overabundance of reward experience-generating chemicals, but additionally, since individuals are unique, they will respond differently to each of the dopamine-burst-creating chemicals and activities. This means that people who become addicted will have preferences not only for "addictive" things but also for specific things – they will develop substance or activity preferences. Naturally, what that particular substance or activity then comes to *mean* to the susceptible individual is fundamentally different in many ways from what it means for others, including positive expectations, importance, relation to other experiences, and relative value to other activities, as well as its call for action in specific circumstances. Again, as we have said, the larger social milieu in which one is exposed to rewarding substances, activities, or experiences has significant influence on the meaning that that thing comes to have for an individual or group. Remember the heavy drinking bouts among Korean men that, due to the social context of their occurrence, are not amenable to being understood as addictive behaviors, however unhealthy they might be.

Furthermore, since our concepts hang together to form our individual worlds, all meanings change (at least to some degree) together. A feature that atomic linguistic theorists find to be a weakness in the holistic prototype understanding of concepts is that the latter suggests that any changes anywhere involve changes everywhere. This is problematic, atomic linguistic theorists think, because it implies that the world is not stable, but is rather constantly shifting as our concepts are refined and change. This seems to be a strength of the view, however, rather than a fault, for the whole world does change as we grow from babies to toddlers to children to adults. Can you imagine inhabiting the world of a seven-year-old? The world also changes as one becomes addicted, as many who have experienced that transformation will attest. Not only does the role and significance of a particular substance or activity change in a person's meaning structure as he becomes addicted but so do the roles and relative value of people who can procure it, the places where the addiction can be indulged, and people and places who might thwart use. Ultimately, this can mean that the value and relative place of all other things in the world are affected as well. The concept of the addictive substance or activity in some cases can take on such importance, although it doesn't always, that it can color the meanings of every other thing that formerly held pride of place in the addict's life. Musical instruments and baseball card collections become means to get money, whereas before they may have been outlets for stress, means of self-expression, or beloved souvenirs. If addiction becomes central in one's life, certain places may become opportunities or obstacles, as can people, activities, and other objects, in addition to whatever other layers of meaning they may carry. Since in a holistic system all things are defined in relation to everything else, when one thing moves or changes, others move or change with it, at least to some extent. In some patterns of addiction the people, activities, and objects that had previously held relatively more central places in a person's world can come to be marginalized and changed in import, perhaps even coming to be conceived of as threats or obstacles.

Meaning flips, recovery, and triggers

When an addict has had it, when she is "sick and tired of being tired," "hits bottom," or, as Gene Heyman argues is the case most of the time, when she is motivated by professional, health, family, or financial concerns, she will transition out of addiction.[22] She will come to see her addictive behavior differently. In fact, she will come to see everything differently. This has been called in some frameworks a "spiritual awakening," and surely it must feel like it, because it is a revolution in one's conceptual framework, a complete gestalt shift. It would not even make sense to speak of an addict quitting her substance or activity as long as its meaning remained intact. The very act of quitting use, even if as the result of imprisonment or other involuntary circumstances, would change the meaning of the object of addiction. In order to stop voluntarily, the positive emotions, expectations, and importance of the substance or activity would have to be changed. All of a sudden, although it may be the result of a long process of experiencing negative physical and social consequences, and emotional experiences associated with the addictive behavior as well as other factors, things can just seem different. The addict sees the substance or activity "in a new light." Unsurprisingly, this shift is often prompted by extreme emotional and physical suffering associated with an indulgent episode, but this isn't necessarily the case, because a shift in *meaning* is what is essential, not the objective consequences evoked by continued use. Some people will use throughout their adult lives, and even to death, if they never come to see their preferred substance or activity as a thing that can be abandoned. And some people will simply give up use because some other source of meaning or value grabs their attention. Either way, the conceptual shift that comes with transition out of addiction is essentially emotional. The substance or activity is drained of its appeal. Likely, it is imbued instead with negative connotations. It can come to be conceived as merely uninteresting, or as poisonous perhaps, or even as evil. Other things take prominence in the addict's world, with the contours of the whole shifting accordingly. And, as with the shift into addiction, inputs from one's social environment both contribute to this shift and help sustain it.

The meanings that things have for us operate in important ways outside of our conscious awareness. We may never know what our concept of a given thing is until we turn our attention to an analysis of it. Since the meanings that things may have for us may not be fully known to us, we are perfectly capable of providing ourselves with reasoned accounts of what we're doing and what we believe and what we plan to do, while those accounts may have little to do with what we actually want, believe, or plan to do.[23] Even after an individual with a history of addiction has abstained from his preferred substance or activity for a significant amount of time, resisting temptation under all kinds of circumstances, and has consciously worked to reframe the activity or substance of addiction in negative terms, even as "impossible," the world can shift back. As certain "triggers," or associated meanings, in an addict's environment bring to the forefront feelings and responses that may have been consciously put aside, the world can suddenly and unconsciously revert to its previous structure. In a complete reversal of the original gestalt-type shift, the meanings that constitute the addict's world can return to the structure in which the substance or activity of choice takes a central place and influences all associated concepts. This may result in the individual's having thoughts totally unconnected to the substance or activity of addiction (such as "I hate my boss, my job is overwhelming, I'm so exhausted..."), but which lead nevertheless to the experience of world shift, in which return to use is rated as preferable to abstinence. Anticipation of imminent relief, satisfaction, or pleasure, as the behavioral economist tells us, predictably evokes this response, and the more so, the more the anticipation is entertained, and the more proximal it appears. These facts about our concepts and beliefs operating unconsciously can be frightful for those struggling with addictive patterns, since they imply that a person's concept of her preferred substance or activity might be associated with many triggers that she has never thought of. *Knowing* this fact, however, seems to provide a counterbalance to the power of unconscious effects, for it suggests that anyone can work daily toward consistently increasing awareness of her own associations, and thus her own vulnerabilities.

Some objections and responses

The view of meaning that has been presented in this chapter has been expressed in light of its main opponent, the atomic linguistic theory. Although it seems to stand up well in the face of familiar objections, not all of them have been adequately answered. A couple of issues remain. One we have already encountered: according to those who hold something like the atomistic informational view of meaning, prototypes and meaning holism are doomed from the start because the meaning of anything affects the meaning of everything. So, the argument goes, anytime anybody learns anything new, or one meaning is changed in any way, all meanings are thereby changed. This is seen as unacceptable on the grounds that no one would ever have a firm grip on his own beliefs and desires, much less could two people ever understand each other. I have expressed these results as features of the perspective, rather than as bugs in it, for it is a fact in need of an account that our concepts are constantly changing, subtly shifting, depending on the context in which we consider them, and so are the beliefs and desires that are constructed of them. Within constantly changing internal and external contexts, our conceptual state space (the "space" within which concepts can be carved out) is constantly morphing, although not to the extent that our opponents might want to make us think. Our concepts of people, events, and objects remain recognizable through change, as their relations to one another remain similar. When my concept of my uncle Joe is significantly altered by new information, so is my concept of my aunt and perhaps additionally even my concepts of dinner, Easter, and tranquilizers. But that does not mean that the world is no longer recognizable. The influence of changes of one concept on another diminishes as the "distance" between them grows. And what is more, when concepts are understood properly, as emerging from minds that in turn emerge from physical processes, it becomes obvious that we don't hold them, but reconstitute them as needed. This means that a little difference goes unnoticed. The concept that we form for a given occasion is close enough to others that we have formed to function just fine. With respect to the likelihood of communication failure on the holistic view, we should observe that this preserves the phenomena: conversations between addicted individuals and those who have never been addicted, and even among a group of self-defined addicts, people with differing preferences and patterns often seem to exhibit more miscommunication than communication. If this is a flaw, it is one that accrues to our nature, not to our theory.

There is another kind of worry to consider as well. The prototype-centered version of meaning holism that we have outlined here may be threatening to people who believe that in order for there to be science or study of anything at all, there must be a single, unambiguous world to which we all have access. Our theory seems to some minds suggest that there is not one body of science, one world to study, one correct theory, and so it may seem to shake our stability as knowers. This implication does not make our theory wrong. Minds, whether human or those of other animals, work to create meanings in much different ways than philosophers and others have portrayed for millennia. Now we must rethink how to account for our beliefs, knowledge, science, and other types of study in light of what we are, rather than trying to think of how we must be in light of dogmatic views about what knowledge, science, and other studies say. This criticism seems to cut against philosophers' assumptions more than it does against meaning holism.

Finally, there is a potential concern, not with respect to prototypes themselves, or to meaning holism, but with respect to what the view we have elaborated on says about addiction. The theory that has been put forward in this chapter is a general theory of meaning, and so the failures to communicate that occur between addicts and nonaddicts are not peculiar to these groups, but apply to any pair or group of individuals with different conceptual frameworks. Moreover, the gestalt shifts that mark transitions out of addiction, and relapses prompted by "triggers," could equally apply to PTSD "flashbacks" or desperation brought on by the discovery of a cheating spouse or by losing one's job. The charge, then, is that the proffered theory of meaning says nothing in particular about addictive patterns. To that I say, these facts rather support the theory's truth than undermine its applicability. The fact that the level of meanings as an emergent feature of addiction works to characterize many diverse human experiences says 1) that the view has a good chance of being correct in showing how the highly complex physical systems that human beings are can be moved by very real nonphysical processes, and 2) that addicts are not so very different from the rest of the population. Addicts are people moved to action by the values inherent in the world that is constructed by them, in interaction with their environments, both local and global. There is no good reason for saying that addicts are addicts because of a disease, or a genetic mutation, although they may well in some numbers have some genetic difference from the nonaddicted population, and they may cause themselves diseases by their addictive behavior. However, there is also no reason to say that addicts resolve to harm themselves and others by obstinately electing to engage in addictive behaviors after weighing their options in the same terms that some others might use. In making their determinations to act, those who suffer with addictions are reasoning within a different conceptual space than are those who would criticize them or treat them. What is more, because meanings are essentially dynamic and interconnected, there is no reason to say that the situation cannot change.

7
Phenomenology and Its Implications

As I sit down to write this chapter, one of my friends who struggled with addiction has just died. He was, like many who considered themselves addicts, a man of many faces. In our conversations he was self-deprecating and funny, but expressed a deep fear of rejection. Every comment or suggestion was qualified with as many as a dozen iterations of phrases such as "this is just my opinion," "I don't speak for everyone," "everyone is different, of course." And yet when his obituary was publicized, it revealed things that most of his friends didn't know, including that he was a highly educated, highly successful professional in at least two or three very diverse fields. He had not used alcohol for over a decade. Unlike the addicts that Gabor Maté profiles so sensitively in his *In the Realm of Hungry Ghosts*, many of the people whom I have met in the groups that I have visited are doctors, lawyers, professors, chemists, judges, actors, and artists, respected in their public lives, reserving their addiction for only those very dark corners of their private lives. Most think that they have no friends, while they are surrounded by supporters and admirers, and although many have underlying social anxiety issues, they are often charming and influential among those with whom they interact. All this is to say that when you think you have a handle on addiction and addicts, you probably don't.

Every addict's story is different, from the inside and from the outside. The account that we have been developing leads us to expect that to be true, given that every addict has unique DNA, activated in a unique environment, and unfolding under a unique developmental trajectory. Any given theory of addiction may well explain some varieties of addictive experience, or several, such as the susceptibility of trauma victims to become drug or activity dependent, but that same theory might falter at connecting that background to the economic or other circumstances associated with whether that susceptibility is actualized. Choice theories might track preference reversals relative to proximity of opportunity for use, but what do they have to say about the personal anguish of sober moments, and the giddy heights of freedom, confidence, and fearlessness of drugged exhilaration? Neurobiological theories may well explain how some addicts come to respond to certain cues virtually automatically with reward-seeking behavior. But what does incentive sensitization tell us about why people in different social contexts respond differently when exposed to these cues? And how do any of those explanations help us understand the role that addiction plays in the shaping of one's identity, or how it feels to have a craving, or to be high "in just the right way," or what we ought to do to help a person change her own psychology?

Why care about phenomenology?

When Bill Wilson took his first drink, it "produced in him instant feelings of completeness, invulnerability, and an ecstasy that approached the religious."[1] Similarly, when philosopher Owen Flanagan was twelve years old and had his first drink of hard cider, what he remembers is an immediate, powerful feeling: "I felt release from being scared and anxious. It was good. I did not know, I would not have known to say if asked at the time, that I was a scared and anxious type." But he knew quite well that after imbibing the cider, "a certain eighth-grade boy was released for a little time from a certain inchoate fear and anxiety."[2] These two experiences are paradigmatic of what we have come to expect from addicts. These stories are quite different, though, from those who choked on cigarettes for months, attempting to fit in with the crowd, only having it slowly dawn on them perhaps years later that they had difficulty quitting when they finally decided that they no longer wanted to smoke. They are different as well from the stories of those who gamble because it is exciting and fun, the same reasons that draw others to video games – not reasons or feelings anything like those that moved Wilson and Flanagan. And the Wilson/Flanagan type stories are different from the experiences related by those who drank or gambled for many years without any major consequences, only to have serious difficulties crop up all of a sudden in midlife as a result of their indulgence.

Flanagan is surely correct when he says that we want to know whether there are any commonalities among the experiences of addicts (he focuses particularly on alcoholics). He is also right when he says that we want to know "how the socio-cultural-political ecology normalizes, romanticizes, pathologizes (and so forth)" addictions and related patterns of behavior.[3] That is in fact part of what we have been trying to do throughout this book. Flanagan also recognizes that the power and influence (what he calls the "phenomenal authority") that AA in particular has enjoyed in determining the assumptions governing the direction of discourse on the subject may be undeserved. In fact, it is undeserved and it has worked to misguide analysis of addiction for decades. AA's phenomenal authority, as we have seen, is the result of accidental historical facts, such as the way that the central text, the "Big Book," was put together, with its collection of stories of people hitting "rock bottom," having experiences of God, and so forth, not to mention the way in which AA was formed out of a Christian perfectionist orientation based in Wilson's own family's history. Because of these coincidental facts, together with the way in which AA was advertised from the beginning, as highly successful, and the fact that no ready alternatives presented themselves, and because of AA's consequent embrace by the medical and insurance industries, assumptions about what it means to be an alcoholic or addict have been driven by characteristic AA discourse, distorted and restricted though it may be. What is actually a wide variety of human experiences has been skewed, smoothed into a recognizable pattern and reified into a diagnosable disease with an inevitable progression. As a consequence, little attention has been paid in the discourse on addiction to the drastic differences among real individuals' experiences. The phenomenal authority of AA has shaped people's thinking about their own stories, not least because the authoritative voice that has become so pervasive in self-help rooms as well as in treatment facilities says that it is "what we have in common" that matters. Focusing on what differentiates members is usually referred to pejoratively as symptoms that are destined to propel people into failure and despair. Members, as Flanagan rightly points out, are told outright to find what they can "identify" with in the stories of others.

We will discuss some other implications of this kind of instruction later, but for now it should help us recognize that most of the accounts of addiction that we encounter in popular literature and in people's anecdotes are based on "folk-tale" experiences of addicts, ones that fit within the formula driven by a particular cultural structure. How does this happen? An empirical study led by Rebecca Hammer in which sixty-three individuals in treatment centers gave personal narratives of their addiction found that the stories told were "a combined product of individual agency and socialization from treatment program ideologies."[4] As argued in Chapters 4 and 5, meanings are generated from individuals' physical and emotional experiences in a largely socially constructed world. This means that lived experience is unique, but it is conditioned by the social milieu in which those experiences unfold. If one begins to write one's narrative while in treatment, it will be significantly influenced by the rhetoric used in the treatment center in which one resides. Hammer's group found this to be true at least of their interviewees. Likewise, if that story is constructed from within the walls of 12-step rooms, it will be informed by paradigmatic AA narratives. Since the 12-step approach dominates treatment, both in professional facilities and in church basements, the assumptions of that orientation can be expected to exert significant influence on addicts' stories, and even more so when the person has been immersed in such programs.

The power of the voice of 12-step programs has driven the development of the numerous theories of addiction we have considered. Since many stories gathered by clinicians and studied by researchers seem similar in type, the similarities have been focused on at the expense of the diversity. Further, those who have worked at the neurological end of the explanatory continuum have gone looking for, and have found, brain change correlations in addicted subjects. As discussed in Chapter 1, however, it is not clear in which direction the causal arrow goes with respect to these brain change analyses: do these changes cause the addiction or follow from it? The theories that we have considered, including the hedonistic theory, the avoidance of withdrawal, the salience sensitivity approach, the ego depletion theory, the trauma-based developmental theories, and the psychodynamic theories, each resonate with some addicts' experiences, but fail to resonate with others. When researchers ask the question of whether "real" addicts have this or that characteristic, it is clear that they mean people who meet their own criteria for addiction. For the purposes of doing focused research on an aspect of the phenomenon, this is absolutely necessary. No science proceeds without its assumptions.

Nevertheless, the diversity of addicts' experiences is greater than is the universality. Since the project of studying addiction is not merely a theoretical exercise in trying to characterize it, or in attempting to determine the degree of responsibility that people would have if addicted, but is rather a preliminary step to finding ways to prevent and escape suffering, we need to reflect on the particular things that individual addicts have had to say about their experiences. We need to take time to focus on the details of individual experiences, rather than relying only on abstracted prototypes of addiction or individuated aspects of the phenomenon. As Hammer's group put it, it is important that individual addicts' voices "not be disenfranchised from the research done for their supposed benefit."[5] What is it that makes one drug or activity the indulgence of choice for one person, but not for another? How is it that some people can have one drink as a youth, and be altered for life, when others can sometimes have just a glass of wine, and at other times behave as though obsessed? Why are some people apparently addicted to everything that can be overdone, while others only experience addictive attachment to one substance or activity – able to gamble just a little, or use cocaine only at parties? We have seen how the social construct of addiction has expanded so much that virtually any activity can be deemed an addictive one, and we have discussed how the psychological pattern of addiction can be characterized in terms of a hierarchy of dynamic levels within complex dynamic systems. But we have not yet considered addiction from the subjective side that emerges out of all this complexity. To that we now turn, for it is in light of individuals' descriptions of their real-world addictive experiences that we need to evaluate our account and its potential for actually helping people lead more satisfying lives.

Two systems and ego depletion

One of the more promising ways of thinking about addiction considered earlier was based in the dual systems understanding of our thought processes, according to which we have on the one hand a fast, intuitive, undemanding and simplifying way of thinking, which operates by default (System 1), and on the other hand a slower, more deliberate, kind of thinking (System 2) that requires more mental resources. According to this theory, when individuals become depleted of cognitive resources, either through having exerted self-control chronically for some time or through being stressed in some way, System 2's control of their behaviors may be overwhelmed, resulting in a switch to the much less taxing System 1 mode of thinking. In this mode, people accept bad arguments, or just do whatever is most habitual or whatever is closest to hand. They escape the difficulty presented to System 2 by switching out of that effortful, deliberate kind of thinking into the more automated mode, with the result that they decide that indulgence is the preferred action.

Many experiences described by addicts seem to accord with the ego depletion theory. Take, for example, the group of subjects in the Hammer study whose responses are loosely collected under the theme that the authors call "punctuated equilibrium." This was the most common theme found among interviewees' responses. The title is employed in order to describe addiction "as a problem that oscillates along a static equilibrium, flaring only with specific triggers." Punctuated equilibrium is the paradigmatic pattern of struggling addicts, the one that inspires the characterization of addiction as "a chronic relapsing disease." A man whom the authors call Joe experienced his alcohol abuse as connected to the amount of stress in his life, particularly in connection with his employment status and his relationship with his wife:

> I resigned one job due to the stress and then I would start another one and that is the one I'm at now and I enjoy the job, but the increase in work duties just kept piling up where the stress was built up again for me... You know, in this day and age, they try to put as much responsibility as they can on people... I mean management does, basically to cut costs and that hurts the blue-collar people. I mean, and the stress just got worse and that is why I started again... My support has always been my wife. She pointed out that if I didn't quit, she would leave... I just quit, and, you know, just go for awhile and then the tension would build up, the stress would build up again and I would go back to it.[6]

This ego depletion theory seems to explain key elements of Joe's experience in a way that the simpler reward-seeking, withdrawal-avoiding, and mere habituation models that we have considered cannot. Joe's experience and the ego depletion analysis of it seem to accord with the incentive salience phenomenon, according to which the pull that the substance or activity of use seems to have emerges when stress rises, even absent any anticipated pleasure. Joe just seemed to return to the "solution" of alcohol use every time the pressure built up.

Lance Dodes, a Harvard psychiatrist who was a leader in the development of the psychodynamic approach to treating addiction, describes a similar response in one of his clients. This man was a business owner who had a history both of alcoholism and of being the victim of embezzlement by his own son. "When he discovered that the son's thefts from the company were far greater than he had known, Dodes says, "he ended many months of sobriety in a two-day alcoholic binge."[7] Very often we see cases in which someone is capable of controlling his use of his favored substance or activity for days, weeks, months or even years. He can control it right up to the point at which the emotional issues, physical exhaustion, financial issues, or some other major stressor is just too much. Then he capitulates. It seems plausible to conclude that in these situations the automatic thinking of System 1 takes over.

People who have this sort of experience in addiction often make deals with themselves, swear off for a time, and are successful for a time, but how long that time is ranges widely. In some cases, decades go by with the promise made good before something incites the switch. In other cases, it is remarkably short. Caroline Knapp, for instance, tells in her bestselling memoir, *Drinking: A Love Story*, of making such a promise to herself and to her mother at one point, after her drinking had become disturbing for both of them: "'I'll cut down. Two drinks a day. No more than that. I promise.' I'd meant it." But by the end of that same day, back in Boston, not feeling well and observing people relaxing in deck chairs, sipping beer from plastic cups, she capitulated.[8] When the physical raggedness that she was feeling due to a hangover combined with images of people relaxing and enjoying beers, her promise went by the board in favor of her default response: to drink.

Sometimes the return to use doesn't seem to be related to anything, though. So it seems that even in this most prototypical of addictive patterns – the one most particularly amenable to the dual systems and related theoretical approaches – many people's experiences are not captured. As actress and comedian Kristen Johnston put it, the return to use sometimes "sneaks up on you and all of a sudden you're boozing at the bar, or whatever. And it doesn't have to be because of you or pressure or this-or-that. It can just *be*."[9] No system switch seems to have happened here, no turn to an easier way of thinking seems to have occurred because of stress, pressure, or any identifiable cognitive load. Kristen just found herself drinking.

A day in the life

It seems from Kristen's experience that the dual systems approach cannot account for all the kinds of experiences that people have with their addictions. In fact, it cannot begin to do so. In a critique of the dual systems approach, Jeanette Kennett suggests that some people simply have no concept of a good life that is available to them.[10] These individuals never reach the point of being on their way to a life they envision, only to hit an obstacle and return to habitual patterns; instead, they remain in the habitual patterns always. In order to explain this situation, Kennett distinguishes between what she calls intentional self-control, which is the kind of self-control that we exert in order to perform individual actions of our choosing, and normative self-control, which is necessary for directing one's actions over time toward the kind of life that one takes to be good. Addicts, like anyone else, must and do exert intentional self-control, whether to purchase drugs, drive to a casino, or solicit sex. It is the failure of normative self-control that characterizes addiction, Kennett argues. This kind of failure could happen, she suggests, for one of two reasons: an individual might be deprived of a conception of the good life to begin with, either because of life circumstances or because of addictive indulgence itself, or one might have a real conception of the good life but in such a way that it exercises no real power over one's choices. Rather than accepting a breakdown in System 2 (due to ego depletion or cognitive load) as the explanation for this second reason for failure of normative self-control, Kennett thinks it is "more likely that in these cases the person does not see the life he would value having as available to him," given his emotional experiences of self. That is, for some reason he just can't see the life that he would truly wish to live as available to *him*.

The individuals whose stories are loosely connected by the theme that Hammer's group labels "What's Normal?" seem to experience something like the first reason that Kennett offers for the failure of normative self-control. That is, they seem to be deprived of a conception of the good life to begin with. A sad, difficult, disadvantaged life for these people seems to be the unquestioned norm. Many of physician and author Gabor Maté's patients in Downtown Eastside, Vancouver, for example, expressed little understanding of the potential for a better life. In one case, a young woman named Celia had a difficult time trusting anyone – for one thing, because she was sexually exploited from the time she was five. Her abuser for eight years was her stepfather, who regularly spat on her, among the many other indignities that he inflicted. She was pregnant at the time that Maté first saw her. She had been involuntarily committed to a psychiatric ward, had a long medical history of bone fractures, bruises, and black eyes, as well as abscesses, dental infections, recurrent fungal infestations of the mouth, and other manifestations of HIV infection. After the baby was born, Celia left the hospital, unable to resist the allure of cocaine.[11] Although the baby was born dependent on opiates, and so faced an uncertain future of its own, it at least was placed in a foster home, with some hope for a better life. Celia hadn't ever had that chance. For Celia, like for many of Maté's patients, it was as if "an invisible barbed-wire barrier surrounds the area extending a few blocks from Main and Hastings in all directions. There is a world beyond, but to them it's largely inaccessible."[12]

Some people, though, seem to experience a much less diminished conception of a good life, and nevertheless see the addictive pattern as the norm. Allison Moore, for instance, a young vice cop who became addicted to methamphetamine, expressed the normality of addiction in her family life without the kind of hopelessness characterized by Celia's situation. Moore says in her memoir that

> [m]y family has a long history of addiction, mostly to alcohol. My mother, two uncles, and both maternal grandparents were alcoholics ... my uncles were at the height of their alcoholism, my cousin was a heroin addict, and my mom, after enjoying fifteen years of sobriety during my childhood, had relapsed into alcoholism during her divorce ... The rampant alcoholism was hardly a big secret; it was just something everyone laughed and joked about. No one in my family treated it seriously. No one thought it was a big deal.[13]

In this case, the very normality of addiction within the family seems to have played a role in Moore's falling into her own addictive pattern. Not every situation, however, in which the presence and use of substances is taken as normal seems to have much to do with Kennett's suggestions for why people fail to exert normative control over their lives. Knapp, for instance, who grew up in a world starkly contrasting with Celia's and Moore's, says that in her life drink was "just always there." The daughter of a psychoanalyst and an artist, a graduate of Brown University, and a successful writer, this woman was surely not deprived of a concept of the good life. Nevertheless, in one way, her experience is similar to those just described. She found the availability of alcohol and daily drinking the norm: "In my parents' house the Scotch and the gin sat in a liquor cabinet, to the left of the fireplace in the living room, and it just emerged, every evening at cocktail hour. I never saw it run out and I never saw it replenished either: it was just there." This experience sounds much like one of Hammer's interviewees, Jill, who said, "I really thought everyone had a cocktail at five. And when I think back, I think, well, [so and so]'s parents never did that ... but all of my parents' friends did."[14] Although these stories do not seem to be illuminated by either a dual systems analysis or by the self-described addicts' lacking a concept of the good life, they are similar in revealing what an impact the presumption of use can have on the development of addictive practices.

But even without this presumed normality of substance use, some who do see a very good life as available to them nevertheless become addicts. Consider the future that Johnston saw for herself:

> Despite that my life at this point was sort of a bummer (for an upper-middle-class, Midwestern kid with plenty to eat, lots of fun vacations, a

> beautiful home, and parents who loved her, that is), I knew something none of my classmates did. Deep inside, I knew someday I'd win.[15]

As with Knapp, given her privileged family and all the attendant expectations, one can hardly draw from Johnston's description of her experience that her inability to exert normative control over her life was a function either of her not having a conception of the good life or of her not being able to see such a life as available to her. And, from the other side, even after successful treatment, Moore did not appear to be able to see herself in a meaningful life: "Once, I had had the opportunity to have a wonderful, normal life, and now I never would. It was over. I was done. I would carry on being detached and cold, pretending that none of these things had happened."[16] And yet, Moore did go on to a life of sobriety and continued success. Just like the other stories, hers tells us that the theories we have examined are sometimes unnecessary and sometimes insufficient for, and sometimes irrelevant to, providing satisfactory explanations of the huge variety of manners and circumstances in which addiction actually occurs in individual lives.

Like a light switch

Another theme that Hammer's group found that tied together a few of their subjects' narratives is what the authors call "Pedal to the Metal." This type of narrative has as its focus the striking experience that we saw in Bill W.'s story, and in fact in most of the stories from the book *Alcoholics Anonymous*. In these stories, the addictive draw of a substance was apparent from the first encounter. We see this pattern illustrated vividly in the memoir of Allison Moore, when she first was exposed to methamphetamine. After being handed some confiscated meth for processing, and after confiscating a small line for herself that kept her up for more than three days, Moore was hooked:

> I had told myself when I did that line that I would only try it once. I would never do it again. But when I started to come down I couldn't face being plunged into the icy cold water of my real life. I couldn't bear to have those feelings return. I did another line, bigger than the first. It made me feel calm, confident, excited about my future. Meth was the answer to all my problems.[17]

Although Hammer's group found that this theme was the least common of all those expressed by their interviewees, Moore's experience seems closest to what is often offered up as the prototype of addiction. At least it is the pattern that is most often described with respect to heroin and meth, perhaps to deter the public from ever using it the first time. As opposed to the *punctuated equilibrium* pattern, this version of addictive behavior seems to be characterized by little control from the start, and attended by physiological withdrawal symptoms when use is discontinued. One of Hammer's interviewees, named Bill, became a smoker in a single day. He said in his interview that

> there was a carton of cigarettes on top of the refrigerator and I decided to try it and the next thing you knew, I was stealing all of her parents' cigarettes ... I heard that you can't smoke like a pack the first time you smoke a cigarette, you know. But I smoked three packs the first night! That is how much I loved it.[18]

None of the theories that we have discussed can explain such experiences. There can be no issue of a brain "hijacked" by drugs here, no question of withdrawal or of interpersonal bargaining. Although it could be the case that there was trauma early in Bill's life, it doesn't seem to be that he experienced any relief from his first use of tobacco; rather, it is expressed as a purely pleasurable experience. Perhaps, then, the by-now largely discounted hedonic theory captures Bill's experience better than do any of the others. After that initial use, he kept up his smoking, with a vengeance, and he "could smoke six or eight" packs of cigarettes if he were to stay up all night. But pleasure doesn't seem to be the key factor in all people who feel immediately addicted to a substance or activity.

Many people who experience addiction in this particular way feel that it is more a matter of pure urge far more than a matter of any particular pleasure. These individuals, most of whom admittedly have gone through a treatment program using this model, seem to understand themselves in terms of the disease model, specified either as genetically programmed or as psychologically predisposed to addiction. Hammer's group interviewed a woman named Nora who explained her experience in these terms:

> I was an addict before I ever even had that first drink. And that first drink just sucked me in. I don't feel like I would have had the same unmanageability if I had never drank [sic], but I believe that I was an addict and an alcoholic waiting to happen ... I always wanted more of everything. Anything if it was like a food that I liked or whatever I want *more* than one ... I think it is part of my personality, but there

> was not a lot of progression for me. I was hooked on alcohol the minute I drank.

For those who experience addiction in this immediately powerful and all-absorbing way, use of one substance or activity can often only be managed by substituting a different one. Individuals who experience this sort of addictive process seem to be those who benefit most from participation in the external control of 12-step programs, even to the extent of using them as their substitution addiction, because the prospect of having no addiction at all seems inconceivable. Moore also experiences herself, after treatment for her meth addiction, as having an "addictive personality," as being doomed to addiction:

> If I had stopped to think about it at the time – if I had stopped to think about *anything* – I would have seen that I had always been an addict. Throughout my life, my addiction had never been a substance. I was addicted to *more*. More work, more control, more exercise, more sex. I'm one of those people who has a bottom-less bottom. Whatever it is, bring it on. I will go until I die. Original emphasis[19]

It is difficult to tell whether these people would have described themselves as diseased, either genetically or psychologically, had they not been through 12-step-based treatment. In any case it is interesting that the description of themselves as having always been addicts is made in retrospect. Like medieval occult qualities, such as "soporific," used to explain the sleep-inducing qualities of certain substances, "addictive personality" is an epithet without explanatory reach. Nevertheless, the words are chosen by the women themselves to describe their experiences, and so the characterization cannot be dismissed.

In these cases it might be helpful to look to a genetic contribution as part of the explanation of the experiences portrayed. Even so, as we have discussed, no more than 50% of the tendency toward addiction is attributable to this contribution, and so other things must be operating as well. And those other things don't seem to be accounted for by hedonic, withdrawal, or dual systems analyses. Again, we seem to get a partial explanation of the phenomena through one or more of the proposed theories. We can't discount that these women experienced trauma earlier in their lives, in addition to other things that might have contributed to their plight. The lesson again, though, is that no theory illuminates the entire range of these experiences, while every theory shines some light on some parts of some of the stories.

The snowball effect

In certain cases a person can use a drug or engage in an activity for years without any discernible negative consequences, and then at some point, things begin to spin out of control. Hammer et al. found this pattern in about a third of their respondents. Isaac, for instance, a forty-seven-year-old man, said that becoming addicted was a long process for him:

> It took me a long time to become an alcoholic. I had to work really, really hard at it... I have been around people who drink, like all of my working life, and I can drink and not drink. It was never a... there was never any kind of associative, addictive behavior. I mean I could drink on weekends and then not drink all week. I knew where there would be consequences to drinking and not do it. I would never plan or necessarily look forward to it. And, I mean that was 25 years. I mean, and then all of a sudden it just run tough. At that point, you are making conscious choices to drink rather than do something else.[20]

Individuals describing experiences like Issac's, of drinking or smoking or doing some other activity for years, only to find it careening out of control quickly after all that time, Hammer's group found, and quite understandably, tended to be more intellectual in their talk about addiction. They comprised a generally older group, and they had more experience with their addictions than did others. This group tended to be more philosophical about what counts as addiction, which also seems reasonable, since behaviors imperceptibly different from long-standing customs seemed for them to come suddenly to have different meanings and different repercussions than they had had previously. For Mary, a news manager in her forties, the change was from being on the job 24–7 to having no job at all. "I was so shocked that I ended up the way I ended up and I went downhill so quickly" (Hammer, p. 728). Like many who experience this kind of sudden change with substances or activities, Mary was totally blindsided by her addiction.

These experiences don't seem to be accounted for by any of the theories that we have so far encountered. If these self-described addicts' problems were due to changes in the reward system in the brain, one would expect those changes to have been effected in fewer than the twenty to forty years that it seems to have taken. But these experiences aren't any better explained by hedonic, withdrawal, or dual systems theories. Certainly neither of the first two explains this pattern. Nor, however, does this kind of situation describe someone who employs System 2 to control something until the system is overwhelmed and the quick and habitual sort of thinking takes over. Moreover, genetic inheritance and trauma seem to have little to say about this kind of sudden change in substance use patterns. Perhaps age itself changes the way in which people react to the effects of certain substances (there may be cases of gambling or shopping that follow this pattern, as well). But if age is the issue, then the question arises why in the prototypical story, as in Knapp's experience, the progress of addiction has "the feel of a swan dive, a long slow curving arc,"[21] while for people who fit into this group the experience is more like falling off a cliff.

Isolation and love stories

One relatively common phenomenon related in the stories of addicts is the feeling of total isolation. Whether self-imposed or because of a reserved nature or shyness or something else, we often find that those who exhibit addictive behavior do so in light of an inability or unwillingness to ask for help or depend on others. For instance, even after spending extended periods of time in the hospital due to a series of potentially fatal health problems resulting from her addictive behavior, Kristen Johnston realized that in order to change her life she would have to change her relationship to herself. Of the time that she was hospitalized, she says,

> I would rather lie alone, hour after hour, day after day, week after week, for almost *two months*, than to have to tell anyone I needed them. You see, if I needed them, that would mean I was weak, which would mean I was flawed. And *that* would be unacceptable. A fate far worse than death Original emphasis.[22]

Likewise, Allison Moore, the vice officer whose police culture didn't allow one to "just go and talk about your problems," kept her troubles to herself. She says, "I had spent my whole life keeping my own secrets, believing that if I didn't tell anyone my story, it couldn't possibly be happening to me."[23] Addicts who speak in support groups often talk about isolation as a major problem, even after they have transitioned out of active use, because it is such a temptation to take on the world alone. The reasons that people give for isolating themselves, though, vary. Sometimes the issue is an overblown sense of one's own power and responsibility, but sometimes the emphasis seems to be on an "out of sight, out of mind" motivation. If the problem is never shared, the person reasons, its reality can be denied.

In some cases, the secrecy, isolation, and fundamental shame that attend addictive vulnerability and addictive behavior are so great that the addiction itself comes to be experienced as a friend. Many, including the man in a recent Chantix commercial, characterize the very thing that they are attempting to eliminate from their lives as their best friend. Knapp subtitled her book *A Love Story*. She says that her story is about "saying good-bye to something that you can't fathom living without." In the end, she says her relationship with alcohol "was the single most important relationship in my life."[24] Things can even reach a point at which the power and poignancy of the relationship between an addict and her substance or activity cannot be overstated. Kristen Johnston experienced her addiction in that way:

> When He's got His evil talons in you, you don't care. You will lie to protect Him, no matter what happens. He's your most devoted better half, your longtime lover. He's adoring and reliable and He's never let you down. It's certainly not His fault that He's killing you. Like a battered wife, you take Him back even though He just knocked out your two front teeth. You lie to your weeping mother even though He's convinced you to steal the painkillers she actually *needs* after a knee-replacement surgery. You will die protecting Him, no matter what. Because no one will ever, ever love you as much as He does.[25]

This is a part of the phenomenon that none of the received theories touches. Even the psychodynamic theory, which, instead of focusing on genetic or neurophysiological analyses, operates purely at the psychological level, has nothing to say about this kind of personal experience. Is there an account to be given of why some people would come to see themselves as having this kind of powerful relationship that can be categorized as a behavior pattern, a rational choice, or a disease? While it is true that the incentive salience approach can give us a brain-based account of the importance that an activity or substance can come to have in someone's life, it can tell us little about why certain people come to experience this kind of personal struggle as an entity, even a love. That is a function of meanings, for which we have developed a sketch of a theory. A full analysis at this level, however, is still needed.

Medicating pain

Of all the approaches to understanding and treating addiction, the dynamical psychological approach most appreciates the unique experiences of individual addicts. Pain is personal, and relief can be sought and experienced in an almost infinite variety of ways. On this approach, it is neither the reward nor the avoidance of withdrawal, nor failures of either System 1 or conceptions of the good life that drives consistent, and sometimes constant, indulgence in addictive behavior. In this case, it is not a loss of self-control that accounts for use, but rather of the only kind of control that a person might have. Those who take the self-medication view of addiction focus on the suffering that addicts undergo more than do any other theorists. Indeed, researchers who take this approach tend to be clinicians, rather than lab researchers or theorists. Maté, for instance, a defender of the self-medication view, in addition to being a researcher and author, has for decades been treating street addicts.

Those who ascribe to the self-medicating hypothesis believe, and have research outcomes to show, that individuals tend to use specific substances to self-medicate particular kinds of psychological suffering. For instance, several researchers found that many of those who have experienced trauma self-medicate with opiates. They use these painkillers to kill their own pain, and to manage the rage and aggression that results from it.[26] However, stimulants and cocaine have been used to self-medicate depression, and, paradoxically, in "high energy" individuals with greater than normal need for excitement and euphoria, to elicit an ongoing experience of the energizing effects that they crave.[27] Finally, sedating drugs, including alcohol, have been found to be used by individuals who have difficulty acknowledging emotions, feel psychologically defensive and anxious, and tend to overrepress anger.[28]

Surely Moore's use of meth seems amenable to this type of analysis. She was working hard, overwhelmed, and worn out by the constant demands of the environment in which she was working, and she tried to handle everything alone: "It was an unspoken rule in most departments that you don't just go and talk about your problems. Instead, you fix them by going out drinking with your buddies. I was drowning in my depression, exhausted from lack of sleep, but I didn't ask for help."[29] She was exhausted and depressed, and the stimulant meth seemed to her at first trial to be the answer to all her problems. Likewise, the famous opium eater Thomas De Quincey found that in opium

> was the secret of happiness, about which philosophers had disputed for so many ages, at once discovered; happiness might now be bought

> for a penny, and carried in the waistcoat-pocket; portable ecstasies might be had corked up in a pint-bottle; and peace of mind could be sent down by the mail.[30]

And surely no one denies that use of alcohol can relax strongly repressed emotions; indeed, the disinhibiting effect is what makes it such a central feature at parties and other social events. One alcohol abuser, though, put it in intellectual terms, of the sense of "rightness" and confidence that accompanies use:

> The thing that the non-addict needs to know is that there is a zone, for the addict, equivalent to the zone of athletes, writers, artists...where you are ok. You don't feel threatened by all the problems that you know face you, and will face you later, with greater strength. You can enjoy doing anything or nothing. You feel perfect. The fact that there is a place like that never leaves an addict, like the feeling of certainty, like the feeling of perfectly excited adrenaline for thrill-seekers (funny that they're called that, and not thrill addicts, even though their yearning for adrenaline can kill them just as easily as our yearning for the feeling that we want).[31]

In this case, the relief described as coming from alcohol use is experienced as a truth, amounting to a certainty, in the face of all facts to the contrary, that life will be ok. Again we have a case that seems amenable to analysis by the self-medication approach. The kind of alleviation of anxiety and production of confidence, as we have seen all too often on the news, can have tremendously negative effects, from drunk-driving accidents to dancing like a fool at the office party. This certainty, or feeling of "rightness," even in things purely intellectual, seems to be as powerful as that brought about through seeing the proof of a theorem. It is patently obvious that the feeling of certainty that what one is doing is good and right is no indicator that it actually is good or right. In fact, when the source of the feeling is a substance or behavior from which one has often received short-term pleasure followed by long-term pain, it is ironic that the impression of certainty can be a characteristic experience.

The same kind of confident feeling of certainty can be brought about by cocaine, however, and for Moore was brought about by meth. What is more, many anxious people will not medicate themselves with alcohol, no matter how uncomfortable they feel, because the threat of loss of control presents an even greater source of anxiety. Further, even if it is true that those who are prone to anxiety and emotion repression turn to sedatives, we would need to ask why among that population some prefer alcohol to the exclusion of any other sedating substance, while others experience the converse, and some get the same measure of relief from any number of substances. It seems that in light of the research, the claims of the self-medicating thesis may be defensible in broad, general terms, and indeed, some components of it are intuitively reasonable, but given the range of experiences that individuals report with respect to the substances they favor, the story must be far more complicated. Kyle Keegan, for example, in his memoir, *Chasing the High*, thinks of himself as an addict, plain and simple. He speaks of one dark evening on which he had failed to secure the heroin he wanted: "instead of getting the fix I had hoped for, I was offered a match-head of cocaine. Against my better judgment, I accepted it and made my way to my roof. You see, though I knew that cocaine without heroin would only make me feel sicker, I was an addict, and therefore unable to turn down any drug."[32] The sentiment "I would take anything you put in front of me" is often echoed in 12-step rooms. Like Nick, for example, one of the first patients we encounter in *The Realm of the Hungry Ghosts*, it is common to hear that "[t]he reason I do drugs is so I don't feel the fucking feelings I feel when I don't do drugs. When I don't feel the drugs in me I get depressed."[33] But Nick was both a heroin and a meth addict. If the self-medicating hypothesis were accurate in its specifics, Nick ought to be seeking only the meth. Perhaps, though, Nick was treating himself for both rage and depression. He mentioned that his father had drilled into him as he was growing up that he was useless, so he certainly had reason for experiencing both. Likewise, Celia, whose baby was taken from her, was addicted to both cocaine and heroin. In fact, many of Maté's patients would use anything they could get their hands on.

It is difficult to see, then, how this diverse collection of individuals can be grouped, other than through the fact that they all suffered significant pain and, due to living in Vancouver's worst drug slum, all had ample reason to want to feel differently. But that means that, like the other theories we have considered, the self-medicating hypothesis on its own cannot do much explanatory work. Not all those even in Downtown Eastside were heroin users, despite their pain, although most in that area were. Most were traumatized, neglected, and sometimes abandoned as children, which is surely at least part of the explanation for their urge to self-medicate, and for their strong responses when they did so. But trauma has been associated with every kind of drug use, not just that of heroin or alcohol. Further, many of these patients, according to Maté, had undiagnosed and/or untreated psychological problems. But even within this restricted population, not all were addicted to the same thing. What's more, some of the people in the Vancouver Hotel, although clearly suffering psychologically, were not addicted at all.

The transition out

There is a paradigmatic story about most elements of addiction, including the transition out of it. While we have numerous examples as well – particularly with respect to those patients whom Maté encounters in Vancouver – of those who never escape the addictive cycle, research show us that the majority do. In 12-step informed narratives, the story often follows the shape of the swan dive, as described by Knapp. The trajectory is of increased use over time, with increasingly bad consequences: broken relationships, illnesses, financial and legal difficulties, debauchery, and sometimes violence, to the point of some dramatic "rock bottom." Moore tells that kind of story, in which, after being rescued from being held captive at a meth dealer's house, her mother takes her to a treatment facility. Flanagan says that at the end of his drinking days, he was driving to the gas station every morning to secure enough beer to get him through classes, after which he could obliterate himself with vodka. The esteemed philosopher was "a wretched, worsening train wreck of a person – a whirling dervish, contaminating, possibly ruining the lives of my loved ones."[34] And then he turned to treatment. For Knapp, the downward spiral hit bottom when she fell while carrying two children who could have died from the fall, although even then it took a couple of months and a career-ending blackout before she drove herself to a rehab facility.

This is the kind of story that we hear again and again, and that the treatment industry and self-help groups tout. But this is not the only kind of transition out of addiction that happens. Sometimes, people just decide to stop. In fact, according to a significant body of research, that is actually the norm, as we saw in Chapter 1. In the case of Edie, for instance, a cocaine user and dealer, it was her husband's bizarre behavior and sexual disability, but particularly the strain that his behavior put on his relationship with their children that caused her to put a stop to her drug use.[35] For Henry, the unpleasant aftereffect of stuffy sinuses attending his cocaine use together with his worry that his law career might be at risk was enough. "As cocaine conflicted with people and plans in which he was invested, Henry just stopped."[36] And Patty had a much more difficult time quitting cigarettes than she did cocaine, drinking brandy to help her to sleep (but not becoming addicted to it) through the cigarette cessation, but not requiring anything to stop the cocaine use.[37]

There are experiences at every possible place on the continuum of difficulty in transitioning out of addiction, from the lightning bolt-type of event that began Wilson's move away from alcohol to those like Henry's, in which use just seemed to interfere with other things that he wanted to do. In any case, it seems that the diversity of experiences of transition out of addiction shows that we have no adequate theory of it.

Conclusions

The very different experiences described by not just the self-identified addicts mentioned in this chapter but also by the vast population who for one reason or another include themselves under that umbrella, render inevitable the conclusion that we do not as of yet have a workable theory of addiction. Nor may we need one. For what we have seen is that no single theory of addiction has the ability to explain all facets of the phenomenon. Not even a single type of theory will be able to explain all addictive experiences. Some of the accounts we have seen seem to call for an explanation of the kind of background that sets up vulnerability to addiction; some seem to give an explanation of how addiction progresses with respect to behaviors, attitudes, and self-images; and some seem to describe what the reward, or the pull, of addiction is like. An explanation, of whatever kind, only makes sense against a particular contrast set. An explanation can be judged as better or worse only relative to other theories attempting to answer the same question. The theories on offer in the addiction literature seem to presuppose that there is only one question to be answered, one phenomenon to be explained. Neuroscientific theories seem to think that they are getting at what is "really real" in addiction. Responsibility/control theories focus on the question of whether "real addicts" are responsible for their actions, and, by extension, what the essence constituting addiction is. Others, such as the self-medication theorists, investigate the suffering of the addict and suggest that cases of addiction are actually cases of other disorders masked by attempts to alleviate their symptoms. In this case, the theory makes the question of addiction one that reduces to other psychological questions.

The fact is, there is no essence of addiction. If these phenomenological explorations have shown us anything, it is that. Different theories of addiction answer different questions, and speak to different issues associated with the phenomenon of addiction. That is not problematic. In fact, it is just what is to be expected if the complex dynamics analysis approach is right. The problems associated with the addictive syndrome exist at a variety of levels, each of which has its own constraints and descriptions, and its own responses to the question of what can be done to improve an individual's situation. Moreover, much of what counts as problematic in addiction is subjective. When many people consider themselves satisfied with their transition out of addiction, and yet continue to smoke or to need their coffee, it seems clear that what is a problem is what counts as a problem for the individual. Many 12-step groups disapprove of the use of any "mind-altering chemicals," and they insist that no one who continues to use them is truly "sober" (or really "in recovery"). Others find that the use of such chemicals as Suboxone or THC to control pain in opiate addicts, or the use of antidepressants or stimulants to treat psychological problems that may coexist with or underlie the addiction, are essential tools for establishing and maintaining "sobriety" or "recovery." In the next chapter, we consider the wide variety of approaches that might be used to transition out of an undesirable addictive pattern and into a more satisfying and valuable life.

8
Possibilities for Change

Addicts appear both to themselves and to others to be stuck in a particular pattern of action, and it must be admitted that getting out of such a pattern is difficult. On many accounts, none of the well-known treatments has a higher than "spontaneous remission" rate of transitioning people out of addiction. That said, many people do make that change, and new approaches to helping them are being tested every year. Although some treatment programs self-report high rates of success in helping individuals achieve desired behavior and improved quality of life, and they even claim that it will work every time "for those who work the program," no such unconditional success has been demonstrated. In fact, such claims are virtually meaningless, since they are essentially untestable. Since any failure to sustain sobriety can be attributed to a failure by the addict to "work" some aspect of the program, according to the pervasive 12-step method of treatment, the claim that the program succeeds in the vast number of cases in which the individual "works the program" is self-affirming.[1]

In contrast to the optimism of 12-step proponents, the National Institute on Drug Abuse's (NIDA) finds that around 60% of those treated for addiction experience relapse (these numbers are optimistic compared to other studies). Whether and for how long a course of treatment for addiction succeeds, according to NIDA, is determined by numerous factors, such as the substance or activity involved, the length of treatment participation, the motivation level of the addicted person, and the amount of external support that is available to and accessed by the addicted person.[2] Given our analysis of addiction as an emergent phenomenon arising from complex, self-organizing, and mutually interdependent causal systems operating on a variety of scales, this variety of factors, as well as many others, would be expected to influence whether an individual can transition out of addiction. Addiction cannot be reduced to any single pattern of neurotransmitter interaction, or changes in brain structure or function. Nor can the "getting stuck," even lethally, in a thinking and behavior pattern, as happens in some cases, be understood outside of the normal distribution curve that describes the range of behavior in any aspect of a human population. Since no two people are the same physiologically, psychologically, or socially, to think that a one-size-fits-all program could be the answer to the suffering of all addicts is shortsighted, as is the attribution of relapse to a "failure" on the part of the addict.

None of this is to say, however, that addiction involves no identifiable general patterns, nor is it to suggest that there are no ways to make inroads toward improving any one individual's chances of achieving lasting change. In fact, the implication is the opposite: there are many and varied ways to disrupt the patterns that characterize addiction, and they arise at as many levels as does the phenomenon itself. While prevention is always easier than change of an established pattern, both approaches can succeed, and both must be available. Although once an individual feels stuck in what we call an additive pattern – and she will have to struggle to some extent to get out of it (but even this happens on a very broad continuum) – it may seem that she is helpless. However, any syndrome that involves memory and habituation can be interfered with and redirected, since the effective units of organization in the addictive pattern are all dynamic. Interventions at the synaptic, neural, neural systems, psychological, and local and global social levels can all be used to bring about disruption of addictive patterns of thinking and behaving.

Manipulating neurotransmitters

As we have seen, an individual's specific experiences alter the probability of the activation of specific neural networks. The more a particular group of neurons has fired together, the higher the probability is that, given the activation of a subset of its member neurons, a similar group will be activated again. Above, we characterized the probability that a given neural network will be activated in terms of attractor wells. A group of neurons that has fired together in the past will be more likely to fire together again when a subset of them is stimulated. Likewise, at a higher level in the hierarchy we would speak of mental association, wherein the more often a particular situation has been connected with use or engagement in an addict's preferred activity, the more likely she is to "feel like using" or repeating the activity when she encounters those familiar cues. And again, at the level of habitual behavior, the more often one has followed a particular pattern of action, once that action is activated, the greater the probability that that pattern of action will be followed through to completion. But each of these is only a probabilistic tendency, and the probability of each can be diminished.

For those who reject the medical model of addiction, the habitual element looms large. From this perspective, addiction can be addressed in the same way as any other undesirable habit: by doing something else in place of the addictive activity. Going to meetings with like-minded others at the time of day when thoughts stray to use has helped innumerable individuals. This is often at the end of the day. After the stresses of a normal day of work, whether at school, at the office, at home, or on a building site, many people are looking for relief. Addicts have unconsciously developed a default setting that their brains will automatically resort to for this purpose, and the sensitized pattern will be set off all the more automatically, the more often they have used their preferred addictive activity for coping. What's more, the more their physiological and psychological state has become used to relief from the day's difficulties, the greater the likelihood that the deep attractor well of their habituated response will send them into that default pattern. Finding something else that provides a significant reward, whether social support, meditation, or a massage, to substitute for the addictive behavior can diminish the likelihood of pursuing the undesired behavior.[3]

But addiction involves more than mere habituation. Most habits that we engage in do not involve an increased sensitivity to the salience of a particular thing. People generally tie their shoes automatically once they have the strings in hand, directed by unconscious habit, with the associated set of neural firing patterns involved later in that process being set off by those occurring earlier in the process. This happens, at the neural level, by the operation of a well-established attractor. But the habituation involved in tying one's shoe does not result in an urge to tie one's shoes every time one sees someone else doing so, nor does tying one's shoe once result in the urge to do it again and again, in the same way that an addict's imbibing a single dose of her substance or engaging in a single instance of her activity of choice often results in a "binge," or at least in a strong desire for further use or continuation of the activity. The addictive case is much more like the obsessive-compulsive disorder case, a cyclical disorder in which a strong attractor is developed to certain thoughts or emotions, which bring about anxiety that leads to an urgent need to engage in particular behaviors. Capitulation to that need only satisfies it for a brief while. When the thoughts or emotions inevitably return, so does the overwhelming need to engage in the behavior. Addiction has the added feature, however, that heightened neurological sensitivity to both the cues and the effects associated with the preferred substance or activity sometimes persists years beyond instances of previous use.

Given this increased biochemical sensitivity, perhaps it is important to add to any attempts at habit shifts the option of changing the neural activation patterns directly. It is possible, at the neural level, to interrupt the circuits that seem to subserve the hallmark craving and seeking associated with addiction. Opiate addicts are already receiving benefits from Soboxone (buprenorphine and naloxone), a drug that occupies opiate receptor sites. The result is that ingestion of opiates does not result in the expected feelings. Campral (acamprosate) has been found to be somewhat effective in promoting abstinence from alcohol.[4] In two different studies, Naltrexone has shown promise for treating alcohol abuse. First, in 1992 Naltrexone was shown to be effective in reducing opioid and alcoholic relapse frequency and reducing heavy drinking by blocking stimulation of opioid receptors.[5] Additionally, a 2006 National Institute on Alcohol Abuse (NIAA) study showed that, in combination with medical management, Naltrexone was the most highly effective of nine different approaches for treating alcohol problems.[6] It is widely used in Europe, and has been approved for use in the United States since 1996, with a physician's prescription. Chantix (varenicline tartrate) has been shown to be more effective at supporting long-term abstinence from smoking than bupropion hydrochloride (Wellbutrin SR or Zyban SR), which is also used as an antismoking aid. Both these and other pharmacoptherapeutic approaches have demonstrated some effectiveness in interrupting the neural pathways involved in the cycle of addiction to nicotine. Even anxiolytics (antianxiety drugs) such as clonodine, diasepam, meprobomate, and others have been shown to have some effectiveness as an aid in smoking cessation.[7] Nicotine replacement, provided through an array of delivery systems, has also been shown somewhat effective in these efforts. Most recently, research into oxytocin administration has proven very promising, at least in animal models. This naturally occurring molecule, when present in sufficient amounts in the brain, seems to block the specific receptor cites responsible for alcohol's ability to induce intoxication.[8] Preclinical and clinical studies, moreover, have shown that oxytocin might also minimize alcohol consumption, craving, and even withdrawal symptoms, which are more dangerous with respect to alcohol than any other substance. How any of these substances will work for any given individual can only be determined by trial, because, as we have seen, every organism is unique. Nevertheless, the pharmaceutical approach is one tool in the box.

One problem with this approach, however, is that many of the treatments available even now are not employed, because publicly funded treatment facilities, and even private ones associated with 12-step programs, discourage use of "any mind-altering chemicals," including those that exhibit excellent experimental results with respect to countering addictive responses. Soboxone, for instance, the safer and more abuse-resistant successor to methadone as a treatment for opioid addictions, has been used by thousands of addicts, often for many years, with no relapses and no addictive behaviors observed in association with its use. According to Mary Jeanne Kreek, pioneering researcher in the use of methadone, the standard treatment, used in approximately 90% of treatment facilities, continues to be abstinence, residential detention, and immersion in 12-step practices, despite the fact that abstinence-based treatment works in fewer than 10% of opiate addicts. [9] Dogma and prejudice in this case effectively block the use of the most effective treatment available. To be fair, there is an argument that, when used only in the short term, Soboxone fares no better than abstinence-based treatment, and weaning former addicts off Soboxone is more difficult than weaning them from heroin. That argument raises a question: since Soboxone seems to be capable of being administered for years on end without ill effects to the body, why would anyone insist on using Soboxone only as a short-term treatment, while lifelong insulin use is expected for diabetics? In both of these cases, the drug can be very dangerous to those who do not need it, but for those who do, it is analogous to taking a daily vitamin, in terms of addictive effects, liver damage, or other types of toxicity.

With any psychopharmacological approach, though, the devil is in the side effects. As the low murmur of quickly stated warnings on the commercials show, most of the drugs touted by researchers for their ability to aid in diminishing cravings and addictive behaviors have their own effects on the bodies and mental states of those taking them. It would be impossible to show that any drug can do all and only what we want it to do in the body, and, in fact, with respect to most drugs that act on the brain, the mechanism of action is unknown. Drugs are substances that, introduced into vastly complex systems served by our circulatory systems, have effects wherever they are carried (throughout our whole bodies, and affecting the psyches that emerge from them), and what those effects might be we can only know after treating humans with them. Even then, we cannot extrapolate from the effects that substances have had on some percentage of people included in trials to the effects they will have on a particular person. This is not to say that some of these drugs, or ones that might be developed in the future, might not be extremely helpful for assisting some addicts with one level of their problem. Soboxone is a good case in point. However, treatment at the level of neurotransmitters and their receptors can never be the whole answer. Claims such as those made in the National Center on Addiction and Substance Abuse's 2012 report, that "addiction is a disease" and that physicians must "diagnose, treat, and manage addiction just as they do all other diseases," are just as wise and biased as are treatment approaches that refuse to include pharmacology at all in the treatment of addiction.[10] Every drug has side effects, and each one can fail to be effective. In the case of Soboxone, although it is safer than methadone, it is still possible for those who do not have a high tolerance for opiates to use it to purposefully become intoxicated, and it is possible to overdose and die from it. For other pharmacological treatments of everything from smoking cessation to alcoholism, the story is the same.

Altering neurological systems

Even when there is not the problem of drug infusion throughout the body, therapies targeting neurocircuitry alone cannot be the whole answer to providing relief from addiction. In one extreme study involving four very hard-core alcoholics, for instance, electrode implants were placed directly into the basal ganglia for the explicit purpose of interrupting the seeking, motivational circuit, and nothing else in the body. In this case, as long as the electricity was flowing into the specific areas into which the electrodes had been implanted, these four men's cravings disappeared, but as soon as the electricity was turned off, the cravings returned to their previous levels, and so there was no extrapolation of the experiment's results in the lab to real-world conditions.[11] The fact is, though, that interrupting neural circuits simply will never be sufficient alone to stop addictive patterns in highly complex organisms like us. Even when Chinese surgeons ablated (burned away with electricity) the cells in the "pleasure centers," or nucleus accumbens areas in some 1,000 opiate-addicted patients, reminiscent of the 1950s practice of frontal lobotomy in America, only 47% of the patients remained free of opiates five years later, with 53% relapsing, a consequence no better than chance.[12] Unsurprisingly, large numbers of the Chinese patients experienced side effects, including memory loss, loss of motivation, and changes in personality.

If directly interrupting the brain's craving response is in fact to be of use in treating addiction, it would be better to try less catastrophically destructive ways than ablation of the nucleus accumbens. Versions of transcranial magnetic stimulation have exhibited some promise in this regard. In transcranial magnetic stimulation (TMS), a noninvasive treatment, electrical coils are drawn across the outside of the cranium. Repetitive TMS, and more recently and most promising, deep TMS – in which the electrical current reaches further than the 2cm inside the cranium than the previous types of TMS did, penetrating the emotional centers beyond the cortex – have been discovered to be effective in curbing cravings and lowering consumption of both tobacco and alcohol. The probability that particular sensory cues will result in the repetition of addictive behavior has been discovered to be diminished through this process by what is thought to be increasing the functionality of the prefrontal cortex. Increased activity in this area is thought to result in greater inhibitive ability. Even if these procedures are helpful, however, and should be investigated enthusiastically, failing to recognize that neural systems are dynamic systems integrated within an organic hierarchy of such systems is bound to result in falling short in the treatment of addiction.

What is more, strengthening the functionality of that "executive" part of the brain can be done without drugs or surgery at all. Conscious activities, such as training in various sorts of mindfulness practices, have become very popular in both addiction treatment and many other types of psychotherapy. While there are many types of mindfulness exercises, and many kinds of meditation practices, let us consider as an example an approach that involves both. Mindfulness meditation has been shown to be effective in increasing the ability to avoid ego depletion, or the exhaustion of executive control. Research indicates that this happens by affecting different types of brain processing, or, on another level of description, of mental processing. For instance, one study performed at the Waisman Laboratory for Brain Imaging and Behavior, using Tibetan Buddhist monks, showed that meditation in which attention is focused on a particular object, as for instance the breath or a mantra, enhances the ability to sustain attention even when one is not meditating.[13] The explanation for this is offered in terms of the "entrainment of neuronal oscillations to sensory input rhythms." In other words, the rhythmic breathing or reciting of a mantra entrains the rhythms of neural firing patterns. In accord with our complex dynamics analysis, in this case "top-down" processing, or focusing mental energy, is shown to change "lower-level" processing, in terms of brain structure and function. Since attention, as we have seen, is a finite resource, it costs to use it. It is important, then, for those who want to change a particular behavior pattern that they have attention available for that purpose. Focus meditation has been shown to increase that resource, apparently by changing the way in which the brain operates. Corroborating this hypothesis, another group of researchers showed in a 2010 experiment that long-term meditators have significantly greater cerebral blood flow in the prefrontal cortex and the midbrain, among other locations.[14] And yet another study produced evidence that intensive meditation practice makes attending to one object of focus *easier* (again reducing brain-resource allocation), so that greater resources remain available for dealing with other issues.[15] As discussed earlier, the ego depletion view of addictive relapse suggests that people who try to control urges in one area for a sustained period of time are more susceptible to giving in to temptation elsewhere, to give up on difficult cognitive tasks sooner, and to display less physical and intellectual fortitude. Attention and self-control are expensive, resource-demanding activities, but these studies show that both of these important resources can be strengthened – a claim that is demonstrable at both the physical and mental levels.

Not only can humans train the brain through meditation but working memory exercises as well have been shown to be correlated with diminished drinking activity in heavy drinkers. In one study, a group of psychologists trained individuals whose behavior constituted hazardous drinking, according to the Alcohol Use Disorders Identification Test, in simple working memory exercises. For twenty-five sessions over at least twenty-five days, these volunteers participated in working memory exercises. Over the period of the study, not only did their working memories improve but their drinking also diminished by as many as ten drinks per week on average, and stayed at that level when tested a month later. The effects of this training seemed to be greatest in those who also scored high on an impulsiveness scale with respect to drinking behavior – in other words, those who were not managing to inhibit urges. While this is just one study, given its tendency to corroborate the findings of the meditation researchers, it seems that, since the prefrontal cortex is generally recognized to be responsible for decision-making, planning complex behavior, and impulse control, anything that one might do to increase prefrontal activity could be a useful asset in addressing addictive patterns of thinking and behavior at the physical level. Since psychological experiences and behaviors emerge from this level, strengthening its influence would seem to be a simple and cheap way to assist those who wish to transition out of addiction to do so. Given the expense and difficulty of administration that often attend other approaches to assisting addicts, it would seem that these methods would be ideal for widespread dissemination. Free yoga and meditation classes are already available in public parks, churches, and other places where middle-class individuals gather. Why not make these opportunities readily available in halfway houses and homeless shelters as well? Without doubt, success in this direction would require social acceptance of these opportunities in the communities into which they were introduced. That is to be expected, and must be addressed. Understanding the rhythms and values that emerge at higher levels of organization in the systems that we are considering is essential to creating effective change at lower levels.

Natural systemic approaches

Even something as broadly systemic as exercise, whether aerobic or resistance based, can increase an individual's chances of transitioning out of addiction. For one thing, exercise increases dopamine levels in just the areas of the brain that are depleted of that neurotransmitter in withdrawal. Not only that, but consistent exercise increases dopamine storage in the brain, and stimulates the production of enzymes that create dopamine receptors, which, as we have seen, are diminished with the chronic overproduction that substances and activities associated with addictions cause. As if that weren't promise enough, consistent exercise increases neurogenesis, the creation of new neurons, a process that is halted in the addictive cycle. Brain derived neurotropic factor (BDNF), a substance that helps existing neurons thrive and encourages the growth and differentiation of new neurons, is also stimulated by vigorous exercise.[16] The brain is plastic, and it is precisely that plasticity that allows for the changes that result in addictions, but it is that same plasticity that allows for people to transition out of addiction and regain feelings of control and well-being.

Appreciating the organic, integrated nature of our body/brains both with respect to individuals and with respect to the larger environment can provide additional tools for those seeking to transition out of addictive behavior. Not only can actively working our bodies enhance our overall health, and our ability to withstand the evocative cues that will inevitably incline addicts toward their default behavior but so can merely taking in experiences of nature. The power of our organic and essentially embedded nature is highlighted in research that indicates the positive influence that simply being around nature can have on our well-being. One very large study (of 345,000 people), for instance, reported that those who live within one kilometer of a park or wooded area suffer lower rates of depression and anxiety than those who face only concrete every day. In areas with mostly concrete surroundings (10% green space), about 2.6% of the population experienced anxiety disorders, and 3.2% dealt with depression, whereas only 1.8% of those living in areas with abundant green space (90%) experienced anxiety, and 2.4% experienced depression.[17] While these differences are small, and the specific causes of the results unknown, numerous studies performed since then support the findings, and anything that makes a difference in occurrence rates of these conditions is worth investigating further. Looking for a single factor to explain the effect is probably wrongheaded. Human organisms are more likely to flourish in the natural environments of which we are a part, and that is for a complex set of reasons. The good news is that even for those living in dense urban areas, there are ways to take advantage of the positive effects that exposure to nature is shown to have. Even if we don't live amid trees and greenery, we can always take a walk through a park, even if it requires some effort to get there, and thereby enhance our exposure to both a healthful environment and to exercise. Commenting on this research, Dr. Kathryn Kotrla of the Texas A&M College of Medicine agreed with the approach of this book that such research "highlights very clearly that our Western notion of body-mind duality is entirely false. The study shows that we are a whole organism, and when we get healthy that means our body and our mind get healthy."[18] Where we start is not the issue; many places will do as well as others. The point is that addiction is a human problem, but one for which there are many potential opportunities for intervention, and so much reason for hope.

Healing the trauma

As we saw in Chapter 3, the experience of trauma significantly increases the likelihood of an individual's becoming addicted. According to the authors of the long-running ACES, who have studied over 17,000 subjects, "addiction overwhelmingly implies prior adverse life experiences."[19] Among patients in substance abuse treatment, it is estimated that 33%–59% of women and 12%–34% of men suffer PTSD.[20] The standard of treatment for this disorder in the recent past has been cognitive behavior therapy (CBT), in which patients are taught to isolate and evaluate stressful thoughts. Next most popular is exposure therapy, in which patients discuss the traumatizing events repeatedly in a safe environment until those events lose their emotional power. Another, similar therapy involves eye movement desensitization and reprocessing therapy (EMDR). In this final method, distractions are employed to minimize emotional response while patients talk about a traumatizing event, so that they can reassociate the memory with diminished emotional reactivity. The idea is to capitalize on the fact that memories are changed each time we experience them. If attention is focused on vision while a patient brings up a traumatic memory, then the affective response that typically attends that memory should be lessened. Often these therapies are provided in conjunction with antidepressants or anxiety medications, to help patients reprocess memories with lowered affective association. The advice generally given in treating traumatized addicts, though, has been to address the addictive behavior first, and only then, after some period (often a year) of abstinence has been achieved, should the PTSD be tackled. This approach has been less than optimal, however, because as discussed in Chapter 3, PTSD symptoms themselves, such as hypervigilance and hyperreactivity are highly predictive of addiction and relapse.

For this reason, some researchers have turned their focus to the functioning of the autonomic nervous system. Lisa Najavits, for example, observed in a 2013 interview that

> [w]hen we were invited to China, Japan, India, and Africa to deal with trauma there, I started to realize how much in Western psychology we value thinking by figuring things out and how much other cultures primarily emphasize self-regulation. For me and many of my colleagues, going to those places has helped us discover ways of regulating autonomic arousal by techniques like breathing, Qui gong, drumming, or yoga. I have been surprised that something that is so obvious to me is not central in our pursuit of effective treatments: learning to regulate your autonomic arousal system is maybe the single most important prerequisite to dealing with PTSD. Physiological arousal needs to be calmed down before you can even access your executive functioning and the rational part of the brain.[21]

Likewise, Saj Razvi and colleagues at the Love and Trauma Center in Denver, Colorado, focus on treating trauma at the level of the autonomic nervous system (ANS). In trauma, the sympathetic nervous system, the activation portion of the ANS, is overcharged because, unlike in normal emergencies, there is nothing that the organism can do to resolve the situation (we can understand this particularly with respect to the kind of complex, ongoing traumas that often affect people from childhood).

In its turn, the deactivation portion of the ANS, the parasympathetic nervous system, responds in an equally powerful way. As a result, withdrawal, dissociation, lethargy, and other shut-down types of reactions occur. Normally, when stressful experiences are just moderate, the ANS system can return to its set point. When the stressful experience amounts to trauma, however, and particularly in trauma that persists for years, there is no opportunity for the ANS to return to a relaxed state. Getting there would require going back through the high-level activation, which is painful, frightening, and threatening. Therefore, according to this model, people retain the stress from the trauma and cope with it by moving around, attempting to physically distract themselves, or by mentally distracting themselves by reading, watching television, trying to reframe in their minds what happened to them, or becoming engaged in any number of other activities. The therapy in this case operates by helping clients stop the natural impulse to abandon the process of moving back through the high level of activation in order to complete the stress response cycle and return to the natural resting level of calm, alert integration with oneself and one's body. By first building resources for clients to rely on when they are most agitated, including both intrapersonal grounding skills and a reliable interpersonal attachment between the client and the therapist, the client can face the somewhat daunting task of recalibrating the ANS system, and integrate the story of her trauma into her self-story in a productive way.

To maximize the speed and efficacy of this approach, called containment therapy, researchers have been studying what happens when MDMA is added into therapy sessions. Supported by the Multidisciplinary Association for Psychedelic Studies (MAPS), four Phase II studies are currently ongoing in Israel, Canada, South Carolina, and Colorado. Because of its effects on certain neurotransmitters and hormones, MDMA has the effect of creating experiences of attachment and trust toward oneself, others, and the world, of feelings of being valued and loved, while producing a sense of intimacy with one's own experience. What might have taken several months to achieve without the MDMA can be achieved in a single drug-accompanied session along with three integrative sessions, and the studies completed so far have shown that the results are lasting. In the South Carolina trial, patients using Zoloft scored six points lower on the Clinicial-Administered PTSD Scale (CAPS) scale (the generally used measure of intensity of PTSD) than did users of a placebo; patients undergoing MDMA-assisted therapy by contrast experienced a CAPS score drop of 30–70+ points. What is more, 83% of the participants no longer met the criteria for PTSD even 3.8 years after treatment. Additionally, CAPS scores dropped an average of ten additional points between a two-month follow-up and the 3.8 year follow-up exams, indicating that healing begun in the MDMA session continued to operate even after treatment had ended.

MAPS supports research into the use of other psychedelic drugs as well, for healing trauma, mitigating anxiety, and treating addiction. Phase II trials using psilocybin that recently concluded at both Johns Hopkins University and New York University (NYU) achieved significant success in alleviating anxiety about death in cancer patients. One would imagine that these results would extrapolate to others with deep-seated generalized anxiety, which, as we have seen, is strongly associated with the onset of addictive behavior. Another Johns Hopkins group has recently found that smokers using psilocybin as part of a smoking cessation treatment program fared substantially better at quitting compared to those undergoing other behavioral and/or pharmacological therapies in similar studies.[22] Whereas the typical number of individuals who manage to remain free of cigarettes six months after treatment with other protocols generally is less than 35%, and often far less than that, these researchers found that 80% of those in the psilocybin-assisted program remained abstinent after six months. The distinctive thing about hallucinogenic treatments is that, rather than attempting to depress the sting of negative feelings by dulling them repeatedly, but temporarily, treatments with hallucinogens seem instead to bring about in just two or three sessions a fundamental shift that remains in effect long after the treatment is over. Moreover, patients experienced very positive side effects from these treatments. For example, 87% of the patients in the Johns Hopkins studies rated at least one of their psilocybin sessions among the ten most meaningful experiences of their lives, and 73% counted at least one of their psilocybin sessions among the five most spiritually significant experiences of their lives. The vast majority also said that their personal well-being increased "very much" as a result of their experience, and this lasted for a significant period after treatment. The outcomes that illustrate most vividly the difference between this kind of treatment and others, though, include that 73% of participants in the Johns Hopkins study reported that the psilocybin increased their belief in their ability to stop smoking, while 68% indicated that they had experienced shifts in life priorities and values in such a way that smoking just wasn't as important anymore. Due to the quite positive results in their early studies, both Johns Hopkins and NYU are now preparing to move into much larger (400-participant) Phase III studies.

The connection to 12-step programs

The switch to a representation of self and world that values sobriety and self-control over use and indulgence is a true revolution in the thinking of the addict. As we saw in Chapter 5, it often comes like a gestalt shift in the way in which one's world is experienced, or, in another way of putting it, a total shift in one's conceptual state space. The experience of this kind of shift seems in some ways totally inexplicable, and certainly not subject to conscious control. Meanings systematically switch together at once, some say "in a moment of clarity." As in any revolution, this switch cannot be *made* to happen from within the system; rather, such a shift requires stimulation from outside. Perhaps it is for this reason that 12-step programs place such emphasis on "admitting that our lives had become unmanageable," and on "a decision to turn our lives over to the care of God as we understood him," because such an overarching, revolutionary change to many seems to happen without their input, as if by a miracle. This kind of revolutionary change is at the very least mysterious, from our ordinary everyday perspective. But on the present theory, it is the essence of natural. It is simply the result of a far from equilibrium system's being affected by a key input, as when a pile of sand collapses at the addition of just one grain more. Rather than being a function of magic or of the intervention of a supernatural God, an overall addictive pattern is changed by changes made in the patterns that create and sustain it. It may well be that one has been changed through powers greater than oneself, but they are all natural powers of one's own body interacting with its physical and social environment. As discussed above, research is showing that such a shift can be brought about with significant reliability by hallucinogenic or magnetic treatment, or by other indirect methods. But work on emotional reactivity, impulse control, and managing responses to one's motivation-reward system within a social context can also be done by yet other means than those so far mentioned.

An individual who identifies as an addict can improve her odds of experiencing a revolution in her conceptual framework and thinking and emotional patterns by taking an introspective approach, and doing exactly the opposite of trying to seize control of her impulses. In part, this is a familiar story to those who are aware of the 12-step program's "spiritual awakening" experience, which is promised to result from going through the prescribed steps. Although the kind of fundamental shift that I am referring to may sometimes occur after taking such steps, those particular steps are neither necessary nor sufficient for achieving it. They are not necessary, because other kinds of self-reflective and socially supportive dynamics have been demonstrated to help to evoke such a shift. Many people (although no research has been done to determine the precise numbers) have experienced a shift in thinking and feeling, and become happy abstainers through LifeRing Secular Recovery, for example, and Smart Recovery – programs without steps or a higher power. And working the steps is not sufficient for achieving revolutionary change. Many who have wholeheartedly attempted to work through such systems of steps have failed to achieve such a fundamental change in feeling and worldview. The more conservative thing to say is that people who engage in self-revelatory and responsibility-taking measures, along with taking perhaps many other conscious steps involving such things as turning attention away from oneself, practicing conscious gratitude, and helping others, have a higher statistical probability of entering into and sustaining periods of abstinence and freedom from addictive symptoms, including cue-based cravings, and so forth.

Given the level of complexity involved in this kind of worldview change, it won't happen all at once, even if the gestalt-type switch that begins a sober career is of a revolutionary character. The new worldview is held tenuously at first, because holding it necessitates that one resist "flipping" back to the other pattern, which has gained stability and strength through untold numbers of repetitions. But the new perspective can be firmed up over time, with reinforcement and strengthening coming in a variety of ways from a variety of sources. Rehabituating one's thinking, through giving and hearing testimony, speech acts repeated over and over again about the actuality of change, is one of the ways in which the newly established gestalt can be strengthened in an individual. One of the most important things that 12-step programs can do is help people believe that they can change. Repetitive storytelling of how life was during the period in which use was paramount, what happened, and how life is free from the cycle of abuse now can rehabituate one's thought patterns to ones that are more conducive to a happy and peaceful life. Of course, this can happen in many different types of support and other types of groups. There is nothing proprietary about those who endorse 12-steps with regard to this function. Likewise, interacting with people who model the behaviors and attitudes that one seeks to emulate reinforces one's own strength, much as parents do for emotional children, by entraining the weaker, less confident person's patterns with those of the stronger, more habituated by success. In this way, alternative automatic responses can be developed to counter difficult situations.

The essential thing is that the addict comes to believe that ceasing her addictive behavior is possible. Whether addicted or not, people are moved by their beliefs. In fact, one way that philosophers sometimes define belief is in terms of that upon which one is willing to act. We may *say* that we believe all kinds of things, but if we aren't willing to act ("Of course, I trust you!"), that is a clear sign that we don't actually believe. This suggests that one way in which a person might become motivated to abstain from a drug or other addictive activity is to become firmly convinced that if she does indulge, she will certainly end up in jail, or in a mental institution, or dead. This is oft-repeated rhetoric in 12-step rooms. Perhaps those who use it believe it. But if prison or institutionalization is not imminent for a person who nevertheless wants to stop using a substance or engaging in an activity, those kinds of threats will not be believed, and will have no power to help her, and they may even hurt, by driving her away from what might be a very helpful belief, that she would be better off if she were to stop. This brings up another caveat regarding 12-step approaches to treating addiction: there is a clear danger for those who attend meetings of these groups and try to take the steps but do not manage to get out of the cycle of addictive behaviors. The danger rests on the fact that "the program" is based on the self-affirming mantra that it "works for those who work it." In other words, continuing in an addictive pattern subsequent to participating in such a program means personal failure. And this is a failure that singles one out as particularly hopeless, for, as the Big Book says, "Rarely have we seen one fail who has thoroughly followed our path." These programs and the 90%+ of rehabilitation treatment programs that are based on them, as has been mentioned, put the responsibility for transitioning out of addiction squarely on the shoulders of the addict. If she fails to achieve the goal that the vocal members around her have managed, there is a clear danger that she will become even more mired in a negative cycle of self-blame, addictive behavior, remorse, and hopelessness.

Deep psychology

As we have seen, the beliefs that affect motivation need not be true and, more importantly, they need not even be conscious. The fact that many, or even most, of our beliefs are not necessarily (or even probably) conscious has serious implications for addicts. For one thing, as we know, nearly every addict has memories, accessible or forgotten, of the substance of their addiction bringing about undeniable pleasure, peace, satisfaction, or some mix of pleasurable sensations. Without such an effect, it is hardly likely that anyone would continually return to the use of something that ultimately brings with it serious negative consequences (and if there are no negative consequences, then it is questionable whether addiction is involved). Some enterprising addicts have even gone to the effort of writing down their feelings while using, in order to try to get an objective understanding of why they would continue to be so compelled by something that they know in their sober moments to be so damaging.[23] What we find in these writings is sobering (the pun is only partially intended). There is in the words of these addicts the expression of genuine, heartfelt pleasure, relief, or satisfaction linked with the substance of their choice. Those associations have been linked in the writers' brains, for better or for worse, and they will drive behavior if left unattended. This is true regardless of "triggers" of which an addict might be consciously aware, although sights, sounds, and smells associated with these perhaps totally unconscious memories are certainly important, as they will, if not countered, automatically activate the anticipation cycle central to addiction.

So, how can addicts deal with unconscious processes? Fortunately, there are ways, some of them encoded in the formulaic language of 12-step programs, and there are others having to do with rendering the unconscious conscious. For instance, if the belief in a higher power is a live option for her, an addict who believes can have a powerful ally in managing the thoughts that lead to addictive behavior. She can "let go and let God." Rather than entertaining the provocative thoughts that might incite them to action, addicts can focus attention on the higher power, which necessarily shifts their thinking away from the thoughts of use, since attention cannot truly be multifocused – perhaps long enough for the sensitivity to those thoughts to pass. If one truly believes that one has help, one does – just as a weight lifter often manages to lift a heavy weight with the assistance of a spotter, even if the spotter only lightly touches the weight. For those who cannot believe in such a power, there are other options for reinforcing belief in their ability to change. As we have seen, some hallucinations may have that effect. In more natural ways, individuals can perhaps be convinced of their own brain's power to overcome itself, by reading scientific literature (or even books like this one!) regarding the brain's marvelous plasticity, the power to circumscribe the activities of the unconscious, the power of belief, or accounts of meditative monks' achievements, and so on. Skeptics can come by a variety of ways to be "excited by nature" to develop beliefs that can aid in their recovery. They just need something that is demonstrable, theoretically sensible, and replicable.

More universally effective than these options is the "social method" of developing beliefs – the practice of telling and hearing narratives that play upon both the power of "making sense" that we crave, and the power of the actual in bringing about belief in the possible. The testimonies heard in AA, LifeRing, or other self- and mutual-help groups, serve the purpose of instilling belief, for they provide undeniable evidence that relief from the suffering of addiction does happen. No matter how hopeless any newcomer might think his own case, when he hears repeatedly the stories of people who had been as badly off or worse than he, and yet became and stayed sober, he cannot but be buoyed in his belief that his own transition out of addiction is possible. But this process of storytelling carries an additional benefit – of rebuilding one's own life through narrative. As one talks through one's own story of misery and confusion with others, and is heard, one begins to make sense of one's trauma and begins to feel human again. Philosopher Susan Brison asks with regard to surviving a life-changing trauma, "How does one go on with a shattered self, with no guarantee of recovery, believing that one will always stay tortured and never feel at home in the world?" The answer: "one remakes oneself by finding meaning in a life of caring for and being sustained by others."[24] Because those who have been addicted, like those who have suffered other kinds of trauma, have often had their experience of everything, including their own identities, changed, the value of reasserting themselves in the presence and with the assistance of others cannot be overstated. Our memories are constructed over time, and they change with time. In fact, they change each time we re-member them, shining not with the emotional valance and significance that they originally had, but rather taking on the meaning valence appropriate at the time of reconstitution.[25] Through the sense-making process of telling and retelling one's life story, unbearable memories that may define a given individual as one in whom transition out of addiction is impossible, can become memories of events that were not person defining, but instead memories of events that were necessary to bring one to the present point of sobriety. In this way, not only do others' life stories help one entering into the transition out of addiction believe that she can do it, but also her own story, the more she tells it and the more success she sees in it, will become one that fosters the project of sobriety.

Of even further value of sharing narratives orally in groups is the value of being heard. As we explored in the chapter on meaning, discussions between addicts and their loved ones or treatment professionals are often exercises in noncommunication. And as we saw in the chapter on the social sources of addiction, the alienated, the dislocated, the disenfranchised often experience dehumanization as well. Being "treated" for such an already difficult situation could exacerbate the problem, were it not for the fact that treatment usually entails being surrounded by others with similar problems and similar experiences. Telling and retelling one's story to others similarly situated enhances the experience of being heard, an essential human need. Whether in a program with steps or not, many experts agree that the social element of support groups, whether for addiction, cancer survival, divorce, or anything else, is a most effective factor in getting through difficult parts of life. While the social world may contribute any number of causes to the development and maintenance of addictions and other human ills, interaction with particular other human beings seems to be one of the most powerful tools available for dealing with them. Feeling included and genuinely touched by other human beings is just as important for those disentangling themselves from a cycle of misery and shame as it is for babies trying to figure out the world for the first time. Communication is difficult to achieve, but for those who have suffered the experience of being "out of sync" with the rest of the world, it can be the key to rediscovering, or discovering for the first time, how to live a meaningful human life.

Reframing the social context

A sense of self-worth is essential to any program of self-improvement, and in the case of addicts, that sense is often more than a little ragged. This is why the "tough love" approach advocated so vocally in previous decades by Al-Anon[26] and other programs is so wrongheaded. In order to transition out of addiction, particularly one that has taken a great toll on the addict's health, relationships, and/or professional life, the addict must be reintegrated into the social systems from which she emerged and of which she is a natural part. Even the toughest prison inmates have shown the importance of such reintegration in overcoming personal challenges. Sarah Huggins Scarbrough, a recent PhD from Virginia Commonwealth University, showed the value of continuing support for addressing addictive issues, violence mitigation, and recidivism. In her three-and-a-half-year-long study, participants in a violent wing of the Richmond City Jail showed that making a meaningful life can often begin with taking responsibility for one's actions and absolving oneself of essential guilt. Using a peer-to-peer AA/NA-based treatment program, along with significant postrelease services, the participants who were studied had an 18% lower recidivism rate than did other inmates without such integration services. What is more, "[e]ven for those participants who did recidivate, there was a significant increase in the amount of time between release and re-incarceration." The key to the success of this program is twofold. First, it is a peer-to-peer program, which means that the experiences shared by participants are heard by others who have been in similar situations. Rather than being counseled by yet more professionals who could not understand their feelings of alienation, resentment, anger, and "otherness," these participants are met by others who have been in similar situations. They can speak there of things that cannot be understood elsewhere, and be part of a group with a shared understanding, absolving them of alienating guilt. Addressing other elements of their experience, the program studied by Scarbrough includes, like all Anonymous programs, a spiritual/faith-based element and, in addition, behavior modification practices aimed at helping people deal with things such as "idle time, loneliness, abandonment, dealing with fear, and/or not being comfortable with asking for help." The second key to the success of this program is its after-release component, which includes transportation assistance; assistance in obtaining important documents, such as birth certificates, social security cards, and identification cards; and access to housing and employment services, all elements necessary to successfully transitioning into a stable place in society.[27] With 6.9 million people incarcerated in 2011 (2.3 million in the United States alone), and 80% of those addicted to alcohol or some other drug, Scarbrough's study deserves serious attention.

Another way to avoid the negative, self-reinforcing consequences of incarcerating human beings for their addictive behaviors is to refuse to incarcerate them to begin with, as has become the practice in Portugal, the Czech Republic, and the Netherlands. In 2000, Portugal decriminalized all drugs in a new approach to the "war on drugs." As part of *Law 30/2000*, the usual substances are still illegal, but penalties for possessing personal amounts of them are much the same as a parking violation. Those caught with what amounts to ten days' worth or less of any of the normally criminalized drugs are required to interview with a "dissuasion commission" office, which are lay panels located in unremarkable office buildings, rather than in police stations. The recommendation in 2012 for 67% of those interviewed by these commissions was a "provisional suspension," which means that no consequences followed.[28] Fourteen percent of recommendations were for interviewees to undergo drug treatment. These recommendations do not come without support. The dissuasion commission's task is to "evaluate the personal circumstances of the individual" and refer them to an array of appropriate services, of which there is a nationwide network.[29] Significantly, the assistance provided by Portugal includes employment subsidies, which make it possible for individuals to provide dignified lives for themselves. The result has been striking. In the mid-1990s, 100,000 of Portugal's ten million citizens were considered "severely drug addicted," with a disproportionally high number of them also HIV infected.[30] Since 2001, there have been significant reductions in new diagnoses of HIV and AIDS, and the number of those who repeatedly use "hard" and intravenous drugs has decreased by an impressive 50%.

Other approaches to undercutting the public health problems and dehumanization of addicts have been tried elsewhere, including supervised drug consumption rooms, heroin-assistance treatment (pure heroin, injected by medical professionals, for the deeply dependent opiate user), drug courts, and supply-side regulation of cannabis. While drug courts, unsurprisingly on the present analysis, have provided no evidence of effectiveness, heroin-assisted treatment does seem to improve retention in treatment of deeply entrenched opiate users, and drug consumption rooms have improved health outcomes for drug users and public nuisance problems associated with certain kinds of drug use.[31] The latter face legal battles, however, since they operate in jurisdictions in which the drugs are illegal. The most famous of these, Insite, in Vancouver, British Columbia, was closed in June 2014, with the immediate result that streets and alleys became littered with needles and other injection accoutrements. Importantly, though, the organization that established Insite, the Vancouver Area Network of Drug Users (VANDU), has continued to fight to reform public policy, to establish dignified housing and health care for drug users, and to fight against police brutality and inhumanity. It is in bringing these drug users back into the community that VANDU has had the greatest impact and given them the greatest chance to lead meaningful lives.

Tools in the kit

In any emotional/psychological phenomenon that humans experience, the questions concern complex dynamic systems interacting at many levels, and unique individuals with unique lifetimes of experiences. Attempting to use linear causal analysis to understand why some people succeed in living the lives they want, while others continue to be disappointed, is bound to result in frustration and demoralization for those who fail. A more promising tactic is to approach overcoming unwanted addictions in terms of increasing one's statistical probabilities of avoiding falling into a well-established attractor well. Likewise, it seems more helpful to frame addiction as a temporal problem rather than as an essential one – a disease to which one is doomed for life.

While some number of addictions will resolve on their own (around 5%–8%), the most helpful attitude for the majority of the population is to focus on increasing probabilities in one's favor. Although we cannot alter our DNA or remove the traumas of childhood, predictors of addiction such as anxiety and hypersensitivity can be addressed through medications, meditation, and talk therapy. Trauma can be addressed through a variety of approaches, such as EMDR, cognitive-behavioral therapy, and somatic therapies. The habitual element of addiction can be addressed by changing any single habit, for success in this arena breeds success. If someone begins to exercise regularly, for example, she will have better success in managing her eating, and will create further resources for control in the future. If she determines to attend a mutual self-help group or join friends for coffee at around the time that she would normally begin to drink or smoke cannabis, she will have better success at managing those behaviors. If she begins a course of reflective thinking or therapy to better understand her reactivity to stressful situations, she will be better prepared to deal with them. And if she reaches out to other people and manages to find support, she will increase her personal resources for self-comfort, just as an infant does by regularly appealing to a reliable, comforting caregiver who helps her stabilize and strengthen her own ability to self-soothe. At what may be the most important level of human experience, if a person begins to speak and be heard as a dignified voice within a human community, the resources of that entire community may be brought to bear to stabilize and render meaningful her life.

9
Conclusion

First question: are there "real addicts"?

Whether used as a tool for control and profit, a weapon for accusation, or an excuse for inexcusable behavior, the appeal to addiction seems to be ubiquitous. And yet, as we have seen, it can be applied to virtually anyone given a particular context. Even in the most paradigmatic cases, it depends upon a network of genetic, environmental, developmental, psychological, and sociological factors. The concept "addiction" should be understood not as a defined and settled phenomenon, the scope of which is delimited by necessary and sufficient conditions, but instead as a prototype, a locus within our conceptual state space. Close to that prototype are examples like the individual who lives in an abandoned building, occupying all her time and devoting all her resources to shooting up heroin. Further away, but still within the scope of the concept, is the individual who drinks coffee most days of the week, and is grumpy when he does not, or who hasn't had a drink in months, but continues to think of it daily. Surely some generalizations can be made across cases; otherwise, there would be no agreement that in most cases addiction is unwanted, and there would be no support groups for escaping it. But we do notice that the support groups are legion in variety, suggesting that many individuals who think of themselves as addicted do not recognize their experiences as being similar to those who are addicted to different substances or activities than they are. Shoppers or gamblers may completely fail to understand how alcohol or opiate addicts can use such dangerous chemicals, and the latter two types of individuals may have no interest whatsoever in allures of the casino or the shopping mall. It is simply not possible to get the kind of definition that philosophers (and many others) want, and it is wrong-headed to try.

As Walter Sinnott-Armstrong says, if we are to answer the question of whether addicts are responsible for their actions, "we need to specify what is common to all real addicts that reduces or removes responsibility."[1] And that, he agrees, is just what we will not be able to do. What does "real addicts" mean? Does it refer to those who lack control with respect to use of some substance or tendency to some activity? We have seen the range of problems with attending what "lack of control" can mean. How far does lack of control have to go before an individual can be counted as an addict, and what degree of lack of control are we talking about? As we have said, almost anybody who could be characterized as an addict has control in some ways and not in others, in some contexts and not in others, and in varying degrees. This is true, though, of nearly everyone with respect to something at some period in his or her life. In 2015, for instance, a Pew Foundation study found that 73% of teenagers surveyed reported having smartphones, with about a third of African American and Hispanic teens declaring that they are online "almost constantly."[2] To high school teachers and instructors in introductory level college classes, it appears that these teens are addicted to their phones. Even when they agree to turn them off, and are penalized for using them, these teens do not seem to be able to resist reaching for their phones. Have we created/discovered a new addiction? Or should a new category be created for such behaviors?

A simple, one-shot answer will not capture the phenomenon of addiction. It is as unique in each individual who counts himself addicted as is his psyche, and at each of the levels of analysis that we might wish to make of it, and at any given time. What's more, which level of specificity counts as a basis for explaining other parts of the addicted person's emergent behavior largely depends on the kind of question we are asking. It is a pragmatic question. On the view argued for here, there do not exist entities that are ultimately the basis of the entire system; rather, it is the interactions that are primary. This, as we have seen, includes the individual's DNA as well as the environment in which replication and self-organization of cells takes place, including the gestating mother's stress, nutrition, and exercise levels, and the larger environment with which the mother is interacting, as well as the larger later environment within which the individual develops, which she helps create. Whether a person becomes an addict as a youth or an adult, even if she is born drug dependent, will also then depend upon whether she suffers from attachment irregularities during postpartum development, and if so, when and how. It will depend further upon whether she is exposed to trauma at an early age, and if so, how that trauma is experienced within her personal world, and within the context of what cultural cues she has been sensitized to. And all of this plays against the background of the world of meanings into which she emerges as a self-conscious, reflective being with specific sensitivities and expectations. The responsiveness of her caregivers, the games her mother plays with her or the jokes she plays on her, the role of cigarettes, alcohol, gambling, and other substances of abuse in her environment, as well as age and brain development at the age of first exposure to relevant substances or activities, all contribute to the likelihood of her falling into addictive patterns, as does the safety of the entire family within their cultural environment. This constellation of factors together with a multitude of others influence an individual's attitudes, sensitivities, self-esteem, conception of the future and, in combination with a multitude of other continually interacting elements, constitute the complex dynamic that is the individual operating within her world. The project of attempting to define "real addicts" in terms of one dogma or another seems unhelpful, if not simply self-serving.

Second question: is there "addictive thinking?"

The factors listed above we have described as operating mostly outside of consciousness, and in complex ways that defy any straightforward causal analysis. That is why we can never know in advance who will become addicted, or to what, or what that addiction will mean within the context of that life. Just as little can we predict what might bring about the revolutionary shift that marks the transition out of an addictive pattern. Equally difficult is anticipating returns to use after some period of abstinence, as those events are changes in the same complex systems from which the addictive pattern emerged in the first place. As one alcoholic put it when people asked him the standard questions about his relapse – what had happened, what he had been feeling prior to the relapse, where he had been, and so forth – he replied, "I haven't found the black box yet." In-flight recording boxes often fail to solve mysteries surrounding even such mechanistic events as airplane crashes. It is hardly likely, then, that a person relapsing into an addictive pattern will be able to point to the cause of that return to use. We can say in terms of neural activity that a person's total state on the verge of crisis falls into an old and deep attractor well. That answers the "what" kind of question. We seek the answer, however, to the "why" question. What we find at the psychological level is a set of circumstances and an at least partially confabulated story. What is most likely to be given as a response to such questions, even by the most honest and reflective of addicts, is similar to what most of us will respond when asked to reflect on why we did something: we give a "typical" story, one that fits with the physical, social, and moral expectations of those around us. People give the explanations that they would expect themselves to give. These explanations provide a postevent sense-making narrative, based on some handily remembered facts, not an insight into what actually motivated people in a particular case. This is a common phenomenon, illustrated with studies involving everything from people's positions on conservation issues to individuals' elaborations of their choices of jam and tea, to descriptions of why particular faces were seen as more attractive relative to others.[3] In some of these studies, people often provided full explanations for why they preferred one or another of some proffered option, when in fact the one about which they explained their reasons for preferring wasn't even the one they had originally chosen.

The kinds of filling in, justifying, and apparently giving a false reason, like many of the other quirks that we've found to plague (and assist) human thinking, does not apply to addicts alone. These patterns of thought operate within and as a result of the evolution of human minds within our environment. It's not really fair, then, for families and friends of addicts, or fellow addicts, or even addicted people themselves, to demand after a slip, "Why did you do it?" There is no one story to be told. The story that we experience of our lives, as addicts or not, is ambiguous, because it is sketchy; we are privy to only a tiny amount of the processing that actually goes on within the organism that we are, and all of that processing is always constrained by and constrains the processing going on in the environment of which we are also a part. It is no wonder that there is significant space remaining for "filling in" or "interpretation." Philosopher Daniel Dennett says in this regard that there is no penultimate draft of our story (or of the self that is the subject of so much of our story).[4] On one occasion, or before one audience, who attracts our attention to a previously expressed aspect of our typical behavior, we might give one explanation, and on another occasion, in a different context, we might offer quite different reasons for our choices. And no one of them is definitive.

This is just one example of what is often labeled "addictive thinking," which is actually a case of universal human cognitive biases being employed in particular contexts, either connected with regular abuse of a substance or activity or with the desire to indulge when it is to one's detriment, or with use against someone else's desire to the contrary. Here's another one: denial. A main theme in 12-step based treatment is that the addict is in denial of his addiction. In fact, denial seems to be appealed to regularly in literature associated with this approach as the very essence of addiction: "addiction is a disease of denial" is a familiar slogan. What exactly does this mean? Typically, it means that the addict, while recognizing that certain unhappy consequences have followed from his continued use or abuse, refuses to attribute those consequences to his substance or activity of choice, but rather attributes those consequences to something else. He finds other, particular events or circumstances to explain the negative consequences that he has experienced, rather than chalk them up to the drug or activity. She may deny that there is a problem with the use in general, even if she says publicly that she recognizes there is a problem. This appears to simply be a case of conservatism bias, wherein people, whether addicted or not, demur from revising their beliefs even when presented with new evidence to the contrary. It blinded NASA with respect to problems with the Challenger launch. Conservatism bias is a pervasive bias, found in all dogmatists, and characterizes attitudes of both optimism and pessimism, but it seems to take on special meaning in the case of addiction. In this circumstance, the common conservatism bias becomes a recognized symptom of a disease.

Another way to think of the denial that is supposed to be a hallmark of addiction is in terms of cognitive dissonance. We are uncomfortable when our attitudes, beliefs, or behaviors are dissonant with one another. We will believe whatever it takes to make a consistent story, keeping the components that have the highest value for us and adjusting others. When people experience dissonance between their beliefs and their behaviors, or between sets of beliefs, or between beliefs and values, they try to lessen the dissonance by changing one or more of the attitudes, behaviors, or beliefs – or by securing new evidence that supports the favored beliefs. This is simple enough to do, applying another well-documented trick of our brains, confirmation bias, which results in our finding cases that fit the system of beliefs that we most wish to preserve. In short, we see the evidence that supports our preferred view, while ignoring evidence contrary to it. Employing this naturally occurring bias, we dismiss, or reduce the importance of, the beliefs or attitudes that conflict with a favored or habitual behavior. This bias is so well recognized that experimental science has made it standard practice to ferret out where it might be operating, and put obstacles in the way of its operation. This is the impetus behind experimental protocols such as double-blind studies. But in the context of suspected addictive patterns, it becomes recognized as "addictive thinking."

Also often characterized as "addictive thinking" is the "better than average effect," a bias that allows most people to take themselves to be better than average at everything from driving cars to making moral decisions to resisting seeing themselves as better than average. This effect is quite obvious with respect to parents' characterization of their children, and is not generally seen in a bad light in this context. Likewise, this phenomenon is hardly ever mentioned as a defect when it is observed in the student applying for medical school against stiff competition. Much less is it seen as defective in the soldier who stands with his group against a much larger force. In this case, believing that one is better than average is what makes it possible to summon the courage necessary in such situations. In fact, Ryan McKay and Dennett have even argued that this particular misbelief, or positive illusion is, if any misbelief is, actually adaptive in evolutionary terms.[5] In the case of those who have been labeled as addicts, however, individuals who exhibit this bias are judged to "have a case of terminal uniqueness," an attitude that must be rectified if the individual is to overcome his addiction. Two ironies regarding this labeling are worth mentioning. The first is tragic: those who are struggling to overcome addiction but become convinced that they are not better than, or different from, the average and additionally believe that only those with special qualities can actually change may give up on their efforts to live better lives. The second irony associated with calling out the "better than average bias" as addictive thinking is that those who point the finger are engaging in another cognitive bias: essentialism. Under the essentialism bias, alcoholism (or drug addiction) is an essential property of certain people, and there is no way to ever escape that characterization once it has been applied. As this view says, "once an alcoholic, always an alcoholic." For many involved in 12-step programs, the essentialism bias is a safety feature. If it were ever recognized that many people just stop being addicted, there would be no need for the dependence on "the program" that is accepted by devotees, a situation that would present too great a threat for many who thrive on community strength. In any case, with respect to the cognitive biases themselves, they are widely recognized by researchers in people of all sorts; they are not indicative of any particularly addictive types of thinking.

Attentional bias seems to be the culprit in another kind of "addictive thinking": addictive patterns of thinking, as is generally recognized, result in heightened attention being paid to those emotions, objects, and events that connect to the locus of their most frequently recurring thoughts. Again, this effect is recognized in psychological literature as a cognitive bias and not as an addictive mental pattern, for it is merely one of the characteristics of human thought. This particular bias has been vividly shown in hundreds of studies, including the famous "Invisible Gorilla" demonstration, to characterize a fundamental feature of the way human attention operates. When we are focused on one thing, for example, players in white shirts passing a basketball, we can fail to notice the most obvious of things also on the scene, such as a person in a gorilla suit walking right through the scene, stopping to beat its chest before walking off. Once again, though, when someone has been labeled an addict, both the term used to express the bias (now "triggers") and the strength of its effect (to bring about virtually automatic behaviors) are understood differently. Those who have stopped their unwanted behavior while attending self-help meetings, particularly 12-step meetings, with their particular structured type of sharing (recounting "what it was like, what happened, what it's like now"), exhibit a different kind of attentional bias. Particularly in the "pink cloud" that many say characterizes their first few months of sobriety, but also in the stories of those who have been abstinent for numbers of years, the negative attendants of their addictive behavior, as well as the positive events and feelings accompanying abstinence, loom large. Of course, if the suffering was great, and directly associated with the addictive behavior, then the relief attending cessation would in fact be great. But those very same events might well have been seen as "not that bad," say, prior to an intervention or hospitalization. Which characterization works is a function of whether an individual's focus is on the prospect of using again or on the goal of abstinence. Countless details will escape her awareness in either situation, but which details escape and which are attended to have everything to do with what is uppermost in her mind.

This sort of directed attention operates in combination with hindsight bias, conservatism bias, and the urge to resolve cognitive dissonance, in all of us. Whether or not one has ever had an experience one would label "addictive," human cognition is biased toward telling a story that is consistent over time, both with respect to expectations and in hindsight. Neither any of these kinds of biased thinking nor any of the dozens of others discovered to operate in ordinary healthy human beings is in any way distinctive of addiction in particular, despite the collective wisdom of certain circles to the contrary. The designation "addictive thinking" is more groundless than the label "addict," and yet these terms in common parlance are unquestionably taken to embody something real. This very language promotes particular ways of addressing a continuum of human problems that are both dismissive of the differences among those who have these problems and the similarities between those who are called addicts and those who are not. Far more helpful for dealing with real problems in the real world is to understand the diversity to which complex systems give rise and to deal with the individuals and the social systems creating them and arising from them in terms of what they really are.

The complexity of motivation

The conclusion to be drawn from all this discussion of complexity, levels of analysis, social constructs, and universal psychological biases cannot be that there is no such thing as addiction. No one can doubt that many people ruin their health, their relationships, and their professional lives through the use of substances and activities. And it would be foolish to deny that many of these individuals sometimes seem to have no control over their behavior, or at least feel like they have no ability to control it, or have no motivation to control it. In any case, the task is not to play with definitions. In many areas of science and social life, groups of people make decisions and policies, and research careers go forward without the field's ever coming to consensus about definitions. The task in our case is to discover why it is so difficult to resolve a certain family of human problems. Such resolution can occur, even within complex systems in which the parts are always changing, adapting to the behavior of other parts, creating new constraints within and for the ever-changing and adapting new whole. For one thing, we can assume that none of the higher levels of analysis can contradict lower levels: organisms cannot defy the laws of physics in the operation of cells, any more than the social systems that constrain the development of healthy or traumatized children can defy the laws, whatever they are, that describe the operations of individual psychology. Although systems "on the edge of chaos" like the weather and the human psyche are not predictable for more than a short time into the future, that fact does not imply that they are not deterministic. Causal principles still operate. For another thing, we know that characteristic of all complex adaptive systems is the existence of certain *lever points*, at which small changes in inputs produce significant and directed changes throughout the whole system.[6] This means that seemingly paradoxical revolutionary changes, such as a brain "stuck" in an addictive pattern transitioning itself out of that pattern, are not only possible but also in some cases and in some sense can be easy.

Addictive patterns seem particularly unstable in the sense that they arise and can only be sustained by continued indulgence. What is more, as they progress, and motivations to continue become crowded by motivations to change, they become even less stable. Particularly for those who have established other patterns in the past (we can think of this equally well in terms of neural firing patterns and their attractor wells, or of habits, or of psychological patterns), any number of things might prove to be the lever point that might make the whole addictive pattern collapse. For instance, a DUI experience might be the trigger, or a fall that results in broken bones. One person I met suffered an acute case of pancreatitis that resulted in a five-day medically induced coma. From then on, the desire to drink was nonexistent. From the positive side, something like a new job opportunity, a child, or a new love might prove the critical input. Even a change in habit, apparently in no way associated with the addiction, such as beginning a routine of evening walks or making the bed every morning, can trigger positive changes that then serve as lever points somewhere else until the person experiencing these little changes makes large life changes, ultimately including cessation of the addictive pattern. Simple abstinence itself can create a tipping point in some cases. This may be the reason why the few people who make a permanent change following a residential treatment program do so. "Breathing space" alone may make the difference. What is it about these events that can overcome years of overeating, or smoking, or general indolence? Within the context of a particular complex dynamic system, they serve as the grain of sand that hits just as the pile is in a critical state, resulting in a slide. For a different person, or for the same person on another day, or for the same person with an even slightly different biochemistry, that event may not have precipitated a change. Chapter 7 outlined a number of points wherein changes in input at one level of the system can cause disproportionately large changes in the whole. The question is one of probabilities.

This brings up another concept that is woven through addiction recovery discourse and operates as a point of contention among various groups: hitting bottom. The paradigm of an addictive career, as told in 12-step rooms, memoirs, and the AA's Big Book, is that a person begins to use or do something that is pleasurable, it becomes too much, bad things happen, and then the person finally "hits bottom" and recovery begins. Without this hitting bottom, forward progress cannot begin. The explanation often given when a person relapses into her addictive pattern of behaviors is that she had not yet hit bottom. Some groups, such as Rational Recovery and LifeRing Secular Recovery, however, maintain that hitting bottom is not necessary, that people merely need to get to a perspective from which they can see that they need to change something. Twelve-step endorsers will usually reply that people like this are among the lucky few who only need to hit a "high bottom" in order to be motivated to change. These are probably two ways of saying the same thing. The important observation is that at some stage something will happen, and nobody can know in advance what that thing will be, which will operate as a lever point, triggering huge changes in the person's whole way of seeing things. That doesn't mean that a different life occurs instantaneously, but it does mean that a critical juncture has been surpassed and that large portions of what had been a stable pattern collapse, creating a move into a different one.

The jurisprudence system seems to think that negative reinforcement can motivate people to stop at least certain addictive behaviors. Gambling or shopping in ways that involve unagreed-upon losses of others' money, taking certain drugs, or at least possessing them, and drinking after a DUI are met with still harsher penalties and sometimes incarceration. In recent years, university campuses have experienced rising numbers of their student populations wearing ankle monitors in order to stop the latter. The problem with this attempt at controlling people's behavior is that it depends upon an economic, rather than a psychological, understanding of motivation. And the presumptions of that particular model of human behavior have proven so faulty that even the field of economics has largely discarded them, while the field of behavioral economics, which focuses on how humans actually behave, given our implicit biases, has burgeoned. Rewards have been shown to be more effective than punishments as motivations, as any dog owner who has been to a training class knows. But even rewards are not always effective, and sometimes can undermine the goal. Although we have seen that in some cases drug users can effectively alter their behavior for financial rewards, in the long run rewards may rob them of their sense of autonomy and their confidence in their ability to act for intrinsic reasons.[7]

In any case, it seems that the factors that enter into an addicted individual's ability to change are legion. Short of defining "hitting bottom" as whatever it is that happens just prior to an individual's transitioning out of an addictive behavior pattern, it seems that crashing to earth in some traumatic way is neither necessary nor sufficient to achieve change. On the one hand, many people make a change, as we have said, on the basis of a simple dissatisfaction with the overall feel of their lives, while on the other, thousands and even millions of people have experienced horrific consequences in connection with their use and have persisted nonetheless. In complex adaptive systems that have the ability to create (and perhaps the inability to refrain from creating) a narrative around big life changes, sometimes framing those changes in terms of traumatic crashes might be helpful, and if so, then it should be fostered. The 12-step model and its linguistic conventions do help many people. But for some of those seeking a change, being exposed to the prototypical "bottoming out" as a necessary part of the process might be enough to frighten them away from accepting the value of making a change at all.

Probability is key

Because addiction is a phenomenon that emerges from a complex dynamic system, as we have said, those who wish to effect change in their lives have to play the odds. If there is no "silver bullet," and if instead addiction is understood as a relatively unstable pattern approaching a critical state, no one can predict what will be the tipping point for the addict. As the guiding thinking behind the LifeRing Secular Recovery program suggests, a person's best bet for creating permanent change is to create a "tool box" with as many resources in it as possible. Rather than offering a set program, this support group advocates that individuals create their own paths to change by reflecting on themselves, what has motivated or stressed them in the past, and finding new ways to support positive life changes. In one's "tool box" might be drugs such as Suboxone, Naltrexone, or Campril, meditation, massage, yoga, nutrition improvement, journaling, talk therapy, psychiatric treatment for underlying anxiety, depression, bipolar, or other disorders, or any of the other variety of things that we considered in Chapter 7, as well many other approaches not considered there. If prescribed steps, or Reiki, or praying to Thor seems to help, then any of them can be included in the tool box, because belief, too, is a causal factor in complex dynamic systems, in which "top-down" causation is as real as the "bottom-up" type. For those who are more scientifically minded, only evidence-supported approaches will work. For the more mystical minded, though, amulets and crystals are not out of the question. The point is to stack the odds in favor of a particular attractor well, a slide of the sand pile to the desired side. "Stack the odds in favor of slippage toward sobriety," some formerly addicted people often advise. In addition, encouragement to try, and try again, without shame or guilt is important, because one never knows which attempt will be successful, until one of them is, and even if a person falls back into addictive patterns at some point, every quality day lived counts.

An indirect approach might prove the most valuable of all for bringing about life changes. This may in fact be the point of the "spiritual awakening" of the 12-step model. Many 12-step group members will tell newcomers to work not on the drinking or the drugs, but on other aspects of their lives, such as resentments, character defects, and correcting wrongs that they might have done. Do this, they say, and the addiction will take care of itself. The book central to LifeRing Secular Recovery, if there is one, *Empowering Your Sober Self,* employs an indirect approach as well, focusing on strengthening the aspects of the "sober self" that has always been functional and good, so that it overpowers the "addicted self" that has more recently arisen. For complex systems, in which causation is nonlinear, the intuitions behind these approaches make good sense. Focusing on health, family, and enjoyable work and play activities, as well as on underlying psychological distress and potential goals (not to mention all of us working together to change the social circumstances that foster addiction) might well be more helpful in overcoming addiction than dwelling on the addiction itself. Attention to these other points will certainly be more useful than isolating the suffering person with an "intervention" in which she is held directly and individually responsible for the "disease" that she is accused of having.

If we think and act in different ways, we can effect changes in the oscillation patterns of groups of neurons, and in the ways that various parts of the brain link up. If causation were to operate in the simplistic way that most of us persist in expecting, this would seem to be peculiar to say the very least. But given the reality of mutual and complex causal interactions in systems like us, nothing magical is required to explain the fact that focusing our minds in certain ways, in yoga or meditation, for instance, or experiencing strong emotions, as happens when we fall in love or take on a new and valued project, can and does change the ways that our brains operate. This shouldn't be surprising, even in the long term, since the mind whose focus changes the brain emerges from the same brain that is changed. The brain itself changes the brain in meditation, in developing new projects, and in moving past addictive patterns. Situating our study of addiction in a context that takes seriously the complexities of human beings and the societies that we create and live in provides many more opportunities for discovering effective ways to prevent or intervene in addictive cycles. Some may say that this approach only makes studying addiction unwieldy, creating more problems than it solves. But in some cases it is better to address real problems with all their difficulties than it is to create models of them that are easier to manage, but that don't translate into real-world answers. In our case, given our generation's endemic addictive problems, perhaps it is worth the trouble to take on the harder problems that address our actual lived situation.

Notes

1 Introduction – Dismantling the Catch Phrase

1. American Psychiatric Association Committee on Nomenclature and Statistics, *Diagnostic and Statistical Manual of Mental Disorders* 4th ed. (Washington, DC: American Psychiatric Association, 1994).
2. Gene M. Heyman, "Addiction and Choice: Theory and New Data," *Frontiers in Psychiatry* (May 6, 2013) doi: 10.3389/fpsyt.2013.00031. Here Heyman cites A. I. Leshner, "Science-based Views of Drug Addiction and Its Treatment," *Journal of the American Medical Association* (282), pp. 131413–16; A. T. McLellan, D. C. Lewis, C. P. O'Brien, and H. D. Kleber, "Drug Dependence: A Chronic Medical Illness: Implications for Treatment, Insurance, and Outcomes Evaluation, *Journal of the American Medical Association* (284), pp. 1689–1695; and N. D. Voldow and T. K. Li, "Drug Addiction: The Neurobiology of Behavior Gone Awry," *National Review of Neuroscience* (5), pp. 963–970.
3. Approximately 500,000 people held in US prisons or jails have been convicted of a drug offense, according to the Justice Policy Institute's "Substance Abuse Treatment and Public Safety," (Washington, DC: January 2008), p. 1.
4. For various statements of this view, see Stephen Stitch, *From Folk Psychology to Cognitive Science: The Case against Belief* (Cambridge, MA: MIT Press, 1983); Patricia Churchland, *Neurophilosophy: Toward a Unified Science of the Mind-Brain* (Cambridge, MA: MIT Press, 1986); Paul Churchland, *The Engine of Reason, The Seat of the Soul: A Philosophical Journey into the Brain* (Cambridge MA: MIT Press, 1995); and Daniel Dennett, *Consciousness Explained* (New York: Little, Brown, 1991), among other works by these authors and others.
5. Terrence Deacon, *Incomplete Nature: How Mind Emerged from Matter* (New York: W. W. Norton, 2012, p. 179.

2 Some Philosophical Questions (and a New Theory)

1. American Psychiatric Association Committee on Nomenclature and Statistics, *Diagnostic and Statistical Manual of Mental Disorders* (Washington, DC: American Psychiatric Association, 1994). Although the revised 4th edition (IV-TR) is currently the most cited, some references will be herein made to the 5th edition.
2. World Health Organization, *The ICD-10 Classification of Mental and Behavioral Disorders: Diagnostic Criteria for Research* (Geneva: World Health Organization, 1993).
3. See, for example, *Time*, April 30, 1990, http://content.time.com/time/magazine/article/0,9171,969965,00.html
4. K. S. Kendler, I. M. Karkowski, M. C. Neale, and C. A. Prescott, "Illicit Psychoactive Substance Use, Heavy Use, Abuse, and Dependence in a U. S. Population-Based Sample of Male Twins," *Archives of General Psychiatry*

57 (2000): 261–269; K. S. Kendler and C. A Presscott, "Cannabis Use, Abuse, and Dependence in a Population-Based Sample of Female Twins," *American Journal of Psychiatry* 155 (1998): 1016–1022; C. R. Cloninger, "Neurogenetic Adaptative Mechanisms in Alcoholism," *Science* 236 (1987): 410–416.

5. Until the summer of 2014, that is, when the DSM-V was published, with much attendant controversy.
6. One might try to say that people are addicted, for instance, when they have "addictive personalities"; or when they feel that they can't control themselves, although they are at the same time just the selves that they can't control; or when they suffer from a "spiritual sickness."
7. I. Marks, "Behavioral (non-chemical) Addictions," *British Journal of Addictions* 85 (1990): 1389–1394.
8. Constance Holden, "Gambling as Addiction," *Science 21* 307, no. 5708 (2005): 349, doi:10.1126/science.307.5708.349d; A. Blaszczynski et al. "Withdrawal and Tolerance Phenomenon in Problem Gambling," *International Gambling Studies* 8, no. 2 (2008): 179–192; H. Rachlin, "Why Do People Gamble and Keep Gambling Despite Heavy Losses?" *Psychological Science* 1, no. 15 (1990): 294–297.
9. A. N. Gearhardt et al., "Neural Correlates of Food Addiction," *Archives of General Psychiatry* 68 (2011): 808–816.
10. Matilda Hellman et al., "Is There Such a Thing as Online Video Game Addiction? Across-Disciplinary Review," *Addiction Research and Theory* Early Online: 1–11 doi:10.3109/16066359.2012.693222.
11. APA (February 2010) News Release "DSM-5 Proposed Revisions Include New Category of Addiction and Related Disorders. New Category of Behavioral Addictions Also Proposed" (Release No. 10–08)
12. DSM IV, 176.
13. Gene Heyman, *Addiction: A Disorder of Choice* (Cambridge, MA: Harvard University Press, 2009).
14. Heyman, 112.
15. Heyman, 83.
16. Heyman cites the study by L. N. Robins, J. E. Helzer, and D. H. Davis, "Narcotic Use in Southeast Asia and Afterward: An Interview Study of 898 Vietnam Returnees," *Archives of General Psychiatry* 32 (1975): 955–961.
17. Heyman, 106–108.
18. Adrian Carter and Wayne Hall, *Addiction Neuroethics: The Promises and Perils of Neuroscience Research on Addiction* (Cambridge: Cambridge University Press, 2012) cite several recent studies, the point of which is either to show that drug use in addicts is compulsive or to describe the mechanism behind such compulsion. See, for example, J. Feil, D. Sheppard et al., "Addiction, Compulsive Drug Seeking, and the Role of Frontostriatal Mechanisms in Regulating Inhibitory Control," *Neuroscience and Biobehavioral Reviews* 35 (2010): 248–275; J. D. Jentsch and J. R. Taylor, "Impulsivity Resulting from Frontostriatal Dysfunction in Drug Abuse: Implications for the Control of Behavior by Reward-Related Stimuli," *Psychopharmacology* 146 (1999): 373–390; M. Yucel and D. I. Lubman, "Neurocognitive and Neuroimiaging Evidence for Behavioral Dysregulation in Human Drug Addiction: Implications for Diagnosis, Treatment, and Prevention," *Drug and Alcohol Review* 26 (2007): 33–39.

19. John Monterosso and George Ainslie, "The Picoeconomic Approach to Addictions: Analyzing the Conflict of Successive Motivational States," *Addiction Research and Theory* 17, no. 2 (2009): 115–134.
20. *Nichomachean Ethics.* For this reason, Aristotle says at 1152a18 that the weak of will "is not wicked, since his purpose is good." He simply behaves irrationally.
21. See Donald Davidson's "How Is Weakness of the Will Possible?," *in Essays on Actions and Events*, (Oxford: Clarendon Press, 1970), 21–42.
22. Davidson, 23.
23. Neil Levy, "Resisting 'Weakness of Will'," *Philosophy and Phenomenological Research* 82, no. 1 (2011): 134.
24. Levy cites R. F. Baumeister, E. Bratslavsky, M. Muraven, and D. M. Tice, "Ego-Depletion: Is the Active Self a Limited Resource?," *Journal of Personality and Social Psychology* 74 (1998): 1252–1265, and R. F. Baumeister, "Ego Depletion and Self-Control Failure: An Energy Model of the Self's Executive Function," *Self and Identity* 1 (2002): 129–136. See also Mark Muraven, Dianne M. Tice, and R. F. Baumeister, "Self Control as a Limited Resource: Regulatory Depletion Patterns," *Journal of Personality and Social Psychology* 74 (1998): 774–789; Mark Muraven and E. Slessareva, "Mechanisms of Self-Control Failure: Motivation and Limited Resources," *Personality and Social Psychology Bulletin* 29 (2003): 894–906.
25. Matthew T. Gaillot, Roy F. Baumeister, C. Nathan DeWall, Jon K. Maner, E. Ashby Plant, and Dianne M. Tice, "Self-Control Relies on Glucose as a Limited Energy Source: Willpower Is More Than a Metaphor," *Journal of Personality and Social Psychology* 92 (2007): 325–336; Matthew T. Gailliot and Roy F. Baumeister, "The Physiology of Willpower: Linking Blood Glucose to Self-Control," *Personality and Social Psychology Review* 11 (2007): 303–327; Roy F. Baumeister, Kathleen D. Vohs, and Dianne M. Tice, "The Strength Model of Self-Control," *Current Directions in Psychological Science* 16, no. 6 (2007): 351–355.
26. Keith E. Stanovich and Richard F. West, "Individual Differences in Reasoning: Implications for the Rationality Debate?" *Behavioral and Brain Sciences* 23 (2000): 645–726; Jonathan St. B. T. Evans, "In Two Minds: Dual-Process Accounts of Reasoning," *Trends In Cognitive Sciences* 7, no. 10 (2003): 454–459; John Pollock, "OSCAR: A General Theory of Rationality," in *Philosophy and AI*, ed. Robert Cummins and John Pollock (Cambridge, MA: The MIT Press, 1995), 257–275. The most popular version of this distinction is found in Daniel Kahneman, *Thinking, Fast and Slow* (New York: Farrar, Straus and Giroux, 2011).
27. William James, *Principles of Psychology* (New York: Henry Holt & Company, 1890), 543.
28. Carter and Hall, 47.
29. Bennett Foddy, "Addiction and its Sciences: Philosophy," *Addiction* 106 (2010): 25–31, doi:10.1111/j.1360—443.2010.03158.x.
30. Foddy, 27.
31. In fact there is a significant philosophical literature around this point, and around the converse, that people can be compelled without knowing that they are.
32. Most who argue this, for example Daniel Wegner, *The Illusion of Conscious Will* (MIT Press, 2002) and Sam Harris *Free Will* (New York: Free Press, 2012),

suggest that even without free will there is moral responsibility, and so the fact that free will is an illusion is practically unimportant. Others, such as Patricia Churchland (see, for example, her essay at Newscientist.com, November 18, 2006) has argued that the concept needs to be revised, and Daniel Dennett has argued in numerous essays and books since his 1978 *Brainstorms* (Cambridge, MA: MIT Press, 1981), but most concertedly in his *Elbow Room: The Varieties of Free Will Worth Wanting* (Cambridge, MA: MIT Press, 1984), that human beings have all the free will that anyone could want.

33. James Ladyman and Don Ross, with David Spurrett and John Collier, *Everything Must Go: Metaphysics Naturalized* (New York: Oxford University Press, 2007), 4.
34. Ladyman and Ross, 4.
35. Ladyman and Ross, 4.
36. John H. Holland, *Complexity: A Very Short Introduction* (Oxford: Oxford University Press, 2014).
37. Terrence W. Deacon, *Incomplete Nature: How Mind Emerged from Matter* (New York: Norton, 2012), 244.
38. Five reasons for believing this are listed on p. 4 of Mark Bickhard, "Some Consequences (and Enablings) of Process Metaphysics," *Axiomathes* 21, no. 1 (2011): 3–32. See also Mark H. Bickhard and Richard J. Campbell, "Physicalism, Emergence, and Downward Causation," *Axiomathes* 21, no. 1 (2011): 33–56
39. Ladyman and Ross, 20.
40. These examples are paraphrased from Mark Bickhard, "Interactivism: A Manifesto" *New Ideas in Psychology*, 27 (2009): 85–89, doi:10.1016/j.newideapsych.2008.05.001.
41. Deacon, 177.
42. J. C. Anthony and J. E. Helzer, "Syndromes of Drug Abuse and Dependence," in *Psychiatric Disorders in America: The Epidemiologic Catchment Area Study*, eds. Lee N. Robins and Darrel A. Regie (New York: Free Press, 1991), 116–154; R. C. Kessler, W. T. Chiu, O. Demler, K. R. Merikangas, and E. E.Walters, "Prevalence, Severity, and Comorbidity of 12-month DSM-IV Disorders in the National Comorbidity Survey Replication," *Archives of General Psychiatry* 62 (2005): 617–627; L. N. Robins and D. Regier, *Psychiatric Disorders in America* (New York: Free Press, 1991); F. S. Stinson, B. F. Grant, D. Dawson, W. J. Ruan, B. Huang, and T. Saha, "Comorbidity between DSM-IV Alcohol and Specific Drug Use Disorders in the United States: Results from the National Epidemiological Survey on Alcohol and Related Conditions," *Drug and Alcohol Dependence* 80 (2005): 105–116; L. A. Warner, R. C. Kessler, M. Hughes, J. C. Anthony, and C. B. Nelson, "Prevalence and Correlates of Drug Use and Dependence in the United States. Results from the National Cormorbidity Survey," *Archives of General Psychiatry,* 52 (1995): 219–229.
43. Deacon, ch. 10.
44. Deacon, 291.
45. John Stuart Mill, *System of Logic: Rationative and Inductive.* (1843) *Collected Works*, Vols. 7 and 8 (Toronto: University of Toronto Press: 1996), 371.
46. C. D. Broad, *The Mind and Its Place in Nature* (London: Kegan Paul, 1925).

47. Carl Hempel and Paul Oppenheim, "Studies in the Logic of Explanation," in Hempel's *Aspects of Scientific Explanation* (New York: The Free Press, 1965). Thomas Nagel, *The Structure* of Science (New York: Harcourt, Brace & World, 1061), ch. 11. Cited in Jaegwon Kim, "Making Sense of Emergentism," *Philosophical Studies: An International Journal for Philosophy in the Analytic Tradition* 95, no. 1/2 (1999): 3–36.
48. Kim, (1999).
49. Bickhard mentions this in "Representational Content in Humans and Machines," *Journal of Experimental and Theoretical Artificial Intelligence* 5 (1993): 285–333, and in "The Biological Emergence of Representation," in *Emergence and Reduction: Proceedings of the 29th Annual Symposium of the Jean Piaget Society*, eds. T. Brown and L. Smith (Hillsdale, NJ: Erlbaum, 2002), 105–131, as well as in (2004).
50. Deacon, 265.
51. Deacon, 266.
52. Deacon, 309.
53. Bickhard (2004), 130.
54. Deacon, 535.
55. Deacon, 323.
56. Mark Bickhard, "Consciousness and Reflective Consciousness," *Philosophical Psychology* 18, no. 2 (2005): 218.

3 Addiction and the Individual

1. It was so characterized by T. Trotter in 1788. Reproduced in *An Essay, Medical, Philosophical, and Chemical on Drunkenness and its Effects on the Human Body*, ed. R. Porter (London: Routledge, 1988), and by B. Rush, an American physician, in an 1808 book, *An Inquiry into the Effects of Ardent Spirits upon the Human Body and Mind: With an Account of the Means of Preventing, and of the Remedies for Curing Them* (Philadelphia: Thomas Dobson, 1808), according to M. Valverde, in *Diseases of the Will: Alcohol and the Dilemmas of Freedom* (Cambridge: Cambridge University Press, 1998), 2. According to the Baldwin Research Institute, Rush also believed that dishonesty, political dissent, and being African American were diseases.
2. *Neuroscience of Psychoactive Substance Use and Dependence* (Geneva, Switzerland: World Health Organization, 2004).
3. George F. Koob and Nora D. Volkow, "Neurocircuitry of Addiction," *Neuropsychopharmacology* 35 (2010): 217–138. doi: 10.1038/npp.2009.110.
4. Koob and Volkow, 217.
5. The case that Joseph LeDoux studied was fear, but perhaps the point can be generalized (LeDoux "Emotion, Memory and the Bain: The Neural Routes Underlying the Formation of Memories about Primitive Emotional Experiences, Such as Fear, Have Been Traced," *Scientific American*, June 1994, 50–57).
6. As we will see below, it is not just the amount of pleasure that one experiences that provokes repetition of use or gambling but also the pleasure that one anticipates. See Hans C. Breiter, Itzhak Aharon, Daniel Kahneman, Anders Dale, and Peter Shizgal, "Functional Imaging of Neural Responses

to Expectancy and Experience of Monetary Gains and Losses," *Neuron* 30 (May 2001): 619–639. In some cases, anticipation seems to play an even more provocative role. In some problem gamblers, almost winning may lead them to gamble even more than winning does. See Henry W. Chase and Luke Clark, "Near-win Situations May Encourage Problem Gamblers to Gamble More," *Journal of Neuroscience* 30, no. 18 (2010): 6180–6187.

7. R. L. Solomon and J. D. Corbit, "An Opponent-Process Theory of Motivation. II. Cigarette Addiction," *Journal of Abnormal Psychology* 81 (1983): 158–171; R. L. Solomon, "Addiction: An Opponent-Process Theory of Acquired Motivation: The Affective Dynamics of Addiction," in *Psychopathology: Experimental Models*, ed. J. D. Maser (San Francisco: Freeman, 1977), 66–103.
8. T. E. Robinson and K. C. Berridge, "The Neural Basis of Drug Craving: An Incentive-Sensitization Theory of Addiction" *Brain Research. Brain Research Reviews* 18 (3) (1993): 247–291; Robinson and Berridge, "The Psychology and Neurobiology of Addiction: An Incentive-Sensitization View," *Addiction* 95, Supplement 2 (2000): S91–117; Robinson and Berridge, "Review. The Incentive Sensitization Theory of Addiction: Some Current Issues," *Philosophical Transactions of the Royal Society of London. Series B, Biological Sciences* 363, no. 1507 (2008): 3137–3146; K. C. Berridge, "Pleasure, Pain, Desire and Dread: Hidden Core Processes of Emotion," in *Well Being: The Foundations of Hedonic Psychology*, ed. D. Kahneman, E. Diener, and N. Schwarz (New York: Sage Foundation: 1999), 527–559.
9. K. C. Berridge and Terry E. Robinson, "Drug Addiction as Incentive Sensitization," in *Addiction and Responsibility*, ed. Jeffrey Poland and George Graham (Cambridge, MA: MIT Press, 2011), 21–53. Clayton Hickey, Leonardo Chelazzi, and Jan Theeuwes, "Reward Changes Salience in Human Vision via the Anterior Cingulate," *Journal of Neuroscience* 30, no. 33 (2010): 30(33), 11096–11103 suggests that incentive sensitization is achieved through the dopamine reward system.
10. A. J. Tindell, K. C. Berridge, J. Zhang, S. Pecifia, and J. W. Aldridge, "Ventral Palladal Neurons Code Incentive Motivation: Amplification by Mesolimbic Sensitization and Amphetamine," *European Journal of Neuroscience* 22, no. 10 (2005): 2617–2634; P. Vezina, "Sensitization of Midbrain Dopamine Neuron Reactivity and the Self-Administration of Psychomotor Stimulant Drugs," *Neuroscience and Biobehavioral Reviews* 27, no. 8 (2004): 827–839; N. D. Volkow, G. J. Wang, F. Telang, J. S. Fowler, J. Logan, A. R. Childress et al., "Cocaine Cues and Dopamine in Dorsal Striatum: Mechanism of Craving in Cocaine Addiction, *Journal of Neuroscience* 26, no. 24 (2006): 6583–6588; C. L. Wyvell and K. C. Berridge, "Intra-accumbens and Amphetamine Increases the Conditioned Incentive Salience of Sucrose Reward: Enhancement of Reward 'Wanting' without Enhanced 'Liking' or Response Reinforcement, " *Journal of Neuroscience* 20, no. 21 (2000): 8122–8130.
11. B. J. Everitt, A. Dickinson, and T. W. Robbins, "The Neuropsychological Basis of Addictive Behavior," *Brain Research Review* (2001) 36: 129–138; J. D. Berke and S. E. Hyman, "Addiction, Dopamine, and the Molecular Mechanisms of Memory," *Neuron* 25 (2000): 515–532; T. W. Robbins and B. J. Everitt, "Drug Addiction: Bad Habits Add Up," *Nature* 398 (1999): 567–570.
12. G. D. Logan and W. Cowan, "On the Ability to Inhibit Thought and Action: A Theory of an Act of Control," *Psychological Review* 91 (1984): 295–327.

13. Daniel Wegner, "Who Is the controller of Controlled Processes?," *The New Unconscious*, ed. Ran R. Hassin, James S. Uleman, and John A. Bargh (Oxford: Oxford University Press, 2005), 19–37. John A. Bargh, ed. *Social Psychology and the Unconscious: The Automaticity of Higher Mental Processes* (New York: Psychology Press, 2007); David D. Franks, *Neurosociology: The Nexus Between Neuroscience and Social Psychology* (New York: Springer, 2010), Chapter 4.
14. D. B. Newlin and K. A. Strubler, "The Habitual Brain: An 'Adapted Habit' Theory of Substance Use Disorders," *Substance Use and Misuse* 42, no. 2–3 (2007): 503–526; George Messinis, "Habit Formation and the Theory of Addiction," *Journal of Economic Surveys* 13, no. 4 (2009): 417–442. doi: 10.1111/1467-6419.00089.
15. Daniel J. Siegal, *The Developing Mind* (New York: Guilford Press, 1999), 28–32.
16. Reinout W. Wiers and Alan W. Stacy, "Implicit Cognition and Addiction," *Current Directions in Psychological Science* 16, no. 6 (Dec. 2006): 292–296.
17. A. E. Kelley and K. C. Berridge, "The Neuroscience of Natural Rewards: Relevance to Addictive Drugs," *Journal of Neuroscience* 22 (2002): 3306–3311.
18. A. E. Kelley and K. C. Berridge, "The Neuroscience of Natural Rewards: Relevance to Addictive Drugs," *Journal of Neuroscience* 22 (2002): 3306–3311; Steven E. Hyman, Robert C. Malenka, and Eric J. Nestler, "Addiction: The Role of Reward-Related Learning and Memory," *Annual Review of Neuroscience* 29 (2006): 565–598; Koob and Volkow (2010).
19. But even this is not without dispute, as some researchers have argued that more than one "type" of alcoholism exist, and require independent discussion. One sort, it is argued, the susceptibility to lose control after drinking begins, is genetically distinct from the susceptibility to lose control after drinking begins, and requires a different analysis. While the first kind of alcoholism may be accounted for in terms of dopamine and hedonic experiences, the other, characterized by impulse control problems, is attributed to a dysfunction in serotonin regulation. Both of these "types" of alcoholism, however, are seen as the result of the interaction of genetic and environmental factors. See C. R. Cloninger, "Neurogenetic Adaptive Mechanisms in Alcoholism," *Science* 236 (1987): 410–416; also Christina S. Barr, Melanie L. Schwandt, Timothy K. Newman, and J. Dee Higley, "The Use of Adolescent Nonhuman Primates to Model Human Alcohol Intake: Neurobiological, Genetic, and Psychological Variables," *Annals of the New York Academy of Sciences* 1021 (2004): 221–233.
20. N. D. Volkow, G. J. Want, J. S. Fowler, S. J. Gatley, Y. S. Ding, J. Logan et al., "Relationship between Psychostimulant-induced 'High' and Dopamine Transporter Occupancy," *Proceedings of the National Academy of Sciences USA* 93 (1996): 10388–10392; N. D. Volkow and J. M. Swanson, "Variables That Affect the Clinical Use and Abuse of Methylphenidate in the Treatment of ADHD," *American Journal of Psychiatry* 160 (2003): 1909–1918; A. A. Grace, "The Tonic/Phasic Model of Dopamine System Regulation and Its Implications for Understanding Alcohol and Psychostimulant Craving," *Addiction* 95, Suppl. 2 (2000): S119–S128.
21. T. E. Robinson and K.C. Berridge, "Addiction," *Annual Review of Psychology* 54 (2003): 25–53.
22. T. E. Robinson and B. Kolb, "Alterations in the Morphology of Dendrites and Dendritic Spines in the Nucleus Accombens and Pre-frontal Cortex Following

Repeated Treatment with Amphetamine or Cocaine," *European Journal of Neuroscience* 11 (1999): 1598–1604;

23. G. F. Koob, S. B. Caine, L. Parsons, A. Markous, and F. Weiss, "Opponent Process Model and Psychostimulant Addiction," *Pharmacological Biochemistry and Behavior* 57 (1997): 513–521; G. F. Koob and M. Le Moal, "Drug Abuse: Hedonic Homeostatic Dysregulation," *Science* 278 (1997): 52–58.
24. Wolfram Schultz, Peter Dayan, and P. Read Montague, "A Neural Substrate of Prediction and Reward," *Science* 275, no. 5306 (1997): 1593–1599; K. A. Hadland, M. F. S. Rushworth, D. Gaffan, and R. E. Passingham, "The Anterior Cingulate and Reward-Guided Selection of Actions," *Journal of Neurophysiology* 89, no. 2 (2003): 1161–1164; Celine Amiez, Jean-Paul Joseph, and Emmanuel Procyk, "Anterior Cingulate Error-related Activity Is Modulated by Predicted Reward," *European Journal of Neuroscience* 21 (2005): 3447–3452.
25. B. J. Everitt and T. W. Robbins, "Neural Systems of Reinforcement for Drug Addiction: From Actions to Habits to Compulsion," *Nature Neuroscience* 8 (2005): 1481–1489.
26. Everett, Dickinson, and Robbins (2001), 134.
27. Terry E. Robinson and Kent C. Berridge, "Addiction," *Annual Review of Psychology* 54 (2003): 25–53.
28. Robinson and Berridge, (1993) and (2000).
29. W. D. Yao, R. R. Gainetdinov, M. I. Arbuckle, T. D. Sotnikova, M. Cyr, J. M Beaulieu et al., "Identification of PSD-95 as a Regulator of Dopamine-Mediated Synaptic and Behavioral Plasticity," *Neuron* 41 (1004): 625–638.
30. N. D. Volkow, J. S. Fowler, G. J. Wang, and J. M. Swanson, "Dopamine in Drug Abuse and Addiction: Results from Imaging Studies and Treatment Implications," *Molecular Psychiatry* 9 (2004): 557–569.
31. A parallel assumption, which we will address later, is made about the resemblance of effects in animal models to those in human beings.
32. Martin Sarter, Gary G. Berntson, and John Cacioppo, "Brain Imaging and Cognitive Neuroscience: Toward Strong Inference in Attributing Function to Structure," *American Psychologist* 51, no. 1 (1996): 13–21; Karl Friston, "Beyond Phrenology: What Can Neuroimaging Tell Us about Distributed Circuitry?," *Annual Review of Neuroscience* 25 (2002): 221–250. doi: 10.1146// annurev.neuro.25.112701.142846.
33. *The New Phrenology: The Limits of Localizing Cognitive Processes in the Brain* (Cambridge, MA: MIT Press, 2001); *Mind and Brain: A Critical Appraisal of Cognitive Neuroscience* (Cambridge, MA: MIT Press, 2011).
34. *Neuropod* (September, 2012), podcast of Nature.com.
35. Donald B. Douglas, "Alcoholism as an Addiction: The Disease Concept Reconsidered," *Journal of Substance Abuse Treatment* 3, no. 2 (1986): 115–120.
36. N. D. Volkow, G. J. Want, J. S. Fowler, S. J. Gatley, Y. S. Ding, J. Logan et al., "Relationship between Psychostimulant-induced 'High' and Dopamine Transporter Occupancy," *Proceedings of the National Academy of Sciences USA* 93 (1996): 10388–10392; N. D. Volkow and J. M. Swanson, "Variables That Affect the Clinical Use and Abuse of Methylphenidate in the Treatment of ADHD," *American Journal of Psychiatry* 160 (2003): 1909–1918; A. A. Grace, "The Tonic/Phasic Model of Dopamine System Regulation and Its Implications for Understanding Alcohol and Psychostimulant Craving," *Addiction* 95, Suppl. 2 (2000): S119–S128.

37. Douglas, 116.
38. Stanton Peel, "Denial – of Reality and of Freedom – in Addiction Research and Treatment," *Bulletin of the Society of Psychologists in Addictive Behaviors* 5, no. 4 (1986): 149–166.
39. Mark R. Hutchinson et al. "Opioid Activation of Toll-Like Receptor 4 Contributes to Drug Reinforcement," *Journal of Neuroscience: The Official Journal of the Society for Neuroscience*, 32, no. 33 (2012): 11187–11200.
40. Mark R. Hutchinson (2012), Press release http://www.colorado.edu/news/releases/2012/08/14/new-study-involving-cu-boulder-shows-heroin-morphine-addiction-can-be.
41. Peele, 154.
42. Stanton Peele, *Diseasing of America: Addiction Treatment Out of Control* (Lexington, MA: Lexington Books, 1989).
43. George Ainslie, *Breakdown of Will* (Cambridge: Cambridge University Press, 2001); also Ainslie, "The Core Process in Addictions and Other Impulses: Hyperbolic Discounting Versus Conditioning and Framing," in *What Is Addiction?* eds D. Ross, H. Kincaid, D. Spurrett, and P. Collins (Cambridge, MA: MIT Press, 2009), 211–245.
44. George Ainslie, "Beyond Microeconomics: Conflict Among Interests in a Multiple Self as a Determinant of Value" in *The Multiple Self*, ed. John Elster (Cambridge: Cambridge University Press, 1986), 133–175.
45. George Anslie and V. Haendel, "The Motives of the Will," in *Etiology Aspects of Alcohol and Drug Abuse*, ed. E. Gottheil, K. Druley, T. Skodals, and H. Waxman (Springfield, IL: Charles C. Thomas, 1983), 119–140; W. K. Bickel, A. L. Odum, and G. J. Madden, "Impulsivity and Cigarette Smoking: Delay Discounting in Current, Never, and Ex-smokers," *Psychopharmacology* 146, no. 4 (1999): 447–454; A. L. Bretteville-Jensen, "Addiction and Discounting" *Journal of Health Economics* 18, no. 4 (1999): 393–407; V. R. Fuchs, "Time Preferences and Health: An Exploratory Study," in *Economic Aspects of Health*, ed. V. R. Fuchs (Chicago: University of Chicago Press, 1956), 92–120); K. N. Kirby, N. M Petry, and W. K. Bickel, "Heroin Addicts Have Higher Discount Rates for Delayed Rewards Than Non-drug-using Controls," *Journal of Experimental Psychology: General* 128, no. 1 (1999): 78–87; G. J. Madden, N. M. Petry, G. J. Badger, and W. K. Bickel, "Impulsive and Self-control Choices in Opioid-dependent Patients and Non-drug-using Control Participants: Drug and Monetary Rewards," *Experimental and Clinical Psychopharmacology* 5, no. 3 (1997): 256–262; S. Mitchell, "Measures of Impulsivity in Cigarette Smokers and Non-Smokers Psychopharmacology 146, no. 4 (1999): 455–464; J. Monterosso, G. Ainslie, J. Xu, X. Cordova, C. P. Domier, and E. D. London "Frontoparietal Cortical Activity of Methamphetamine-dependent and Comparison Subjects Performing a Delay Discounting Task," *Human Brain Mapping* 28, no. 5 (2007): 383–393; R. E. Vuchinich, "Hyperbolic Temporal Discounting in Social Drinkers and Problem Drinkers," *Experimental and Clinical Psychopharmacology* 6, no. 3 (1998): 292–305.
46. George Ainslie, "Free Will as Recursive Self-Prediction," in *Addiction and Responsibility*, ed. Jeffrey Poland and George Graham (Cambridge, MA: MIT Press, 2011), 64.
47. Ainslie (2011), 65.

48. Mark Muraven and Elisaveta Slessareva, "Mechanisms of Self-Control Failure: Motivation and Limited Resources," *Personality and Social Psychology Bulletin* 29 (2003): 894–906; Mark Muraven, Dianne M. Tice, and Roy F. Baumeister, "Self-Control as a Limited Resource: Regulatory Depletion Patterns," *Journal of Personality and Social Psychology* 74 (1998): 774–789.
49. Kathleen D. Vohs and Todd F. Heatherton, "Self-Regulatory Failure: A Resource-Depletion Approach," *Psychological Science* 11, no. 3 (2000): 249–254; also see D. Kahn, J. Polivy, and C. P. Herman, "Conformity and Dietary Disinhibition: A Test of the Ego Strength Model of Self-Regulation," *International Journal of Eating Disorders* 33, no. 2 (2003): 165–171.
50. Neil Levey, "Addiction, Responsibility, and Ego Depletion," in *Addiction and Responsibility*, ed. Jeffrey Poland and George Graham (Cambridge, MA: MIT Press, 2011), 101–111.
51. Levey (2011), 102, original emphasis.
52. G. Loewenstein, "Willpower: A Decision Theorist's Perspective," *Law and Philosophy* 19, no. 1 (2000): 51–76.
53. James MacKillop and Christopher W. Kahler, "Delayed Reward Discounting Predicts Treatment Response for Heavy Drinkers Receiving Smoking Cessation Treatment," *Drug and Alcohol Dependence* 104, no. 3 (2009): 197–203.
54. Bruce D. Perry, "Childhood Experience and the Expression of Genetic Potential: What Childhood Neglect Tells Us about Nature and Nurture," *Brain and Mind* 3, no. 1 (2002): 79–100.

4 The Ecology of Addiction

1. Gregory Bateson, "The Cybernetics of Self: A Theory of Alcoholism," in *Steps to an Ecology of Mind: Collected Essays in Anthropology, Psychiatry, Evolution and Epistemology* (San Francisco: Chandler Publishing Company, 1982), originally published in *Psychiatry* 34, no. 1 (1971): 1–18.
2. Bateson, 4.
3. We agree on this point. The remainder of Bateson's analysis of alcoholism, and in particular his view regarding a higher power, prayer, and etc. stand in stark contrast to the view presented here.
4. This is according to Bateson scholar Peter Harries-Jones, *A Recursive Vision: Ecological Understanding and Gregory Bateson* (Toronto: University of Toronto Press, 1995), 38.
5. Lisa A. Briand and Julie A. Blendy, "Molecular and Genetic Substrates Linking Stress and Addiction." *Brain Research* 1314 (2010): 219–234; S. A. Brown, P. W. Vik, J. R. McQuaid, T. L. Patterson, M. R. Irwin, and I. Grant, "Severity of Psychosocial Stress and Outcome of Alcoholism Treatment.," *Journal of Abnormal Psychology* 99 (1990): 344–348; S. A. Brown, P. W. Vik, T. L. Patterson, I. Grant, and M. A. Schuckit, "Stress, Vulnerability and Adult Alcohol Relapse" *Journal of the Study of Alcohol,* 56, no. 5 (1995): 538–545; P. Ouimette, D. Coolhart, J. S. Funderburk, M. Wade, P. J. Brown, "Precipitants of First Substance Use in Recently Abstinent Substance Use Disorder Patients With PTSD," *Addictive Behaviors* 32, no. 8 (2007): 1719–1727.
6. A. N. Schore, *Affect Regulation and the Origin of the Self* (Hillsdale, NJ: Lawrence Erlbaum Associates, 1994), 12.

7. Megan Gunnar and Karina Quevedo, "The Neurobiology of Stress and Development," *Annual Review of Psychology* 58 (2007): 145–173.
8. Shanta R. Dube, Vincent J. Felitti, Maxia Dong, Daniel P. Chapman, Wayne H. Giles, and Robert F. Anda, "Childhood Abuse, Neglect, and Household Dysfunction and the Risk of Illicit Drug Use: The Adverse Childhood Experiences Study," *Pediatrics* 111, no. 3 (2003): 564–572.
9. These results were corroborated in a later study: Shanta Dube, J. Miller, D. Brown et al., "Adverse Childhood Experiences and the Association with Ever Using Alcohol and Initiating Alcohol Use During Adolescence," *Journal of Adolescent Health* 35, no. 4 (2006): 444.e1–444.e10, and also by Emily F. Rothman, Erika M. Edwards, Timothy Heeren, and Ralph W. Hingson, "Adverse Childhood Experiences Predict Earlier Age of Drinking Onset: Results from a Representative U.S. Sample of Current or Former Drinkers," *Pediatrics* 122, no. 2 (2008): e298–e304, doi: 10.1542/peds.2007–3412.
10. Bruce D. Perry et al., "Childhood Trauma, the Neurobiology of Adaptation and 'Use-dependent' Development of the Brain: How 'States' become 'Traits'" *Infant Mental Health Journal* 16, no. 4 (1995): 271–291.
11. R. S. Falck, R. W. Nahhas, L. Li, and R. G. Carlson, "Surveying Teens in School to Assess the Prevalence of Problematic Drug Use," *Journal of School Health* 82, no.5 (2012): 217–224.
12. Michael D. DeBellis, Andrew S. Baum, et al., "Developmental Traumatology Part I: Biological Stress Systems," *Biological Psychiatry* 45, no. 10 (1999): 1259–1270.
13. B. D. Perry and R. Pollard, "Homeostasis, Stress, Trauma, and Adaptation: A Neurodevelopmental View of Childhood Trauma," *Child and Adolescent Psychiatric Clinics of North America* 7 (1998): 33–51.
14. Darlene D. Francis and Michael J. Meaney, "Maternal Care and the Development of Stress Responses," *Current Opinion in Neurobiology* 9, no. 1 (1999): 128–134.
15. M. Mar Sanchez, Charlotte O. Ladd, and Paul M. Plotsky, "Early Adverse Experience as a Developmental Risk Factor for Later Psychopathology: Evidence from Rodent and Primate Models," *Development and Psychopathology* 13, no. 3 (2001): 419–149; Joan Kaufman, Paul Plotsky, Charles B. Nemeroff, Dennis S. Charney, "Effects of Early Adverse Experiences on Brain Structure and Function: Clinical Implications," *Biological Psychiatry* 48, no. 8 (2000): 778–790.
16. Christian Caldiji, Beth Tannenbaum, Shakti Sharma, Darlene Francis, Paul M. Plotsky, and Michael J. Meaney, "Maternal Care During Infancy Regulates the Development of Neural Systems Mediating the Expression of Fearfulness in the Rat," *Proceedings of the* National *Academy of Science of the U.S.A.* 95, no. 9 (1998): 5335–5340.
17. D. D. Francis et al. (1998), 130; Michael J. Meaney, David H. Aitken, Seema Bhatnagar, Robert M. Sapolsky, "Postnatal Handling Attenuates Certain Neuroendocrine, Anatomical, and Cognitive Dysfunctions Associated with Aging in Female Rats," *Neurobiology of Aging* 12, no. 1 (1991): 31–38.
18. Alison S. Fleming, Gary W. Kraemer, Andrea Gonzalez, Vedran Lovic, Stephanie Rees, and Angel Melo, "Mothering Begets Mothering: The Transmission of Behavior and Its Neurobiology Across Generations," *Pharmacology Biochemistry and Behavior* 73, no. 1 (2002): 61–75.

19. C. M. Berman, "Intergenerational Transmission of Maternal Rejection Rates among Free-Ranging Rhesus Monkeys on Cayo Santiago," *Animal Behavior* 44 (1990): 247–258.
20. Francis Champagne and Michael Meaney, "Chapter 21: Like Mother, Like Daughter: Evidence for Non-Genomic Transmission of Parental Behavior and Stress Responsivity," *Progress in Brain Research* 133 (2001): 287–302.
21. Stanley I. Greenspan and Stuart Shanker, *The First Idea: How Symbols, Language, and Intelligence Evolved From Our Primate Ancestors to Modern Humans* (Cambridge, MA: Da Capo Press, 2004), 102.
22. Greenspan and Shanker (2004), 201.
23. Greenspan and Shanker (2004), 102.
24. Michael J. Meaney, Wayne Brake, Alain Gratton, "Environmental Regulation of the Development of Mesolimbic Dopamine Systems: A Neurobiological Mechanism for Vulnerability to Drug Abuse?," *Psychoneuroendocrinology* 27 (2002): 127–138.
25. Paul Plotsky, "Early Life Adversity, Allostasis, and Resilience," presentation at Culture, Mind, and Brain: Emerging Concepts, Methods, Applications 5th Foundation for Psychocultural Research-UCLA Interdisciplinary Conference. Also see Christine Helm, Paul M. Plotsky, and Charles B. Nemeroff, "Importance of Studying the Contributions of Early Adverse Experience to Neurobiological Findings in Depression," *Neuropsychopharmacology* 29, no. 4 (2004): 205–217.
26. Rajita Sinha, "How Does Stress Increase Risk of Drug Abuse and Relapse?" *Psychopharmacology* 158 (2001): 343–359; George Koob, Mary Jeanne Kreek, "Stress, Dysregulation of Drug Reward Pathways, and the Transition to Drug Dependence," *American Journal of Psychiatry* 164, no. 8 (2007): 1149–1159.
27. Gary W. Kraemer and William T. McKinney, "Social Separation Increases Alcohol Consumption in Rhesus Monkeys," *Psychopharmacology* 86 (1985): 182–189.
28. Claudia Fahlke, Joseph G. Lorenz, Jeffrey Long, Maribeth Champous, Stephen J. Soumi, J. Dee Higley, "Rearing Experiences and Stress-Induced Plasma Cortisol as Early Risk Factors for Excessive Alcohol Consumption in Nonhuman Primates," *Alcoholism: Clinical and Experimental Research* 24, no. 5 (2000): 644–650.
29. B. K. Alexander, R. B. Coambs, and P. F. Hadaway, "The Effect of Housing and Gender on Morphine Self-Administration in Rats," *Psychopharmacology* 58 (1978): 175–179.
30. Bruce Alexander, "The Myth of Drug-Induced Addiction," Report to the Parliament of Canada (January 2001). http://www.parl.gc.ca/content/sen/committee/371/ille/presentation/alexander-e.htm.
31. Marian Logrip, Eric P. Zorrilla, George F. Koob, "Stress Modulation of Drug Self-Administration: Implications for Addiction Comorbidity with Post-traumatic Stress Disorder," *Neurophyarmacology* 62, no. 2 (2012): 552–564; E. G. Triffleman, C. R. Marmar, K. L. Delucchi, H. Ronfeldt, "Childhood Trauma and Posttraumatic Stress Disorder in Substance Abuse Inpatients," *Journal of Nervous and Mental Disease* 183, no. 3 (1995): 172–176.
32. P. V. Piazza and M. Le Moal, "The Role of Stress in Drug Self-Administration," *Trends in Pharmacological Sciences* 19, no. 2 (1998): 67–74.

33. Uri Shalev, David Highfield, Jasmine Yap, and Yavin Shaha, "Stress and Relapse to Drug Seeking in Rats: Studies on the Generality of the Effect," *Psychopharmacology* 150, no. 3 (2000): 337–346; Yavin Shaham, Suzanne Erb, and Jane Steward, "Stress Induced Relapse to Heroin and Cocaine Seeking in Rats: A Review," *Brain Research Reviews* 33, no. 1 (2000): 13–33.
34. Mara Mather and Nichole R. Lighthall, "Risk and Reward Are Processed Differently in Decisions Made Under Stress," *Current Directions in Psychological Science* 21, no. 1 (2012): 36–41.
35. Xiao-li Zhang, Jie Shi, Li-yan Zhao, Li-li Sun, Jun Wang, Gui-bin Wang, David Epstein, and Lin Lu, "Effects of Stress on Decision-Making Deficits in Formerly Heroin-Dependent Patients after Different Durations of Abstinence," *American Journal of Psychiatry* 168, no. 6 (2011): 610–616.
36. Mary-Anne Enoch and David Goldman, "The Genetics of Alcoholism and Alcohol Abuse," *Current Psychiatry Reports* 3 (2001): 144–151.
37. International Human Genome Sequencing Consortium, "Initial Sequencing and Analysis of the Human Genome," *Nature* 409, no. 6822 (2001): 860–921; International Human Genome Sequencing Consortium, "Finishing the Euchromatic Sequence of the Human Genome," *Nature* 431, no. 7011 (2004): 931–945.
38. J. Hirsch, "Some History of Heredity-vs-Environment, Genetic Inferiority at Harvard (?) and The (Incredible) Bell Curve," *Genetica* 99 (1997): 207–224.
39. Heyman (2009), 91.
40. C. Robert Cloninger, Michael Bohman, Soren Sigvardsson, "Inheritance of Alcohol Abuse: Cross-Fostering Analysis of Adopted Men," *Archives of General Psychiatry* 38, no. 8 (1981): 861–868.
41. M. Bohman, S. Sigvardsson, and C. R. Cloninger, "Maternal Inheritance of Alcohol Abuse: Cross-fostering Analysis of Adopted Women," *Archives in General Psychiatry* 38, no. 9 (1981): 861–868.
42. Jay Joseph, "The 'Missing Heritability' of Psychiatric Disorders: Elusive Genes or Non-Existent Genes?," *Applied Developmental Science* 16, no. 2 (2012): 72.
43. R. Plomin, R. Corley, A. Caspi, D. W. Fulker, and J. C. DeFries, "Adoption Results for Self-Reported Personality: Evidence for Nonadditive Genetic Effects?," *Journal of Personality and Social Psychology* 75 (1998): 211–218.
44. Gabor Maté, *In the Realm of Hungry Ghosts: Close Encounters with Addiction* (Berkeley, CA: North Atlantic Books, 2010), 433–437.
45. Maté (2010), 438.
46. Maté (2010), 439.
47. Joshua P. Smith and Sarah W. Book, "Comorbidity of Generalized Anxiety Disorder and Alcohol Use Disorders among Individuals Seeking Outpatient Substance Abuse Treatment," *Addictive Behaviors* 35, no. 1 (2010): 42–45.
48. F. R. Schneier, T. E. Foose, D. S. Hasin, R. G. Heimberg, S. M. Liu, B. F. Grant, and C. Blanco, "Social Anxiety Disorder and Alcohol Use Disorder Co-morbidity in the National Epidemiologic Survey on Alcohol and Related Conditions," *Psychological Medicine* 40, no. 6 (2010): 977–988.
49. D. A. Regier, M. E. Farmer, D. S. Rae, B.Z. Locke, S. J. Keith, L. O. Judd, and F. K. Goodwin, "Comorbidity of Mental Disorders with Alcohol and Other Drug Abuse: Results from the Epidemiological Catchment Area (ECA) Study," *Journal of the American Medical Association* 264 (1990): 2511–2518.

50. Joseph M. Boden and David M. Fergusson, "Alcohol and Depression," *Addiction* 106, no. 5 (2011): 906–914.
51. David A. Shoham, Liping Tong, Peter J. Lamberson, Amy H. Auchincloss, Jun Zhang, Lara Dugas, Jay S. Kaufman, Richard S. Cooper, and Amy Luke, "An Actor-Based Model of Social Network Influence on Adolescent Body Size, Screen Time, and Playing Sports," Public Library of Science ONE, published June 29, 2012.
52. B. F. Grant and D. A. Dawson, "Age at Onset of Alcohol Use and Its Association with DSM-IV Alcohol Abuse and Dependence: Results from the National Longitudinal Alcohol Epidemiologic Survey," *Journal of Substance Abuse* 9 (1997): 103–110; B. F. Grant and D. A. Dawson, "Age of Onset of Drug Use and Its Association with DSM IV Drug Abuse and Dependence: Results from the National Longitudinal Alcohol Epidemiologic Survey," *Journal of Substance Abuse* 10, no. 2 (1998): pp. 163–173.
53. B. F. Grant, "Age at Smoking Onset and Its Association With Alcohol Consumption and DSM-IV Alcohol Abuse and Dependence: Results from the National Longitudinal Alcohol Epidemiologic Survey," *Journal of Substance Abuse* 10, no. 1 (1998): 59–73.

5 The Culture of Addiction

1. James Barber, "Alcohol Addiction: Private Trouble or Social Issue?," *Social Service Review* 68, no. 4 (1994): 521–535
2. David T. Courtwright, *Forces of Habit: Drugs and the Making of the Modern World* (Cambridge, MA: Harvard University Press, 2001136–139.
3. Jan Rogozinski, *Smokeless Tobacco in the Western World, 1550–1950* (New York: Praeger, 1990), ch. 4.
4. Courtwright, 135–138.
5. World Health Organization, "The Tobacco Epidemic: A Global Public Health Emergency," http://www.who/int/inf-fs/en/factus8.html, June 29, 2000.
6. Courtwright, 19.
7. Courtwright, 59. He notes that "it is probably no coincidence that the rapid growth of European distilling, and the explosive growth of tobacco imports, took place during what historians call 'the general crisis of the seventeenth century,'" a period in which Europeans suffered "inflation, unemployment, pestilence, frigid weather, crop failures, riots, massacres, and warfare with parallel since the grimmest days of the fourteenth century."
8. Courtwright, 75.
9. T. Smollett, *The History of England from the Revolution in 1688, to the Death of George the Second* (Philadelphia: M'Carty and Davis, 1839), 452.
10. Gerda Reith, "Consumption and Its Discontents: Addiction and the Problems of Freedom," *The British Journal of Sociology*, 55, no. 2 (2004): 283–300.
11. Reith, 287
12. S. Ewen and E. Ewen, *Channels of Desire* (New York: McGraw-Hill, 1982), 250.
13. Daniel Bell, *The Cultural Contradictions of Capitalism* (London: Heinemann, 1976), 31.

14. Robin Room, "Treatment-seeking Populations and Larger Realities," in *Alcohol Treatment in Transition*, ed. Griffith Edwards and Marcus Grant (London: Croom Helm, 1980), 205–224.
15. C. M. Weisner and Robin Room, "Financing and Ideology in Alcohol Treatment," *Social Problems* 32, no. 2 (1984): 167–184.
16. Substance Abuse and Mental Health Services Administration, "Projections of National Expenditures for Mental Health Services and Substance Abuse Treatment 2004–2014," http://store.samhsa.gov/product/SMA08-4326
17. Elayne Rapping, *The Culture of Recovery: Making Sense of the Self-Help Movement in Women's Lives* (Boston: Beacon Press, 1996), 69.
18. Michelle Alexander, *The New Jim Crow: Mass Incarceration in the Age of Colorblindness* (New York: The New Press, 2010), 59.
19. G. D. Jaynes and R. M. Williams, Jr., eds., *A Common Destiny: Blacks and the American Society* (Washington: National Academy Press, 1989).
20. William Kornblum, "Drug Legalization and the Minority Poor," *Milbank Quarterly* 69, no. 3 (1991): 415–435.
21. Kornblum, 426
22. Sam Mitrani, "Stop Kidding Yourself: The Police Were Created to Control Working Class and Poor People," *Laboronline* (December 29, 2014), Labor and Working-Class History Association. Lawcha.org/wordpress/2014/12/29/stop-kidding-police-created-control-working-class-poor-people/.
23. Alexander, 4.
24. Alexander, 4. To illustrate Alexander's point, we have only to consider the numerous cases of brutality against black young men that have surfaced in recent months, including those involving the deaths of Trayvon Martin at the hands of George Zimmerman, Freddie Gray at the hands of the Baltimore police, and Walter Scott, shot in the back by North Charleston police officer Michael Slager.
25. J. E. Helzer, G. J. Canino, E. K. Yeh, R. C. Bland, C. K. Lee, H. G. Hwu, and S. Newman, "Alcoholism – North America and Asia: A Comparison of Population Surveys with the Diagnostic Interview Schedule," *Archives of General Psychiatry*, 47, no. 4 (1990): 313.
26. Martin Levine and Richard Troiden, "The Myth of Sexual Compulsivity," *The Journal of Sex Research* 25, no. 3 (1988): 347–363.
27. Levine and Troiden, 347.
28. Levine and Troiden, 351.
29. Levine and Troden, 360.
30. Heyman (2009), 2.
31. I. Nelson Rose, "Compulsive Gambling and the Law: From Sin to Vice to Disease," *Journal of Gambling Behavior* 4, no. 4 (1988): 240–260.
32. Credit Suisse AG, Paradeplatz 8 P. O. Box CH-8070, Zurich, Switzerland, redia. relations@credit-suisse.com.
33. Data from New York City Department of Homeless Services.
34. National Alliance to End Homelessness, National Coalition for the Homeless, the National Health Care for the Homeless Council, the National Association for the Education of Homeless Children and Youth, the National Law Center on Homelessness and Poverty, National Low Income Housing Coalition, and National Policy and Advocacy Council on Homelessness, "Foreclosure to Homelessness 2009: The Forgotten Victims of the Subprime Crisis."

35. Oxfam, "Even It Up: Time to End Extreme Inequality," oxfamamerica.org, http://www.oxfamamerica.org/static/media/files/even-it-up-inequality-oxfam.pdf.
36. Amy Goodman, video interview, "Drugs Aren't the Problem": Neuroscientist Carl Hart on Brain Science and Myths About Addiction," *Truthout*, (Tuesday 7 January 2014), http://www.truth-out.org/news/item/21078-drugs-arent-the-problem-neuroscientist-carl-hart-on-brain-science-and-myths-about-addiction.
37. Carl L. Hard, Baroline B. Marvin, Rae Silver, and Edward E. Smith, "Is Cognitive Functioning Impaired in Methamphetamine Users? A Critical Review," *Neuropsychopharmacology* 37, no. 3 (2012): 586–608.
38. Gene Heyman, "Addiction and Choice: Theory and New Data," *Frontiers in Psychiatry* 4, no. 31 (2013): p. 3. doi: 10.3389/fpsyt2013.00031.
39. Karamat Ali, "Causes of Drug Addiction in Pakistan," *Pakistan Economic and Social Review* 18, no. 3/4 (1980): 102–111.
40. Ali, 106.
41. Ali, 106.
42. Daniel H. Lende, "Wanting and Drug Use: A Biocultural Approach to the Analysis of Addiction," *Ethos* 33, no. 1 (2005), Special Issue: Building Biocultural Anthropology, 100–124.
43. Judith S. Brook et al., "Pathways to Marijuana Use Among Adolescents: Cultural/Ecological, Family, Peer, and Personality Influences," *Journal of the American Academy of Child & Adolescent Psychiatry* 37, no. 7 (1998): 759–766.
44. Gilbert Quintero and Sally Davis, "Why Do Teens Smoke? American Indian and Hispanic Adolescents Perspectives on Functional Values and Addiction," *Medical Anthropology Quarterly,* New Series, 16, no. 4 (2002): 439–457.
45. Quintero and Davis, 446.
46. Paul Hayes, "Many People Use Drugs – But Here's Why Most Don't Become Addicts," *The Conversation,* US Addition (January 6, 2015), https://theconversation.com/many-people-use-drugs-but-heres-why-most-dont-become-addicts-35504.
47. Lee Fang, "The Anti-Pot Lobby's Big Bankroll: The Opponents of Marijuana-Law Reform Insist That Legalization Is Dangerous, But the Biggest Threat Is to Their Own Bottom Line," *The Nation,* 299, nos. 3–4 (2014): 112–117, https://www.thenation.com/article/anti-pot-lobbys-big-bankroll/.
48. Fang, 14.
49. Barbara Starfield, "Is U.S. Health Really the Best in the World?," *Journal of the American Medical Association* 284, no. 4 (2000): 483–485.
50. Centers for Disease Control and Prevention, "Prescription Drug Overdose in the United States: Fact Sheet," cdc.gov, http://www.cdc.gov/homeandrecreationalsafety/overdose/facts.html.
51. Sasha Knezev and Gregory A. Smith, MD, *American Addict,* directed by Sasha Knezev (Torrance, CA: Pain MD Productions, 2014), DVD.
52. Lende, 105
53. Ali, 104.
54. Timothy S. Paul, "Obesity Kills More Americans Than Previously Thought," report by Columbia Mailman School of Public Health, August 14, 2013, mailman.columbia.edu, http://www.mailman.columbia.edu/news/obesity-kills-more-americans-previously-thought.

55. Kornblum, 422.
56. Kornblum, 433.
57. Alfred Lindesmith, "A Sociological Theory of Addiction," *American Journal of Sociology* 43, no. 4 (1938): 593–613.
58. Darin Weinbert, "Lindsmith on Addiction: A Critical History of a Classic Theory," *Sociological Theory* 15, no. 2 (1997): 150–161.
59. Weinbert, 153.
60. Weinbert, 157.

6 Addiction and Meaning

1. Paul Churchland, *Neurophilosophy at Work* (New York: Cambridge University Press, 2007), 138–140.
2. Jerry Fodor, *The Language of Thought* (New York: Crowell, 1975); also Jerry Fodor, *RePresentations* (Cambridge, MA: MIT Press, 1981) and others. In Jerry Fodor, *Concepts: Where Cognitive Science Went Wrong* (Oxford: Oxford University Press, 1998), he denies the existence of innate *ideas*, or *concepts*, opting instead for innate *mechanisms* (142) – but this is all compatible with classical innatism, at least as put forth in the philosophy of Gottfried Wilhelm Leibniz, and arguably in that of Descartes.
3. Jerry Fodor, "Concepts: A Potboiler," *Cognition* 50 (1994): 107.
4. Fodor (1994), 107.
5. Jerry Fodor, "Semantics, Wisconsin Style," *Synthese* 59 (1984): 231–250, reprinted in *A Theory of Content and Other Essays* (Cambridge, MA: MIT Press, 1990).
6. Jerry Fodor, *A Theory of Content and Other Essays*, chapter 4.
7. Walter J. Freeman, *How Brains Make Up Their Minds* (Cambridge, MA: MIT Press, 1999), 25.
8. Freeman (1999), 41.
9. John Searle, "Minds, Brains, and Programs," *Brain and Behavioral Science* 3, no. 3 (1980): 417–457.
10. Levine and Bickhard, 19.
11. Antonio Damasio, *The Feeling of What Happens: Body and Emotion in the Making of Consciousness* (New York: Harcourt, 1999), 320–321.
12. Churchland (2007), 135. Original emphasis.
13. Damasio, 321.
14. David Hume, *Inquiry Concerning Human Understanding*, Project Gutenberg, section 2, paragraphs 13, 14. www.gutenberg/org/ebooks/9662.
15. Hume, *Inquiry,* paragraph 14.
16. Churchland (2007), 135.
17. Churchland (2007), 135.
18. Greenspan and Shanker (2004), 104.
19. Greenspan and Shanker (2004), 47.
20. Greenspan and Shanker (2004), 48.
21. S. I. Greenspan, *The Growth of the Mind and the Endangered Origins of Intelligence* (Reading, MA: Addison Wesley Longman, 1997).
22. Gene Heyman, *Addiction: A Disorder of Choice* (Cambridge, MA: Harvard University Press, 2009), 84–86.

23. See H. Mercier and D. Sperber, "Why Do Humans Reason? Arguments for an Argumentative Theory," *The Behavioral and Brain Sciences* (April 1, 2011), 57–74, for an argument that the function of reasoning in humans is not to determine optimal behavior or beliefs, but rather to persuade others of what we are already inclined to do or believe. We "look for arguments that support a given conclusion, and ceteris paribus, favor conclusions for which arguments can be found." (p. 57).

7 Phenomenology and Its Implications

1. Susan Cheever, *My Name Is Wilson: His Life and the Creation of Alcoholics Anonymous* (New York: Washington Square Press, 2005).
2. Owen Flanagan, "What Is It Like to Be an Addict?" *Addiction and Responsibility*, ed. Jeffrey Poland and George Graham (Cambridge, MA: MIT Press, 2011), 269–292.
3. Owen Flanagan, "Phenomenal Authority: The Epistemic Authority of Alcoholics Anonymous," *Addiction and Self-Control: Perspectives from Philosophy, Psychology, and Neuroscience*, ed. Neil Levy (New York: Oxford University Press, 2013), p. 67–93.
4. Rachael R. Hammer, Molly J. Dingel, Jenny E. Ostergren, Katherine E. Nowakowski, and Barbara A Koenig, "The Experience of Addiction as Told by the Addicted: Incorporating Biological Understandings into Self-Story," *Culture, Medicine, and Psychiatry* 36, no. 4 (2012): 712–734.
5. Hammer et al., 732.
6. Hammer et al., 720.
7. Lance Dodes, "Psychodynamic Practice: Individuals, Groups and Organisations," *Psychodynamic Practice: Individuals, Groups and Organizations*, Special Issue: *The Psychodynamics of Substance Abuse* 15, no. 4 (2009): 381–393.
8. Caroline Knapp, *Drinking: A Love Story* (New York: Bantam Doubleday Dell Publishing Group, 1996), 4.
9. Clark Collis, "Kristen Johnston Talks about Her Drug Addiction, Her Life-Threatening Illness, Her Recovery, and Her New Memoir, 'Guts,'" *Entertainment Weekly* (January 18, 2015) online supplement, http://www.ew.com/article/2012/03/10/kristen-johnston-talks-about-her-drug-addiction-her-life-threatening-illness-her-recovery-and-her-new-memoir-guts.
10. Jeanette Kennett, "Just Say No? Addiction and the Elements of Self-Control," in *Addiction and Self-Control: Perspectives from Philosophy, Psychology, and Neuroscience*, ed. Neil Levey (New York: Oxford University Press, 2013), 144–164.
11. Gabor Maté, *In the Realm of Hungry Ghosts* (Berkeley, CA: North Atlantic Books, 2010), 64–74.
12. Maté, 20.
13. Allison Moore, *Shards: A Young Vice Cop Investigates Her Darkest Case of Meth Addiction – Her Own* (New York: Touchstone, 2014), 23.
14. Hammer et al., 717.
15. Kristen Johnston, *Guts: The Endless Follies and Tiny Triumphs of a Giant Disaster* (New York: Gallery Books, 2012), 49.
16. Moore, 228.
17. Moore, 86.

18. Hammer et al., 724.
19. Moore, 87.
20. Hammer et al., 727.
21. Knapp, 117.
22. Johnston, 143.
23. Moore, 79
24. Knapp, 5.
25. Johnston, 109.
26. E. J. Khantzian, "The Self-Medication Hypothesis of Addictive Disorders: Focus on Heroin and Cocaine Dependence," *American Journal of Psychiatry* 142 (1985): 1259–1264. Also see E. J. Khantzian, "Psychological (Structural) Vulnerabilities and the Specific Appeal of Narcotics, *Annals of the New York Academy of Sciences* 398 (1982): 24–32.
27. E. J. Khantzian, K. S. Halliday, and W. E. McAuliffe, *Addiction and the Vulnerable Self: Modified Dynamic Group Therapy for Substance Abuser* (New York: Guilford, 1990). See also Khanztian (1985) and Khantzian (1982).
28. J. J. Suh, S. Ruffins, C. E. Robins, M. J. Albanese, and E. J. Khantzian, "Self-Medication Hypothesis: Connecting Affective Experience and Drug Choice," *Psychoanalytic Psychology* 25, no. 3 (2008): 518–532. Also see D. M. Eschbaugh, D. J. Josi, C. N. Hoyt, and M. A. Murphy, "Some Personality Patterns and Dimensions of Male Alcoholics: A Multivariate Description, *"A Clinician's Guide to the Personality Profiles of Alcohol and Drug Abusers: Typological Descriptions Using the MMPI*, ed. D. J. Tosi, D. M. Eshbaugh, and M. A. Murphy (Springfield, IL: Charles C. Thomas Publisher, 1993), 17–30. See also C. Wells, D. J. Tosi, D. M. Eshbaugh and M. A. Murphy, "Comparison and Discrimination of Male and Female Alcoholic and Substance Abusers," 73–73 in that volume.
29. Moore, 79.
30. Thomas de Quincy, *Confessions of an Opium Eater*, open access e-book through Project Gutenberg.
31. Personal communication, in a conversation that happened in the fall of 2013.
32. Kyle Keegan, "Chasing the High" (New York: Oxford University Press, 2008), 8.
33. Maté, 14.
34. Flanagan, 278
35. Dan Waldorf, Craig Reinarman, and Sheigla Murphy, *Cocaine Changes: The Experience of Using and Quitting* (Philadelphia: Temple University Press, 1991), 191.
36. Waldorf et al., 193.
37. Waldorf et al., 202.

8 Possibilities for Change

1. The book *Alcoholics Anonymous* says, "[R]arely have we seen one fail, who has thoroughly followed our path." 4th Edition, online, Chapter 5, p. 58.
2. National Institute on Drug Abuse: The Science of Drug Abuse & Addiction. "Drugs, Brains, and Behavior: The Science of Addiction," drugabuse.gov, http://www.drugabuse.gov/publications/drugs-brains-behavior-science-addiction/treatment-recovery.

3. Charles Duhigg, *The Power of Habit: Why We Do What We Do in Life and Business* (New York: Random House, 2012), 70–72.
4. N. C. Maisel, J. C. Blodgett, P. L. Wilbourne, K. Humphreys, and J. W. Finney, "Meta-analysis of Naltrexone and Acamprosate for Treating Alcohol Use Disorders: When Are These Medications Most Helpful?" *Addiction* 108, no. 2 (2013): 275–293.
5. J. R. Volpicelli, A. I. Alterman, M. Hayashida, and C. P. O'Brien, "Naltrexone in the Treatment of Alcohol Dependence," *Archives of General Psychiatry* 49, no. 11 (1992): 876–880.
6. Raymond F. Anton et al., "Combined Pharmacolotherapies and Behavioral Interventions for Alcohol Dependence/The COMBINE Study: A Randomized Controlled Trial," *Journal of the American Medical Association* 295, no. 27 (2006): 2003–2017. http://jama.jamanetwork.com/article.aspx!articleid=202789.
7. Kristin V. Carson, Malcolm P. Brinn, Thomas A. Robertson, Rachada To-A-Nan, Adrian J. Esterman, Matthew Peters, and Brian J. Smith, "Current and Emerging Pharmacotherapeutic Options for Smoking Cessation" *Substance Abuse* 7 (2013): 85–105.
8. Michael T. Bowen, Sebastian T. Peters, Nathan Absalom, Mary Chebib, Inga D. Neumann, and Iain S. McGregor, "Oxcytocin Prevents Ethanol Actions at ʒ Subunit-Containing $GABA_A$ Receptors and Attenuates Ethanol-Induced Motor Impairment in Rats," *Proceedings of the National Academy of Sciences of the United States of America*, 112, no. 10 (2015): 3104–3109. Published online before print February 23, 2015. doi: 10.1073/pnas.1416900112.
9. Jason Cherkis "Dying to Be Free: There's a Treatment for Heroin Addiction That Actually Works: Why Aren't We Using It?" *Huffington Post*, January 28, 2015.
10. National Center for Addiction and Substance Abuse, "Addiction Medicine: Closing the Gap between Science and Practice," Columbia University, June 2012.
11. Charles Duhigg, *The Power of Habit: Why We Do What We Do in Life and Business* (New York: Random House, 2012), 72–73.
12. N. Li, J. Wang, X. L. Wang, C. W. Chang, S. N. Ge, L. Gao, H. M. Wu, H. K. Zhao, N. Geng, and G. D. Gad, "Nucleus Accumbens Surgery for Addiction," *World* Neurosurgery 80, no. 3–4 (September–October 2013): S28 e9–19.
13. Antoine Lutz, Heleen A. Slagter, Nancy B. Rawlings, Andrew D. Francis, Lawrence L. Greischar, and Richard J. Davidson, "Mental Training Enhances Attentional Stability: Neural and Behavioral Evidence, *Journal of Neuroscience* 29, no. 42 (2009): 13418–13427; B. Rael Cahn and John Polich, "Meditation (Vipassana) and the P3a Event-related Brain Potential," *International Journal of Psychophysiology* 72 (2009): 51–60.
14. Andres B. Newberg, Nancy Wintering, Mark R. Waldman, Daniel Amen, Dharma S. Khalsa, and Alavi Abass, "Cerebral Blood Flow Differences between Long-term Meditators and Non-meditators," *Consciousness and Cognition*, 19, no. 4 (2010), 899–905.
15. Heleen A. Slagter, Antoine Lutz, Lawrence L. Greishar, Andrew D. Francis, Sander Nieuwenhuis, James M. Davis, Richard J. Davidson, "Mental Training Affects Distribution of Limited Brain Resources," *Plos Biology* 5, no. 6 (2007): 1228–1235.

16. John Ratey, with Eric Hagerman, *Spark: The Revolutionary New Science of Exercise and the Brain* (New York: Little, Brown and Co., 2008), 167–190 and 217–232.
17. Jolanda Mass, Robert A. Verheij, Peter P. Groenewegen, Sjerp de Vries, and Peter Spreeuwenberg, "Green Space, Urbanity, and Health: How Strong Is the Relation?," *Journal of Epidemiology and Community Health* 60, no. 7 (2006): 587–592, online.
18. Amanda Gardner, "Green Spaces Boost the Body and the Mind," abcnews.go.com, October 16, 2009, http://abcnews.go.com/Health/Healthday/green-spaces-boost-body-mind/story?id=8835912&page=2.
19. www.acestudy.org.
20. Lisa M. Najavits, R. D. Weiss, and S. R. Shaw, "The Link Between Substance Abuse and Posttraumatic Stress Disorder in Women: A Research Review," *American Journal on Addictions* 6 (1997): 273–283.
21. Bessel van der Kolk with Lisa M. Najavits, "Interview: What Is PTSD Really? Surprises, Twists of History, and the Politics of Diagnosis and Treatment," *Journal of Clinical Psychology: In Session*, 69, no. 5 (2013): 516–522.
22. Matthew W. Johnson et al., "Pilot Study of the 5-HT2AR Agonist Psilocybin in the Treatment of Tobacco Addiction," *Journal of Psychopharmacology* 28, no. 11 (2014): 983–992.
23. Many such memoirs are included among addiction self-help books, including, for example, Caroline Knapp's *Drinking: A Love Story* (New York: Dial Press Trade, 1997).
24. Susan Brison, "Violence and the Remaking of a Self," *The Chronicle of Higher Education,* January 18, 2002, B7. See also Susan Brison, *Aftermath: Violence and the Remaking of a Self* (Princeton: Princeton University Press, 2002; Paris: Editions Chambon, 2003; Munich: C. H. Beck Verlag, 2004).
25. Donna J. Bridge and Joel L. Voss, "Hippocampal Binding of Novel Information with Dominant Memory Traces Can Support Both Memory Stability and Change," *The Journal of Neuroscience* 34, no. 6 (2014): 2203–2213.
26. Al-Anon is the sister organization to AA, created to provide support and its own version of the 12 steps for spouses and others who are in close relationships with addicted individuals. Al-Ateen and Adult Children of Alcoholics are other such programs available in certain areas.
27. Sarah Huggins Scarbrough, "Breakthroughs in Offender Treatment: A Virginia Program Makes Inroads with Peer Support, Behavior Modification," *Addiction Professional* 10, no. 5 (2012): 13–15. The research for this article was done as part of Dr. Scarbrough's dissertation work. Her study is entitled "Drugs, Crime, and the Gateway Effect: A Study of Federal Crime Defendants."
28. UK Home Office Report, "Drugs: International Comparators," www.gov.uk, October, 2014, https://www.gov.uk/government/uploads/system/uploads/attachment_data/file/368489/DrugsInternationalComparators.pdf.
29. UK Home Office Report, 46.
30. Wiebke Hollersen, "'This Is Working:' Portugal, 12 years after Decriminalizing Drugs," *Spiegel Online International*, March 27, 2013, http://www.spiegel.de/international/europe/evaluating-drug-decriminalization-in-portugal-12-years-later-a-891060.html.
31. UK Home Office Report, 5.

9 Conclusion

1. Walter Sinnott-Armstrong, "Are Addicts Responsible?" *Perspectives from Philosophy, Psychology, and Neuroscience,* ed. Neil Levy (New York: Oxford University Press, 2013), 126.
2. Amanda Lenhart, "Teens, Social Media and Technology Overview 2015," Pew Research Center, Internet, Science, and Tech, www.pewinternet.org, April 9, 2015, http://www.pewinternet.org/2015/04/09/teens-social-media-technology-2015/.
3. Richard E. Nisbett and Timothy DeCamp Wilson, "Verbal Reports about Causal Influences on Social Judgments: Private Access versus Public Theories," *Journal of Personality and Social Psychology* 35, no. 9 (1977): 613–624; Richard E. Nisbett and Timothy DeCamp Wilson, "Telling More Than We Can Know," *Psychological Review* 84, no. 3 (1977): 231–359, doi: 10.1037/0033-295X.84.3.231. Petter Johansson, Lars Hall, Sverker Sikstrom, Betty Tarning, and Andreas Lind, "How Something Can Be Said about Telling More Than We Can Know: On Choice Blindness and Introspection," *Conscious and Cognition* 15, no. 4 (2006): 673–692.
4. Daniel Dennett, *Consciousness Explained* (Boston: Little, Brown, and Company, 1991), 115–138.
5. Ryan T. McKay and Daniel C. Dennett, "The Evolution of Misbelief," *Brain and Behavioral Sciences* 32 (2009): 493–561.
6. John H. Holland, *Hidden Order: How Adaptation Builds Complexity* (New York: Helix Books, 1995), 39–40, 93–97, and 165–167.
7. C. L. Hart, M. Haney, R. W. Foltin, and M. W. Fischman, "Alternative Reinforcers Differentially Modify Cocaine Self-Administration by Humans," *Behavioral Pharmacology* 11, no. 1 (2000): 87–91. Also see William W. Stoops, Joshua A. Lile, Paul E. A. Glaser, Lon. R. Hays, and Craig R. Rush, "Alternative Reinforcer Response Cost Impacts Cocaine Choice in Humans," *Progress in Neuro-Psychopharmacology and Biological Psychiatry* 36, no. 1 (2012): 189–193.

Bibliography

Alexander, Michelle. *The New Jim Crow: Mass Incarceration in the Age of Colorblindness*. New York: The New Press, 2010.

American Psychiatric Association Committee on Nomenclature and Statistics. *Diagnostic and Statistical Manual of Mental Disorders IV-TR*. Washington DC: American Psychiatric Association, 1994.

Bateson, Gregory. "The Cybernetics of Self: A Theory of Alcoholism," in *Steps to an Ecology of Mind: Collected Essays in Anthropology, Psychiatry, Evolution and Epistemology*. San Francisco: Chandler Publishing Company, 1982, 315–345.

Bickhard, Mark, "Process and Emergence: Normative Function and Representation," *Axiomathes: An International Journal in Ontology and Cognitive Systems* 14 (2004): 135–169.

Churchland, Paul. *Neurophilosophy at Work*. New York: Cambridge University Press, 2007.

Courtwright, David T. *Forces of Habit: Drugs and the Making of the Modern World*. Cambridge, MA: Harvard University Press, 2001.

Damasio, Antonio. *The Feeling of What Happens: Body and Emotion in the Making of Consciousness*. New York: Harcourt, 1999.

Deacon, Terrance W. *Incomplete Nature: How Mind Emerged from Matter*. New York: Norton, 2012.

Dennett, Daniel. *Elbow Room: The Varieties of Free Will Worth Wanting*. Cambridge, MA: MIT Press, 1984.

Dennett, Daniel. *Consciousness Explained*. Boston: Little, Brown, and Company, 1991.

Dodes, Lance. "Psychodynamic Practice: Individuals, Groups and Organisations," *Psychodynamic Practice: Individuals, Groups and Organizations*, Special Issue: *The Psychodynamics of Substance Abuse* 15, no. 4 (2009): 381–393.

Dube, Shanta R., Felitti, Vincent J., Dong, Maxia, Chapman, Daniel P., Giles, Wayne H., and Anda, Robert F. "Childhood Abuse, Neglect, and Household Dysfunction and the Risk of Illicit Drug Use: The Adverse Childhood Experiences Study," *Pediatrics* 111, no. 3 (2003): 564–572.

Everitt, B. J., Dickinson, A, and Robbins, T. W. "The Neuropsychological Basis of Addictive Behavior," *Brain Research Review* 36 (2001): 129–138.

Everitt, B. J., and Robbins, T. W. "Neural Systems of Reinforcement for Drug Addiction: From Actions to Habits to Compulsion," *Nature Neuroscience* 8 (2005): 1481–1489.

Flanagan, Owen. "What Is It Like to Be An Addict?", in *Addiction and Responsibility*, ed. Jeffrey Poland and George Graham. Cambridge, Mass: MIT Press. 2011, 269–292.

Flanagan, Owen. "Phenomenal Authority: The Epistemic Authority of Alcoholics Anonymous," in *Addiction and Self-Control: Perspectives from Philosophy, Psychology, and Neuroscience*, ed. Neil Levy. New York: Oxford University Press. 2013, 269–292.

Foddy, Bennett. "Addiction and Its Sciences: Philosophy," *Addiction* 106 (2010): 25–31.

Fodor, Jerry. *The Language of Thought*. New York: Crowell, 1975.

Fodor, Jerry. *RePresentations*. Cambridge, MA: MIT Press, 1981.

Greenspan, Stanley I., and Shanker, Stuart. *The First Idea: How Symbols, Language, and Intelligence Evolved From Our Primate Ancestors to Modern Humans*. Cambridge, MA: Da Capo Press, 2004.

Helm, Christine, Plotsky, Paul M. and Nemeroff, Charles B. "Importance of Studying the Contributions of Early Adverse Experience to Neurobiological Findings in Depression," *Neuropsychopharmacology* 29, no. 4 (2004): 205–217.

Heyman, Gene. *Addiction: A Disorder of Choice*. Cambridge, MA: Harvard University Press, 2009.

Kahneman, Daniel. *Thinking, Fast and Slow*. New York: Farrar, Straus and Giroux, 2011.

Kennett, Jeanette. "Just Say No? Addiction and the Elements of Self-Control," in *Addiction and Self-Control: Perspectives from Philosophy, Psychology, and Neuroscience*, ed. Neil Levey. New York: Oxford University Press, 2013, 144–164.

Knapp, Caroline. *Drinking: A Love Story*. New York: Bantam Doubleday Dell Publishing Group. 1996.

Koob, G. F., and Le Moal, M. "Drug Abuse: Hedonic Homeostatic Dysregulation," *Science* 278 (1997): 52–58.

Koob, G. F. et al. "Opponent Process Model and Psychostimulant Addiction," *Pharmacological Biochemistry and Behavior* 57 (1997): 513–521.

Koob, George F., and Volkow, Nora D. "Neurocircuitry of Addiction," *Neuropsychopharmacology* 35 (2010): 217–138.

Ladyman, James, and Ross, Don, with David Spurrett and John Collier. *Everything Must Go: Metaphysics Naturalized*. New York: Oxford University Press, 2007.

Levy, Neil. "Resisting 'Weakness of Will,'" *Philosophy and Phenomenological Research* 82, no. 1 (2011): 134–155.

Maté, Gabor. *In The Realm of Hungry Ghosts: Close Encounters with Addiction*. Berkeley, CA: North Atlantic Books, 2010.

Perry, B. D., and Pollard, R. "Homeostasis, Stress, Trauma, and Adaptation: A Neurodevelopmental View of Childhood Trauma," *Child and Adolescent Psychiatric Clinics of North America* 7 (1998): 33–51.

Perry, Bruce D. "Childhood Experience and the Expression of Genetic Potential: What Childhood Neglect Tells Us about Nature and Nurture," *Brain and Mind* 3, no. 1 (2002): 79–100.

Rapping, Elayne. *The Culture of Recovery: Making Sense of the Self-Help Movement in Women's Lives*. Boston: Beacon Press, 1996.

Ratey, John, with Eric Hagerman. *Spark: The Revolutionary New Science of Exercise and the Brain*. New York: Little, Brown and Co., 2008.

Robinson, T. E., and Berridge, K. C. "The Neural Basis of Drug Craving: An Incentive-Sensitization Theory of Addiction," *Brain Research Reviews* 18, no. 3 (1993): 247–291.

Index